ERIC R. BRAVERMAN, M.D.

Younger YOU

Unlock the Hidden Power of Your Brain

to Look and Feel 15 Years Younger

New York   Chicago   San Francisco   Lisbon   London   Madrid   Mexico City
Milan   New Delhi   San Juan   Seoul   Singapore   Sydney   Toronto

Library of Congress Cataloging-in-Publication Data

Braverman, Eric R.
    Younger you : unlock the hidden power of your brain to look and feel 15 years
younger / Eric R. Braverman.
        p.   cm.
    ISBN 0-07-146613-4 (alk. paper)
    1. Longevity—Popular works.   2. Aging—Prevention—Popular works.
3. Middle-aged persons—Health and hygiene—Popular works.   4. Older persons—
Health and hygiene—Popular works.   I. Title.

RA776.75B737   2007
613.2—dc22   2006026812

1 2 3 4 5 6 7 8 9 10 11 12 13 14 15 16 17 18 19 FGR/FGR 0 9 8 7 6

ISBN-13: 978-0-07-146613-4
ISBN-10:   0-07-146613-4

Interior design by Nick Panos

McGraw-Hill books are available at special quantity discounts to use as premiums and
sales promotions, or for use in corporate training programs. For more information, please
write to the Director of Special Sales, Professional Publishing, McGraw-Hill, Two Penn
Plaza, New York, NY 10121-2298. Or contact your local bookstore.

The information contained in this book is intended to provide helpful and informative
material on the subject addressed. It is not intended to serve as a replacement for
professional medical advice. Before beginning any diet, exercise, or healthcare program, a
healthcare professional should be consulted regarding your specific situation. All nutrient,
hormone, and medication recommendations mentioned in this book are not to be taken
without the advice of a medical doctor, naturopathic physician, registered dietitian and/or
endocrine specialist.

This book is printed on acid-free paper.

For my beloved wife, Dasha, and my children, Stevie, Danny, J.J., and Ellie.
My family is my inspiration, my love, and my comfort.

Contents

Foreword

W e live in a wonderful time, when medical breakthroughs are happening faster than we had ever anticipated, and their direct impact upon health is both real and tangible. Perhaps the most exciting and potentially the most powerful tools now emerging in the science of medicine are derived from our new understanding of genes. When I was in medical school in the late 1970s, genes were considered to be a vast library of information that played out during the course of one's lifetime. We understood that some diseases were genetically based, following well-described inheritance patterns with typical and predictable clinical manifestations. The basic premise was that essentially information from genes, in health or disease, flowed in one direction. Normal genes led to normal physiology while genetic defects were associated with disease.

The pages that follow reveal how far we have come from what now appears to have been a simplistic and almost primitive understanding of how genes work. Science has made a quantum leap in understanding not just what genes do and how they work, but most importantly, what directs our genetic expression in sickness and in health. It is this revolutionary understanding of genetic control so eloquently presented by Dr. Braverman that paves the way for health benefits beyond measure. As Dr. Braverman reveals, every aspect of a healthy lifestyle—from diet to nutritional supplements, hormone replacement, exercise and restful sleep—will ultimately provide you positive and youth-preserving benefits by actually affecting how your genes work. Indeed our new understanding of gene function recognizes that to maintain normal physiology, hundreds of genes are switched on and off every minute, and it is this dance of genetic expression that ultimately determines who will have health and longevity and who will not. The keys to the kingdom are found in this book.

You will learn not only which lifestyle choices are best, but, more importantly, you will gain the knowledge that these choices manifest health by actually choreographing the genetic dance, and in this sense this knowledge is empowering.

David Perlmutter, M.D., FACN
Author, *The Better Brain Book* and
Raise a Smarter Child by Kindergarten

Acknowledgments

The creation of this book could not have been possible without the help of many individuals. I would like to thank my writer, Pamela Liflander, for her unique skills, insights, and attentiveness in helping to get my ideas onto these pages.

I am grateful to my colleagues who have been my most invaluable critics. Tatiana Karikh, M.D.; Alison Notaro, M.A.; John Pillepich, Ph.D.; Oscar Varshavsky, D.O.; and Bruce Scali have all been wonderful assets.

I am fortunate to have assembled a gifted team of medical and administrative personnel at my PATH Medical office in New York, each of whom is integral at turning my philosophies into successful healing work. Their skills are unsurpassed and I am lucky to have them: Michele Caragiulo, N.D., RD; Jackie DiMaria, RPA-C; Anish Bajaj, D.C.; Javier Carbajal; Xudong Fu; Richard Smayda; Ida Feit; Melissa Dispensa; Ellie Capria, RPA-C; Sandy Gelbard, M.D.; and Donna Ruth. I would also like to thank my staff members whose contribution to this book, as well as their loyalty and dedication to helping my patients, cannot go unnoticed: Susan Kaplysh, Sam Ng, Tanya Perepada, Manu Sharma, Vanessa Arcuri, Alisa Cawley, Serdar Cetinbas, Victoria Gibbs, Angelique Williams, Denise Greenridge, Rosina Giaccio-Williams, and Svetlana Tacheva.

I must offer special thanks to John Aherne and the sales, marketing, production, and publicity staff at McGraw-Hill. John in particular has shown great faith in my message and has helped me shape this important book. And special thanks to Carol Mann, my agent, for putting us together.

Finally, I would like to thank my patients, the greatest teachers of all, who are responsible for providing me with their stories and the opportunity to make them younger.

Introduction

Get Younger and Healthier Now

Today's health care is holding us back from living longer and living well. Conventional American medicine is like a Ford assembly line, each specialist looking at one of our "parts" without considering the rest of the body. But this approach is a medical disaster that's affecting our health and longevity today. We all know that our entire body, from the top of our head to the soles of our feet, is intricately interconnected. Our internal organs do not function independently either; each one could be the catalyst that signals the downward cascade of deteriorating health and eventual death. Yet every single day people go to specialists and they are told they are "fine," when their doctor looked at only one part without considering the health of the others. Months later, they are surprised to find that another part has completely broken.

Often, serious disease catches most Americans by surprise. But no more. This book will teach you the age of every part of your body so that you can fix your oldest parts. By doing so, a younger you will emerge with a new abundant life.

If you saw a specialist who said that you were "fine," think again. At age 64, John had recently been to his doctor where he was told that he was in "tip-top" shape. Yet John instinctively knew that he didn't feel quite right. When he explained this to me, I had him come in and I ordered some blood tests. I found that his blood was too thick; he was being overmedicated with testosterone by his previous physician. All of his other tests—including cognitive assessments, bone density, and a psychological profile—appeared normal. I told John that he had to stop taking the synthetic testosterone that his previous physician had prescribed. By doing so, his blood would return to a more age-appropriate state. John did not listen to my warning and, on his own, continued on his regimen of synthetic testosterone because he thought it made him seem younger; it made him look and feel sharp, muscular, energetic, and healthy. Yet, just two weeks later John had a massive blood clot and nearly died. Even though he thought he looked and felt younger, his "old" blood was literally pulling him toward the grave.

Imagine walking into a room full of strangers and being able to predict who is going to live long or die young. Most people would think you are crazy for even trying. However, virtually all illness and disease can be detected from the outside. The biggest risk factors or signs of illness are all brain related, such as obesity, cigarette smoking, alcoholism, depression, anxiety, circles under the eyes, lack of mental clarity, and a large waistline. Other factors or signs include shrinking muscle mass, a slightly hunched spine, sagging skin, age spots, frailty, chronic coughing, yellowish skin or eyes, a slow gait, or nervousness. All of these visible signs are indications that a person is aging; and if this is the case, you can be certain that one or some of his or her organs are starting to fail.

Each section of the body has its known markers or tests of aging. These become the *age codes*. Once they are distorted, aging has now begun at an advanced rate. This book provides you with the tests that identify the aging of each section of your body so you can catch the disease before it catches you. In my office, diagnostic testing pinpoints with incredible accuracy the aging code of every organ in the body. No more will there be surprise illness, surprise deaths, and shocking diagnoses. In fact, I predict in the near future that living less than 100 years of age will be a rarity.

The Weakest Link: Found and Reversed

Illness is rarely isolated. Diseases are usually associated with illness in other bodily systems that starts a domino effect of health problems. If illness starts in the brain, it makes the body sick; if it starts in the body, it can make the brain sick. What's more, illness is now being perceived in a whole new way. The latest research shows that disease itself is a sign of an aging organ. And each of these aging organs sends a signal to the rest of the body that can wreak havoc. For example, if you are diagnosed with diabetes, chances are your body is failing in other ways. Elevated sugar levels damage your blood circulation, skin, eyes, heart, kidneys, nervous system, and the neurons of your brain and also causes weight gain. These issues used to be considered as "independent yet related symptoms of disease." But I know that they are all part of the body's aging code.

Everyone Ages Differently

Aging occurs throughout the entire body from the moment you are born until the day you die, but to varying degrees. As children, we call these changes "development." As adults, we refer to them as "illness." The difference is purely semantic. Even children reach adulthood with poorly developed or aged parts that can be prevented or repaired. Every time an internal system changes—whether it is the heart, bones, kidneys, brain, or ovaries—we age. As one system begins to fail, it sends an aging code to the rest of the body, transmitting a signal that things are falling apart. This code is a death signal that the rest of the body responds to in kind. When one part of the body dies, the rest follow the leader to their death, as if the body has its own herding instinct.

General categories of aging and disease do exist, yet there is no exact trend that occurs for all of us. One person may develop dementia that initially began as heart problems leading to high blood pressure leading to stroke; while another may develop dementia that began as depression, leading to lack of motivation, leading to slowed brain speed. Focus on your oldest parts and you break your aging barrier, reversing the aging code.

A New Paradigm: Internal Plastic Surgery

We live in a society where youth is valued above almost everything else. Many people will try any miracle product or diet that promises to make them look young again. Some are willing to go under the knife and risk serious health complications in the pursuit of youth and beauty. But what if you could not only look 15 years younger but also *feel* 15 years younger?

We all know intrinsically that neither plastic surgery nor the most expensive facial creams will make us feel younger or healthier. The key to a long, full life comes from fixing the inside, not the outside. Just as we can be externally beautiful, we can achieve inner beauty and health, and I don't mean having a sensitive nature or winning personality. I mean the inner youthfulness of good health. You can look and feel like 40 or 50 even when you are 65.

I call this *internal plastic surgery*, and it defines a new paradigm in medicine where we will be able to identify aging organs and repair or reverse them to achieve a younger, healthier you.

Creating a Younger You

The body ages at different rates; the heart, for instance, can get older before the rest of you ages. Or, you may lose your hair "prematurely," or it may turn grey before you are 40. This means that these genes and parts were older than your chronological age. In my medical practice and research, I have decoded the aging process of every part of your body. Whether you are 30, 40, 50, or 60, some part of your body is aging more rapidly than the others. Unless you know the age of every part of your body, you are not taking proper care of your health.

Perhaps you've lost two inches in height. You may be experiencing nagging depression or forgetfulness. These failing parts pull you into old age with their aging code, pressuring the rest of your body to deteriorate. Precise tests can give you the aging code at each section, while bioidentical hormones, medications, nutrients, diet, and lifestyle changes reverse this aging code to a *youth code*.

CODE BREAKER: Look and Feel 15 Years Younger
Without Surgery!
Surgically enhancing your face or body will make you look younger,
but it won't stop you from aging inside.

Aging Chronologically While Becoming Younger

I had a 45-year-old patient named Alisa whom I assessed using various tests. She had been suffering from chronic fatigue, a chemical imbalance, hypothyroidism, and osteoporosis for seven years. By using the tests and mapping techniques that will be explained in the following chapters, I determined that she was currently at least 11 years older in every aspect of her health. Once she began following the protocols outlined in this book, she was able to reverse the age of each organ or system by as much as 20 years. By the time she was chronologically 53 years old, she had the mind and body of a woman in her early 40s. She's 8 years older yet 10 to 15 years younger. This same age reversal can happen to you.

Alisa's Organ or System Age		
Organ	Pre–Younger You	Post–Younger You
Brain	56 years	44 years
Thyroid gland	80 years	40 years
Musculoskeletal	90 years	45 years
Ovaries	70 years	45 years
Adrenal gland	65 years	45 years
Skin	70 years	40 years
Circulation	60 years	45 years

It's hard to imagine that as you age chronologically you can actually get younger. By following my instructions, your parts are getting younger as you yourself age. Here is another example of a patient, Seth, who came to PATH and got younger.

Seth's AgePrint		
	Pre–Younger You	**Post–Younger You**
Patient's age	40 years	32 years
Brain age	28 years	26 years
Mind age	20 years	20 years
Parathyroid age	55 years	45 years
Thyroid age	55 years	40 years
Muscle mass age	85 years	45 years
Prostate age	60 years	50 years
Bone age	70 years	50 years

Breaking the Aging Code

The aging code is our destiny, and it has been broken. We can live longer, look better, and feel younger by understanding our bodies as they truly are: a compilation of ages and stages. My goal for this book is to teach you how to break your own personal aging code so that when you are 40 years old, you can feel like you are just 25; or when you are 80 years old you will look, feel, and be like you are 65 or younger.

CODE BREAKER: Maybe You Were Born Old

Just as the body ages at different rates, some people are born old. You might have old bones, infertility, chronic gastrointestinal issues, obesity, or a heart condition. These are problems related to old age, and you were just genetically unfortunate to get them when you were young. I see many patients who even at age 20 have body parts that are age 40 and 50.

Right now, science has made it possible for us all to have the capability to live to be 120, but only you can determine how you will choose to live your later years. For example, do we have to lose our vitality after age 60? Does a woman's sex life have to end at 55? Do men have to become impotent or plagued with dementia as they age? The era of premature death, disease, and suffering is over, and a new era of the banishment of pain, suffering, and aging and an increased longevity has begun.

I'd like everyone to have a chance to live to 100 years of age but feel the way they did at 60 or younger. By learning how to break the aging code, you will be able to identify illness and disease in their earliest stages. You will learn how to compensate for the failure of modern medicine and coordinate your medical care from your internist to your eye doctor to your dentist, cardiologist, psychiatrist, neurologist, and nutritionist.

Amazing Age Reversals Occur When You Take Care of Your Health

Many of my patients have achieved remarkable medical miracles. These people, and hundreds more like them, are able to feel younger today, as well as get back years lost from illness and disease.

- Joe M. lost 90 pounds, quit smoking, and reversed his dangerously high cholesterol level in one year. By doing so, he increased his life expectancy by 10 years and feels younger than ever.
- Barry L. came in severely addicted to OxyContin, first prescribed to him for chronic pain a few years back. He was successfully able to kick his drug addiction with the help of GABA-boosting medications and supplements. (See Chapter 5.)
- Susie H. had been suffering from clinical depression for 20 years. She had been in and out of treatment centers and had tried almost every antidepressant in the book, all to no avail. It wasn't until I assessed her brain and personality inventories that I determined the root cause of her problem. We started fresh with a stimulant and dopamine-enhancing program, as well as a complete diet overhaul. Within a few months she told me she was happy for the first time in years.
- Mary T. had been diagnosed with heart disease and congestive heart failure and was not expected to live more than six months.

Like Humpty Dumpty her heart sat on the edge of the wall of death. I began her on a treatment program consisting of continued use of heart medications, hormone replacement therapy (HRT), nutrients, and chelation therapy. Three years later, Mary is still alive and well.

- Stuart M. was suffering from chronic lymphocytic leukemia (CLL); his white blood cell count was one million. I wondered how this man was still alive. I immediately started him on megadose vitamin C IV drips. His white blood cell count stood still as death itself was halted allowing him many more years of enjoyable life.
- Jane C. is singing the praises of my skin-rejuvenating program. At age 59 she was placed on Retin-A, Tri-Luma, skin-enhancing nutrients, and a complete internal hydration program of natural estrogen, progesterone, and low-dose testosterone and human growth hormone (HGH), as well as an intense version of my Rainbow Diet. Within six months, Jane looked as though she had a $10,000 face-lift.

Take Small Steps to Reach Lasting Change

Often, getting to a younger you takes time. You can change your health to live younger now and add years to your life by taking small, structured steps. For example, Gabrielle was 52 years old when she first walked into my office, performing her laundry list of illnesses and treatments as if she were performing a well-memorized school poem. She knew she had depression and was taking Effexor. She couldn't sleep and had tried both Ambien and Lunesta. She was having a hard time losing weight, even though she had religiously followed one popular diet plan after another. Gabrielle also knew that she had a thyroid problem and was addressing it with medication. She had cold hands and feet all the time, even in the summer months. She had high blood pressure and just found out that she had a "fatty liver" but didn't know what that meant. She had breast cysts and lumps, which were discovered at her last annual breast exam. She was taking Fosamax for her bones. Her skin was dry as parchment, even though she had tried every moisturizer available, spending hundreds of dollars on lotions from department stores, specialty stores, and the Internet.

Gabrielle thought that by taking all of these medications her health was under control, so she couldn't understand why she was still feeling so lousy. She believed that her specialists correctly identified each one of her health problems and were trying to treat her symptoms. But no one was looking at Gabrielle's aging holistically. There was no blueprint or AgePrint. Neither Gabrielle nor her physicians fully understood the relationship between hormones and her dry skin, that vitamin deficiencies were causing her breast cysts, or that there was a link between menopause and her mood. Gabrielle didn't understand that the loss of growth hormone since the age of 30 had her body creating more and more body fat, or that her bones were losing density because of her inability to produce estrogen, progesterone, testosterone, and growth hormone, and that no amount of cream was going to resolve her dry skin and wrinkles.

Luckily for Gabrielle, I recognized that many of her symptoms could be linked to menopause. Her metabolism completely shut down, and instead of living with a 52-year-old body, she had an 80-year-old waistline. In essence, she lost almost 30 years of health from one faltering organ system: the ovaries. My challenge was not only to restore Gabrielle's health so that she could retrieve those years but to turn the clock back further to extend her life. By fixing her oldest part (her ovaries) first, decoding her health crisis, and tricking her body to stop sending its death code, I knew I could restore her health. This is an important lesson because every organ goes into some type of "pause" as it gets older. Menopause is like a boulder dropped in a lake in which the waves keep battering women, aging their skin and hair, and damaging their memory, attention, and sleep cycles.

As I do with each patient, I began with my typical routine of state-of-the-art medical testing. Gabrielle underwent full-body ultrasound testing, and I discovered that there was more to Gabrielle's condition than she or her specialists were able to assess. She had a thyroid nodule; a Doppler test revealed circulatory problems. Her musculoskeletal results were very weak, and she wasn't gaining muscle mass regardless of how much she worked out. When I did her memory and attention testing, I found that she had no cognitive decline. Gabrielle was a prime example of a young brain trapped in an old, broken-down body.

Gabrielle started taking bioidentical natural estrogen, progesterone, and testosterone, which did wonders for her weight, hair loss, and lack of libido. I also put her on the hormone dehydroepiandrosterone (DHEA), which got rid of her abdominal girth, resulting in a 30-pound weight loss. I gave her N-acetyl cysteine (NAC) and alpha lipoic acid, which cleaned out her fatty liver and increased her odds of avoiding breast cancer. She took thyroxine (T4) and triiodothyronine (T3) natural thyroid hormones, which significantly improved her mood. Her poor circulation was treated with fish oils and vitamin E, which also improved her breast cysts. It took a few years for me to completely reverse Gabrielle's aging, but eventually I was able to restore her body to her age-appropriate state. What's more, her improved skin and leaner body make her look a full 10 years younger. Many patients like Gabrielle have added the controversial treatment of HGH to their regimen and have found that by doing so they were able to add pounds of muscle to their body as well as correct their adult deficiency of growth hormone.

Breaking the Aging Code for a Younger Brain

By the time Gabrielle was back to health, she was able to add as much as 15 years to her life. The same can be true for you, no matter what your illness, symptoms, or previous diagnosis. I can help get your body back to not only where it should be to match your current age, but to a younger, more vibrant place. The secret is simple: it all starts with the brain. If you have the right brain and mind-set, you can take this age-reversing program to the limit for a younger you.

Even so-called healthy aging associated with mild impairments of brain function are reversible, which controls the health of the rest of the body. The most common ailments, including osteoporosis, back pain, arthritis, heart disease, and high blood pressure, are all age-related conditions that are affected by an increasingly aging brain. Added to this list are Alzheimer's disease or dementia and other declines in faculties such as attention, cognitive flexibility, as well as depression and anxiety, addiction, and sleep disorders. Other illnesses affect the heart, immune system, male and female sexual organs, and the skin.

The latest studies, and my own patient work, have also shown that the brain can be taught to break the aging code and actually resurrect the aging body. By balancing the brain with medications, natural hormones, diet, and lifestyle changes, I help my patients delay the progression of many of these diseases so that their life can return to a more normal, age-appropriate state. It's a simple remedy: to restore your health, restore your brain chemistry. And the earlier you start, the better your chances of postponing or completely avoiding the ravages of the aging process.

For example, Alzheimer's disease doesn't occur overnight. Just like heart disease, it's a condition that begins slowly and silently progresses over the years. You already know that if you keep your cholesterol low, you'll reduce the risk of heart attack and stroke. Similarly, if you address those first lapses of memory, there's a chance that you won't totally lose cognitive function later on in life. I have successfully used the same approach for the reversal of such chronic degenerative diseases as osteoporosis, heart disease, high blood pressure, elevated cholesterol, arthritis, and even cancer.

CODE BREAKER: Old Brains Affect Your Personality

If any of your personality traits intensify, it means your brain's aging code has started to advance. For example, if a giving person becomes too giving all the time, his brain chemistry might be challenged. If an aggressive person is too aggressive all the time, her brain code has become distorted. Much like a baseball pitcher who overworks his arm, living too much in one personality pattern gives you a sore brain.

How This Book Works

I have developed a simple system that can teach you everything you need to know to create a younger you. You will be able to connect all your health issues into one solid program of reversal and rejuvenation, returning your body and mind to its optimal state.

Part 1 explains in detail how the brain and body function together to both create and end illness. Through one easy quiz called the AgePrint, you will be able to recognize which part of your body is the oldest and learn how it is affecting your total health. With this information, you can begin treating your illnesses immediately and correctly. The younger body is achieved by knowing your AgePrint and testing for health issues *at the first sign of symptoms,* or even before you become symptomatic. As you've seen, medical miracles can happen, but it's much easier to live longer when you can begin reversing age and disease at the earliest opportunities.

Part 2 discusses how an aging brain affects the rest of the body and how an aging body affects the brain. What's more, I will show how each of the most prevalent diseases ultimately affects the rest of the body; if you can restore your brain power and speed and control your major illnesses, the more minor symptoms will also disappear. There is a simple electronic brain code that, when working properly, keeps you at a normal weight, keeps you thinking clearly, helps you stay calm, and maintains the right balance for your moods and sleep cycle.

The rest of the book highlights the proper medications, hormone therapies, nutrients and supplements, diet, and lifestyle changes to reverse each of the aging systems. Many of my patients have graciously agreed to share their stories so that you can learn from their successes. With this information, you can begin to restore your health and prevent future problems from occurring. Once you begin to treat your oldest part, you'll quickly see how much better the rest of your body and mind feels.

The Promise of a Beautiful You

A younger you will come from achieving a younger brain and coordinating its care with your younger body. You will be a more beautiful you, inside and out. You will be able to coordinate your health care. You will be able to multimodally handle your diet, exercise, and nutritional program and integrate them in a cohesive fashion, so you are not focusing on purchasing the most expensive skin creams while you are dying of cancer inside. If you are not internally young, then you are not truly young or healthy.

Please join me on this adventure in finding the younger, most beautiful you!

PART 1

What's Your AgePrint?

1

Breaking Your Aging Barrier

A wise man once said that the art of living was to survive for as many years as possible. I would modify those clever words to say, "to be able to live a healthy, happy life for as many years as possible." The goal of science and medicine today is not just to live long lives but to live in full health.

We all want the same thing: to enjoy our lives at our peak performance every day. Yet this can mean something different for each of us. Some search for true happiness, some strive for physically beautiful faces and bodies, while others may be working hard toward athletic prowess and strength. Whatever the case, all these states can be summed up in one single word: *youth*. A younger you is a more powerful, quicker, healthier you. No matter how you feel today, a better, healthier, and younger you is achievable.

My goal for each of you is to be able to look and feel 15 to 25 years younger. We've all heard that in today's business world, 50 is the new 30. Well in my office, 50 is the new 35, and 85 could be the new 60! Anyone can look and feel younger. My patients have learned to take care of themselves at the slightest onset of illness. They stop the aging process in their oldest parts as soon as changes occur. And because they are on top of their health, they continue to feel young all over. What's more, their trimmer bodies and supple skin—both mirrors for the internal workings of the mind and body—continue to radiate with a youthful glow.

You're Only as Young as Your Oldest Part

As we age, our bodies deteriorate. We used to think that this weakening was due to the illnesses we were experiencing, but now the scientific community believes that it is just a factor of age. Yet the outcome is the same: any illness that is caused by aged, weakened organs or systems subtracts from our overall well-being and eventually leads to death. I refer to these failing organs as experiencing "pauses": the time markers that identify the wear and tear of every part of the body. Women are familiar with the term *menopause*, which is the model for this theory. Like menopause, all of the pauses occur along with diminishing hormonal production.

During these pauses, the failing organ, or part, becomes older than the rest of your body. At the same time, its associated hormone levels drop, sending a signal or code to the rest of the body whose purpose is to broadcast that the system is failing. This signal also begins the process whereby the whole body will begin to shut down. In essence, when diminished, the hormones of life and the electrical signals of the brain send a wrong or "anti"-signal to the rest of the life.

Aging occurs throughout the entire body through the following codes:

- Biopause: The brain loses its chemical messengers called neurotransmitters.
- Electropause: The brain loses processing speed.
- Cardiopause: The heart rate increases when pumping efficiency decreases.
- Vasculopause: Blood vessel diameter decreases.
- Immunopause: The immune system weakens.
- Thyropause: The thyroid system weakens.
- Menopause: Hormone loss in women starts.
- Andropause: Hormone loss in men starts.
- Osteopause: Bones lose density and become brittle.
- Somatopause: Muscles lose strength and tone.
- Dermatopause: The skin loses collagen and elasticity.

The Pauses and Aging

Our body parts will not pause at the same time. For example, a cardiologist treats a patient with coronary artery disease because her heart has become older than the rest of her organs. When a doctor works on a hip or diagnoses osteoporosis these bones have become old. For a patient with these problems, his heart can be 50 years old, his bones 60 years old, yet his chronological, or real, age and the rest of the body is only 40 years old. Figuring out the *AgePrint* requires us to start by first fixing the oldest part, or identifying the oldest failed system that has paused.

Today's most innovative medical research has finally come to recognize that the most successful way to achieve total health and extend life is to prevent internal aging from occurring. The key then to a younger you are the tests that detect symptoms before a health problem hits you, instead of waiting for medical and surgical intervention. Every aging code currently known is reversible in its early stages. I know of no aging signal that has not been reversed. Can we reverse them all at the same time? It's beginning to happen now.

A Younger You = DNA + the Power of the Brain

Understanding DNA has been an important scientific breakthrough because it is the map to the mind and body. This code identifies and predicts which familial traits and illnesses have been handed down to you. The pauses can be partially determined by our heredity. Our ancestors may have suffered from the illnesses we currently have and passed down their genetic code to us. Our DNA controls how we will emotionally and physically deal with these illnesses. But DNA offers limited information. Genetic testing is mostly valuable for the young, not for the old. By the time we are old, we have already developed into our medical destiny.

A younger you begins with understanding what we're made of so that we can make the necessary fixes. Once we know our DNA, we can work with the one organ that controls all health: the brain. To prevent or reverse aging and sickness, we need to control and enhance the electrical signals that are sent from the brain to the body. The key then is keeping your brain young so that you can have a younger body and a more beautiful you, improving on your DNA and repealing its forecast.

Is Disease All in Your Head?

Brain-body medicine has changed the way we think about and ultimately diagnose disease. The irritable bowel syndrome you thought you had can now be traced to an anxiety disorder; the dementia your grandmother suffered from may have been undiagnosed depression; the carbohydrate addiction you once faced turned out to be a dopamine imbalance; or the fibromyalgia your uncle was diagnosed with was a result of a serotonin deficiency. All of these conditions can improve once the source of the problem is recognized.

Change Your Brain, Change Your Body, Change Your Life

Your skin is repairable, and all your organs are replaceable with transplants or pills. But the complete human life is the brain. The brain is the source of life and is divided into three parts: the cerebrum, brain stem, and cerebellum. The cerebrum is further divided into two hemispheres that are linked by a thick band of nerve fibers called the corpus callosum. These hemispheres have identical areas that are designated as "lobes." Each lobe instructs our bodies to perform specific functions and control the automatic processes such as breathing, heart rate, and digestion, and formulates our total health by managing all our internal systems.

You can think of your brain as a circuit box inside the walls of your home. When you want to turn a light on, you plug in a lamp, and the electricity transfers from the circuit box into the lamp. In much the same way, the brain performs four functions. It generates and sends an electric current throughout your entire body, fuels your internal systems, and orchestrates your health.

The Brain Controls the Body

The following four functions are coordinated by four individual neurotransmitters, or biochemicals, that each dominate in specialized locations within the brain. These measurements determine the relationship between brain function or life and the creation and delivery of human electricity.

- **Voltage:** Voltage measures power, the intensity at which the brain responds to a stimulus, and the effectiveness of the brain's ability to process information. This information can be cognitive as well as physical. For example, voltage determines your metabolism, how your body processes food, and the various states of consciousness, ranging from fully alert to deep sleep. It also controls how you choose to meet your emotional/physical needs. Voltage is controlled by the neurotransmitter **dopamine**, the brain's natural amphetamine.

- **Speed:** Speed measures how fast we think or process information. The speed of your brain determines how quickly the electrical signals are processed. By increasing your brain speed you can improve memory, attention, IQ, and even your behavior. Brain speed is governed by the neurotransmitter **acetylcholine**.

- **Rhythm:** Rhythm measures the balance between the two hemispheres of the brain. A balanced brain creates and receives electricity in a smooth, even flow. When the electricity is generated in bursts, it is called an arrhythmia, and it signifies the beginning of brain dysfunction. Rhythm determines how you handle life's stresses. When your rhythm is affected, you might feel anxious, nervous, or irritable. What's more, rhythm also influences how acutely you feel pain.

When you are out of rhythm, you can be irregular anywhere, such as in your bowels, lungs, or joints. The signal is transferred to the body through the neurotransmitter **GABA**.

• **Synchrony:** The electricity that your brain creates moves through your body in waves. There are four types of brain waves, each providing us with a level of consciousness. Synchrony balances the movement of these four brain waves across both hemispheres. When they are out of balance, you will experience sleep disorders during the night and depression and fear during the day. Lack of sleep can exacerbate any disease in our body, triggering the cycle of inflammation. **Serotonin** is the biochemical that affects synchrony.

The Stages of Diseases

All diseases occur in stages. Each stage represents a slightly older you. Small biochemical and cellular changes occur initially that blood testing may pick up. Then structural changes occur that radiological scanning can pick up. Next, physiological changes occur in the body. It is not until the disease is so far progressed that a human physician can pick up the changes.

A Faulty Brain Code Accelerates Aging

Subsequently, each biochemical also controls the related main age accelerators. For example, dopamine controls the brain's voltage, or power. This is related to the rest of the body in terms of metabolism, which regulates our weight. When our dopamine levels fall, we can become overweight, sending a code to the rest of our body to begin the pauses, and a cascade of health symptoms begins. Our heart now needs to work harder to function properly; our digestive system becomes stressed, leading to diabetes; cholesterol builds in our vascular system;

our immune system becomes compromised; depression mounts as we cannot lose weight; and our sex drive diminishes because we have no energy or libido.

Each of the biochemicals works in much the same way. They each control a few specific age accelerators. When out of balance, they can wreak havoc on the entire body, as shown here.

Brain Age Accelerators	The Effect on the Body
Dopamine	Obesity, addiction, fatigue
Acetylcholine	Dementia, Alzheimer's disease, learning disorders
GABA	Anxiety, pain, mood swings
Serotonin	Depression, sleep disorders, fears

Your Lifestyle Is Hazardous to Your Health

While it is best to limit unhealthy behavior, if you are having trouble with any of these age accelerators—excessive weight, addiction, anxiety, depression, lack of sleep, or thinking decline—you can bet it will take away 7 to 10 years of your life *and* will exacerbate any current medical conditions you have.

Your Hormones and the Brain Code

The brain regulates, translates, and interprets its code as hormonal output from the various other organs of the body. After the age of 30, the brain code becomes less effective in sending messages to the other organs to produce hormones. This forces the organs themselves to age. We start to lose our health in small steps, just like taking a walk down a flight of stairs. For example, growth hormone production diminishes at age 30; by age 40 progesterone begins to decline and women begin to lose estrogen and men lose testosterone; then we lose DHEA, and calcitonin. The order of these losses, as well as the exact timing, will vary from one individual to another. Yet the more we age the more hormones we lose. Our organs get to a point where they can no longer produce a particular hormone on their own. Without supplementation, that organ will die and drag the others down with it. The brain tries desperately to resurrect the dying parts of our body by sending more and more electrical signals to the pituitary gland, which begins to secrete all sorts of stimulating hormones to our body parts such as the ovaries, testicles, adrenal glands, pancreas, and liver in an attempt to save it. Until you begin to take bioidentical hormones, the entire cascade will continue.

Conversely, the aging of various organs directly affects the workings of the brain. For example, Alzheimer's disease and senility are both related to the loss of acetylcholine, the biochemical that controls hydration. When this occurs, the brain literally dries out, its speed diminishes, and the brain ages faster than the rest of the body. We now know how to stop the process.

Typical Chronological Age	Hormone Changes
Age 30	Human growth hormone (HGH)
Age 40	Testosterone, estrogen, progesterone
Age 50	DHEA, thyroid
Age 60	Insulin, parathyroid
Age 70	Calcitonin, erythropoietin

Aging can be like falling down a descending hormonal flight of stairs. Supplements can reverse the "fall of aging."

Boosting Your Brain

When optimally functioning, the same four neurotransmitters are also the great age decelerators. By boosting each of them, you can build up your brain power, speed, synchrony, and rhythm. By increasing your dopamine, you can achieve weight loss; by increasing acetylcholine, you can improve your memory; by increasing serotonin, you can give yourself, and your brain, the rest you deserve.

What's more, the latest medical studies suggest that the brain can be taught to reignite your hormone systems and actually resurrect the aging body. Increased amounts of these biochemicals can send new messages to the body to produce more hormones. By regulating this connection, we can delay—or possibly even stop—the premature aging of the brain or body. We can teach the body to restore health in affected areas and enhance health in the organs and systems that have not been damaged. Like walking back up this same flight of stairs, each step that reverses this process becomes a code breaker. By taking these small steps, you can become younger.

You are only one program away from becoming a younger you. Once you recognize when your pauses are occurring, you can take control of the aging process.

The human body works in real time, and at this point we cannot turn back the clock and completely eliminate each and every problem. However, we can stop these pauses from progressing, and in many instances, with proper treatment, reverse their effects on the mind and body.

Any single pause has the ability to take 10 to 20 years off your life. For example, a "healthy" 50-year-old man might "suddenly" have a heart attack. However, the pause model proves that when it comes to our health, nothing just "happens." Instead, this man was in "cardiopause" for many years and just didn't know it. While his chronological age was 50, he was living like an 80-year-old because of the age of his heart. What's more, his disease wasn't sudden; it was just not detected early enough. The makings of heart disease can be brewing in your body for decades. Everyone who faces a titanic crisis of health had many opportunities with early diagnostics to stop the illness in its tracks. Unfortunately most of us are not made aware of the opportunities of preventive medicine. By checking aging codes in each of the organs or symptoms before symptoms occur, you can reverse the codes. Most diseases progress by 80 percent before anyone notices them.

The earlier you start to deal with aging, the better results you will achieve. What's more, if you can detect each of the pauses before symptoms occur, and keep each organ as well as your brain young, you will get total health. By following my protocol, together we can get you to look and feel younger.

Step 1: Early Testing and Diagnosis Is the Key

You may not know it, but by the time you are 30, one part of your body may already be breaking down. You won't feel this breakdown happening, but it is and the only way to find it is with diagnostic screening tests. Specific blood tests, ultrasounds, cognitive tests, and other scans that can detect disease in its earliest stages before symptoms occur are available today in doctors' offices. The goal in my office is to find aging organs before they damage the rest of the body, treat them, and reverse aging to make you look and feel younger. Each abnormal test, symptom, or illness is an aging code that signals the death process to a part of the body; then the whole begins to die.

Most doctors do not perform sufficient testing, which leaves their patients vulnerable to all sorts of deadly surprises. But in my new paradigm of preventive medicine and with the currently available and advanced diagnostics, we can obtain the aging code of almost every part of your body.

The first step to becoming younger is to assess your current health and determine which of the pauses you may be experiencing. The quiz in Chapter 2 is all you need to determine your unique AgePrint. This simple quiz will assign an age—or AgePrint—to every part of your body. The AgePrint can identify your oldest parts and see which ones are creating your cascade of poor health. The oldest part is your weakest link and would require immediate treatment.

Reversing One Pause Results in a Domino Effect to a More Abundant Life

With this information, you and your doctor will be able to work together not only to identify the source of the problems you are experiencing today but to predict what will happen to your health in the future. What's more, your doctor will be able to correctly treat your subsequent symptoms and illnesses more efficiently. For example, my patient Marty was 40 years old when he came in with the beginning stages of andropause. His symptoms included hair loss on various parts of his body, erectile dysfunction, fatigue, and a decreased libido, all of which most men usually do not experience until they are in their 50s. After taking the quiz, Marty realized that his AgePrint for andropause was 55. By following the rest of the Younger You program, Marty was able to increase his testosterone production and delay the progression of andropause. In time, his body returned to a more normal, age-appropriate state in many ways.

Do You Know Your Real Age?

Many of you may already have a good idea what's aging you. Take the test anyway, just to confirm your suspicions. And if you can't automatically identify your oldest part, and you believe that you are in good health already, the AgePrint becomes more important than ever.

Step 2: The Best Treatment Is the Right Choice

Once you've identified your AgePrint, you can begin to address your pauses in the right order. The approach is not one size fits all. Some people respond best to traditional drug regimens, while others will improve through different therapies. I'm a huge proponent of finding the right treatment for each patient. This can range from creative uses of medications to hormonal therapies, nutrient supplementation, or even physical tools. Or, the best option might be a combination of many therapies. This is called a *multimodal approach*.

The choice of treatments is best left for you and your doctor to decide together. Don't disregard traditional medicine as a viable option. My choice is based on 30 years of experience, and a basic rule for me is to try to kill two problems with one stone. For example, an individual with a sleep problem in conjunction with depression should choose an anti-depressant and nutrients that help both sleep and mood. And it does not stop there. If you can select a hormone, a medication, and nutrients that help three or four problems, then you've addressed a far greater issue. Throughout this book, I've outlined dozens of treatment options for each of the pauses for you and your doctor to evaluate.

Step 3: Natural Hormone Therapies Support Longevity

A younger you depends on maintaining appropriate hormone production and, in many cases, boosting your existing levels to those of a younger age. The good news is that a decline of any hormone is neither irreparable nor permanent. In fact, the fix is often easy and painless. Through natural hormone supplementation, we can trick the body into thinking that the organ that produces this particular hormone has not died. Over time, the organ's death sequence slows and then eventually, with total repair, stops.

Multimodal Means a Younger You

Over and over I see the same basic trends; my patients who beat their illness and got younger were the ones who followed a multimodal treatment approach. Besides taking their medicine, they diligently used nutrient and natural supplements, natural hormone replacement therapy, as well as dietary and lifestyle changes.

For example, human growth hormone (HGH) supplementation is one of the biggest breakthroughs in antiaging medicine and may well be the medical community's proverbial fountain of youth. Thousands of studies confirm that raising HGH levels can help prevent and even reverse the aging process. Raising HGH levels has also been known to reverse a decline in memory and cognitive performance, as well as create sharper vision and improved sleep.

Bioidentical Hormones Don't Cause Cancer

Synthetic estrogen has been linked to cancer, as have other pharmaceutical hormones such as methyltestosterone, diethylstilbestrol (DES), conjugated estrogens, medroxyprogesterones, cadaver growth hormones, and birth control pills. Natural, bioidentical hormones, on the other hand, are much safer and generally not linked to cancer at all. These are often plant-based hormone supplements with the exact same molecular structure as those that come from the human body and have the same effect on our bodies as the ones we naturally produce. What's more, I also believe that a lack of hormones can also cause cancer. With age, virtually every hormone decreases and yet cancer increases. The loss of hormones results in a distortion in your DNA copying mechanisms, and, combined with radiation and environmental toxins, all contribute to cancer.

Bioidentical Means Resurrection of Dead Body Parts and Reversal of the Aging Code. I believe that bioidentical hormone therapies are probably the most integral antiaging tool necessary to combat each one of the aging codes. Most of these bioidentical hormones are not new on the market; they have been available for more than 20 years and are so lacking in side effects that they are frequently sold over the counter as supplements, including vitamins D_2 and D_3, pregnenolone, progesterone, DHEA, and melatonin.

Stop Horsing Around. Women are routinely given estrogen supplements made from horse urine (Premarin) for treating menopause or as birth control pills. But would you take a horse's skin for your skin graft? Why would you use horse urine to supplement your estrogen? The Younger You Plan insists on going bioidentical whenever possible.

There is no match between a horse and a human. Introducing the wrong type of hormone in the human body can be dangerous. With bioidentical hormones, there is a perfect match, human to human. The structures of bioidentical hormones are identical to those of the actual hormones produced by the human body.

Stay away from nonbioidentical hormones, such as:

- Methyltestosterone
- Diethylstilbestrol (DES)
- Conjugated estrogens
- Medroxyprogesterones
- Cadaver growth hormones
- Birth control pills

Reverse aging with these bioidentical hormones:

- Androstenedione
- Calcitonin
- Dehydroepiandrosterone (DHEA)
- Erythropoietin
- Estradiol
- Estriol
- Estrone
- Human growth hormone (HGH)
- Hydroxycortisol/aldosterone
- Insulin-like growth factor (IGF)
- Incretin (at least 50 percent bioidentical)
- Insulin
- Melatonin
- Parathormone
- Pregnenolone
- Progesterone
- Testosterone
- Thyroid: T3, T4
- Vitamins D_2, D_3

Step 4: Supplementing with Nutrients Does Make a Difference

Nutrients and supplements are essential tools for becoming a younger you. They can increase your brain power and speed, as well as address specific illnesses. Throughout the rest of this book you will find information on which supplements are right for each of the pauses and the quantities you need to take them in. You'll also see lots of overlap, where some nutrients can benefit many pauses at the same time. For example, a recent study showed that children and adults who were frequently given vitamin D not only had better muscle strength and exercised more vigorously, but also had even fewer diagnoses of fibromyalgia. Vitamin D has been shown to benefit your skin, protect your bones, and enhance your immune system.

You can boost your vitamins in one of two ways. First, you can increase your intake of specific vitamin-rich foods. Or, you can supplement vitamins in pill form or in teas. Each pause requires specific dosages, so you will need to determine a reasonable method to get the right amounts of these nutrients. The fresh foods we buy are often drained of important nutrients, mostly because the soil they are grown in has been depleted. That's why supplementing with vitamins is such an important part of my program.

Zinc Is an Aging Code Breaker for All the Pauses

Certain nutrients are pause busters that reverse aging all over the body. Take, for example, zinc. This essential mineral is naturally found in every cell in the body, and it stimulates the activity of more than 100 enzymes.

Supplementing with additional zinc can create good health all over. The latest research shows that zinc can protect us against specific immune diseases, such as esophageal cancer. Individuals who suffer from gastroesophageal reflux disease, or GERD, have a higher incidence of developing esophageal cancer and should take at least 15 milligrams of zinc daily. Zinc has also been found to impact the secretion of growth hormone in children when administered in the first three years of life.

I have been prescribing zinc for more than 20 years, and it was a significant focus of my research done with the late Carl Pfeiffer, M.D., Ph.D. Furthermore, my clinical work with Robert Atkins, M.D., and Carlton Fredericks, M.D., had further validated the use of zinc for a variety of medical illnesses. I consider the essential nutrient zinc to be a super aging code buster because it is able to achieve all of the following:

- Maintains a healthy immune system
- Accelerates wound healing
- Maintains sense of taste and smell
- Maintains sight
- Helps synthesize DNA
- Supports normal growth and development
- Helps sperm develop
- Promotes ovulation and fertilization
- Protects against prostate problems
- Helps protect against cancer
- Helps decrease cholesterol deposits
- Is good for hair and skin health
- Helps preserve mental faculties in the elderly
- Detoxifies and removes lead, cadmium, aluminum, and other toxins

Want Smart Children

Fish oils are another super nutrient pause buster. Unlike zinc, fish oils are obviously not something the body naturally produces. Instead, beneficial fish oils come from cold-water fish, such as mackerel, salmon, black cod, albacore tuna, sardines, and herring. The active ingredients in fish oils are essential fatty acids known as omega-3 fatty acids. Fish oils benefit both adults and children, and it's never too late to begin supplementing these additional nutrients. But what if you, or your children, won't eat fish? Not to worry. You can purchase these powerful brain-boosting oils in convenient, easy-to-swallow capsules.

CODE BREAKER: Vitamins and Supplements Are Almost Never Recalled

Occasionally, supplements have been recalled, as in the case of tryptophan, when a single manufacturer produced a contaminated batch. However, I know of no other vitamin recalls that amount to the drug recalls like Rezulin, Baycol, cytisus solution (for cataract surgery), Bextra, Seldane, Vioxx, Diethylstilbestrol (DES), and thalidomide.

These oils have been used for many years (remember cod liver oil?) in helping to prevent heart disease, increase circulation, and lubricate joints. Recent studies also show that fish oils can boost mental processing by increasing acetylcholine, dopamine, and serotonin levels in the brain.

CODE BREAKER: Nutrient Supplementation Is Now More Important than Ever

The nutritional content of our fruits and vegetables has declined over the past 50 years. To ensure that you're getting what you need, supplementing may be the way to go. For example:

- The amount of vitamin C in fruits and vegetables has dropped 20 percent.
- Riboflavin, or vitamin B_2, has fallen 38 percent.

Step 5: Adopt the Rainbow Diet

Often, simply by adjusting your diet, you will be able to get larger amounts of important vitamins and minerals that are key to younger living. A diet high in colorful fruits and vegetables has been shown to provide many benefits to your overall health. The Rainbow Diet offers high-nutrient, low-density menu options. It is considered to be a volumetric food plan that offers high-nutrient, low-density foods and is based on eating the right amounts of vitamin-rich, colorful fruits, vegetables, spices, teas, whole grains, and lean proteins in any given week. While this is not a typical weight-loss regimen, following the Rainbow Diet will get you back on track to making healthier, more natural food choices that are both good for you and lower in calories than processed junk foods.

I have identified a wide array of foods and supplements that benefit many parts of the body. Even if your AgePrint is normal, you can still benefit from eating Rainbow foods by following the diet's guidelines and increasing the nutrition in every one of your meals. If your AgePrint shows pauses that require reversing, I will teach you how to incorporate the concepts of the Rainbow Diet so that it directly relates to your specific AgePrint. You'll see that certain nutrients are directly correlated to reversing each pause. You will learn how to choose the right foods and prepare delicious and healthy meals, while reversing your AgePrint and generally contributing to a younger you.

Creating a Rainbow Plate

The Rainbow Diet allows for all foods that are low fat, complex carbohydrates, and lean proteins that occur in any of the colors of the rainbow, except for white, since there is no white color in the rainbow. Each of your three meals, plus one snack, should be at least 80 percent plant based and no more than 20 percent animal based. Your plate should always look like a rainbow: not too much of any one color and always a variety. All of your food choices and supplements should be from natural food sources and organic when possible.

By eliminating extreme foods, this diet does not allow any white foods: no salt, white sugar, white salt, white flour, soy milk, white rice, white potatoes, or white pasta. Instead of white foods, choose more colorful versions:

- Instead of white rice, choose brown rice.
- Instead of white sugar, try brown sugar or honey.
- Instead of white potatoes, eat sweet potatoes and yams.
- Instead of white flour, use whole-grain flour.
- Instead of salt, season your meals with spices.

Rules of the Rainbow Diet

1. Most of your meals should contain a variety of brightly colored foods.
2. Don't skip meals. Eat three evenly spaced meals a day, plus one late-morning or late-afternoon snack. Make sure to finish your dinner in time to have three full hours to digest before going to bed.
3. Avoid canned foods.
4. Avoid saturated fats.
5. Read labels carefully; some "fat-free" foods are high in sugar and salt.
6. Avoid pickled and smoked foods.
7. Choose lean meats, and trim fat wherever possible.
8. Increase your fiber intake.
9. Drink a variety of colored teas.
10. Drink only fresh-squeezed juice, not from concentrate.
11. Drink eight glasses of water each day.
12. Avoid processed foods, such as white flour, salt, sugar, and soft drinks.
13. Eat yogurt daily.
14. Chew raw, crunchy foods such as celery, carrots, apples, and pears to feel satisfied.

Top 20 Rainbow Antioxidant Fruits and Vegetables

Red	Cranberries, raspberries, cherries, red beans, beets
Orange	Sweet potatoes, oranges, orange bell peppers
Yellow	Squash, artichokes, yellow bell peppers
Green	Kale, spinach, broccoli, green bell peppers
Blue	Blueberries, grapes
Indigo/violet	Prunes, blackberries, plums

The Natural Colors of the Rainbow

Studies show that increasing your fruits and vegetables while lowering overall calorie consumption is the best way to lose weight. The following is a comprehensive list of color-coded fruits and vegetables, along with their power nutrients.

Reds. Many red foods contain antioxidant compounds that protect your body from the damaging effects of free radicals. The red pigments protect your blood vessels, cartilage, tendons, and ligaments from damage. These pigments may reduce the likelihood of cancer by preventing tissue degeneration that sometimes follows chronic irritation.

Cranberry	Anthocyanins, quercetin, resveratrol
Red cabbage	Anthocyanins, glucosinolates, indole-3-carbinol, lutein
Red globe onions	Allyl propyl disulfide, fructooligosaccharides, glucosinolates, pectin, quercetin
Red peppers, all varieties	Capsaicinoids, carotenoids
Red potatoes	Catechols, chlorogenic acid
Tomatoes, all varieties	Beta-carotene, chlorogenic acid, citric acid, fructooligosaccharides, lycopene, malic acid
Red apple, all varieties	Caffeic acid, chlorogenic acid, d-glucaric acid, ellagic acid, ferulic acid, pectin, quercetin
Red bananas	Fructooligosaccharides, pectin, potassium
Raspberries	Anthocyanosides, ellagic acid
Strawberries	Anthocyanosides, ellagic acid
Red cherries	Anthocyanosides, ellagic acid, malic acid
Red grapefruits	D-glucaric acid, lycopene, naringin, naringenin
Red grapes	Ellagic acid, lycopene, oligomeric proanthocyanidins, pectin, resveratrol

Watermelon	Cucurbocitrin, lycopene
Rhubarb	Anthraquinones, emodin, ferulic acid
Kidney beans	Galactomannans, lectins, protease inhibitors

Orange. Orange fruits and vegetables are high in carotenoids, which have anticancer and antioxidant properties. Carotenoids lead to an increase in the number of white blood cells circulating throughout the bloodstream, having basically the same effects as the well-known immune booster echinacea. Try to eat at least two to three different orange foods daily.

Carrots	Alpha-carotene, beta-carotene, lignin, lutein, lycopene, mannitol, pectin, xanthophyll
Spanish onions	Allyl propyl disulfide, fructooligosaccharides, glucosinolates, pectin, quercetin
Parsnips	Furocoumarins
Pumpkin	Alpha-carotene, beta-carotene, lutein, zeaxanthin
Sweet potatoes	Alpha-carotene, beta-carotene, chlorogenic acid, lutein, protease inhibitors
Apricots	Alpha-carotene, beta-carotene, cryptoxanthin, lutein, lycopene, zeaxanthin
Calimyrna figs	Furocoumarins, lignin
Mangoes	Alpha-carotene, anacardic acid, beta-carotene, cryptoxanthin, ellagic acid, lutein, zeaxanthin
Casaba	Beta-carotene, lutein, zeaxanthin
Crenshaw	Beta-carotene, lutein, zeaxanthin
Nectarines	Beta-carotene, cryptoxanthin, lutein, zeaxanthin

Oranges, all varieties	Beta-carotene, cryptoxanthin, cyanidin, delphinidin, d-glucaric acid, hesperidin, tangeretin
Tangerines	Beta-carotene, hesperidin, nobiletin, tangeretin
Peaches	Alpha-carotene, lignin, lutein, zeaxanthin
Kumquat	Citric acid
Pumpkin seeds	Cucurbitin

Yellow. Yellow fruits and vegetables contain large amounts of phytochemicals including allicin, as well as carotenoids and bioflavonoids, which have anticancer and antioxidant properties. Try to eat at least two to three different yellow foods daily.

Yellow snap beans	Alpha-carotene, coumestrol, lignin, lutein, quercetin
Corn	Lutein, zeaxanthin
Cashew nuts	Anacardiol, fatty acids
Walnuts	Alpha-linolenic acid, linoleic acid, phytosterols
Peanuts	Isothiocyanates, resveratrol, saponins
Chickpeas	Gamma tocopherol, protease inhibitors, saponins
Yellow globe onions	Allyl propyl disulfide, fructooligosaccharides, glucosinolates, pectin, quercetin
Pineapple	Bromelain, protease inhibitors
Yellow bell pepper	Beta-carotene, capsaicin, capsanthin, capsorubin, cryptoxanthin, lutein, lycopene
Golden zucchini	Beta-carotene
Butternut squash	Alpha-carotene, beta-carotene, lutein, zeaxanthin

Bananas	Fructooligosaccharides, pectin, potassium
Golden apples	Caffeic acid, chlorogenic acid, d-glucaric acid, ellagic acid, ferulic acid, pectin, quercetin
Grapefruit	D-glucaric acid, lycopene, naringin, naringenin
Lemons	Citric acid, citronellal, diosmin, limonene, p-coumaric acid
Papayas	Ellagic acid, lutein, papain
Jerusalem artichokes	Inulin
Soybeans	Alpha-linolenic acid, beta-sitosterol, daidzein, gamma tocopherol, genistein, isothiocyanates, phosphatidylcholine
Sesame seeds	Sesamin, sesaminol
Pine nuts	Fatty acids
Macadamia nuts	Monounsaturated fatty acids

Green. Chlorophyll, present in all green plants, has anticancer and detoxifying properties. Green fruits and vegetables are high in lutein and indols, which are currently being studied for their antioxidant properties. Green leaves are high in carotenoids, bioflavonoids (bonus vitamins and minerals found in many foods that naturally reduce inflammation), vitamins, and organic mineral complexes. It is recommended that you eat at least one serving daily of green, leafy vegetables.

| Artichokes | Apigenin, caffeic acid, chlorogenic acid, cosmoside, cyanidine, cynarin, cynaropicrin, cynaroside, hesperidoside, hesperitin, inulin, luteolin, maritimein, mucilage, pectin, quercetin, rutin, scolimoside |
| Asparagus | Asparagosides, zeaxanthin |

Green snap beans	Alpha-carotene, coumestrol, lignin, lutein, quercetin
Italian green beans	Alpha-carotene, coumestrol, lignin, lutein, quercetin
Fava beans	Beta-carotene, protease inhibitors, saponins
Lima beans	Alpha-carotene, gamma tocopherol, lutein, protease inhibitors
Broccoli	Glucobrassicins, indole-3-carbinol, isothiocyanates, quercetin, sulforaphane
Brussels sprouts	Alpha-carotene, coumestrol, dithiolthiones, isothiocyanates, lutein, protease inhibitors
Cabbage, all varieties	Glucosinolates, indole-3-carbinol, lutein
Celery	Coumarins, lutein
Cucumbers	Protease inhibitors, silicon
Fennel	Beta-sitosterol, coumarins, limonene, pectin, stigmasterol, terpineol, urease, volatile oils
Turnip greens	Beta-carotene, calcium, iron, folacin, vitamin C
Collards	Beta-carotene, calcium, iron, folacin, vitamin C
Kale	Alpha-carotene, beta-carotene, indoles, isothiocyanates, lutein, quercetin, sulforaphane, zeaxanthin
Dandelion greens	Lactucin, lactupicrin, taraxacin
Mustard greens	Isothiocyanates, lutein, zeaxanthin
Lettuces, all varieties	Alpha-carotene, lacturcarium, lutein, vitamin K, zeaxanthin
Leeks	Allicin, allylic sulfides
Okra	Mucilages, pectins

Green bell peppers, all varieties	Beta-carotene, cryptoxanthin, lutein, lycopene
Spinach	Alpha-carotene, beta-carotene, caffeic acid, coumestrol, ferulic acid, lutein, neoxanthin, zeaxanthin
Chives	Beta-carotene, fumaric acid, sulfur
Zucchini	Beta-carotene
Green apples, all varieties	Caffeic acid, chlorogenic acid, d-glucaric acid, ellagic acid, ferulic acid, pectin, quercetin
Avocados	Beta-sitosterol, glutathione, mannoheptulose
Plantains/bananas	Gums, mucilages
Green grapes, all varieties	Ellagic acid, pectin, resveratrol
Kiwi	Actinidin, alpha-carotene, beta-carotene, lutein, zeaxanthin
Limes	Bioflavonoids, citral, citric acid, furocoumarins, nobiletin
Pears, all varieties	Citric acid, pectin
Mung beans	Protease inhibitors

Blue. Many of these foods contain anthocyanins and phenolics, two powerful phytochemicals currently being studied for their antiaging benefits. Blue fruits and vegetables are extremely high in antioxidant compounds that protect your body from the damaging effects of free radicals.

Black radishes	Diastase, gallic acid, methanethiol, pelargonidin, protease inhibitors, sulforaphane
Blueberries	Anthocyanidins, anthocyanosides, ellagic acid, myrtillin
Blackberries	Anthocyanidins

Dark grapes, all varieties	Ellagic acid, lycopene, oligomeric proanthocyanidins, pectin, resveratrol
Currants	Anthocyanidins, anthocyanosides, ellagic acid
Black beans	Galactomannans, protease inhibitors
Black walnuts	Alpha-linolenic acid, linoleic acid, phytosterols
Brazil nuts	Alpha-linolenic acid, ellagic acid, lignin, selenium

Indigo/Violet. Similar to blue fruits and vegetables, indigo and violet also contain an abundance of antioxidant compounds. Dark blue and indigo foods reduce "oxidative stress," one of the main factors that causes aging. They also contain high levels of resveratrol, believed to reduce the risk of heart disease and cancer.

Purple wax beans	Alpha-carotene, gamma tocopherol, lutein, protease inhibitors
Beets	Betaine, fumaric acid, glutamine, succinic acid
Purple broccoli	Glucobrassicins, indole-3-carbinol, isothiocyanates, quercetin, sulforaphane
Red cabbage	Anthocyanins, glucosinolates, indole-3-carbinol, lutein
Chinese purple eggplant	Anthocyanidins, coumarins, gallic acid, protease inhibitors, saponins
Purple kale	Alpha-carotene, beta-carotene, indoles, isothiocyanates, lutein, quercetin, sulforaphane, zeaxanthin
Turnips	Glucosinolates, indoles, isothiocyanates, phenethyl isothiocyanate, sulforaphane

Ruby seedless grapes	Ellagic acid, lycopene, oligomeric proanthocyanidins, pectin, resveratrol
Plums, all varieties	Alpha-carotene, beta-cryptoxanthin, lutein, malic acid, pectin, zeaxanthin
Prunes	Alpha-carotene, beta-cryptoxanthin, lutein, malic acid, pectin, zeaxanthin
Passion fruit	Anthocyanidins, harmala alkaloids
Purple artichoke	Apigenin, caffeic acid, chlorogenic acid, cosmoside, cyanidine, cynarin, cynaropicrin, cynaroside, hesperiodoside, hesperitin, inulin, luteolin, maritimein, mucilage, pectin, quercetin, rutin, scolimoside

Fiber

Our digestive systems need 40 to 45 grams of fiber per day to function properly. We can get our fiber from a variety of sources, including fruits, vegetables, breads, and cereals. Check labels for fiber content in baked goods, and choose breads, cereals, and pastas made from whole grains. Leafy greens, root vegetables, beans, and lentils are all good sources. Other recommended fiber-abundant foods are quinoa, millet, bulgar, buckwheat, seeds, and nuts. Seaweed, wild cold-water algae, dark leafy greens, organic produce, and properly prepared grains are good sources of trace minerals. Eat seaweed and algae every day. Add seaweed and leafy greens to every pot of soup or vegetable dish you make.

Rainbow Grains

Amaranth	Calcium, fiber, folacin, iron, phosphorus, potassium, protein, vitamin B_6, zinc
Arborio rice	Iron, zinc, folacin, niacin, phosphorus
Corn pasta	Folacin, high-protein fiber, potassium, vitamin B_6, zinc

Couscous	Folacin, high-protein fiber, potassium, vitamin B$_6$, zinc
Egg pasta	Folacin, high-protein fiber, potassium, vitamin B$_6$, zinc
Hulled barley	Fiber, magnesium, phosphorus
Millet	B vitamins, copper, iron, phosphorus
Oat bran	Iron, magnesium, phosphorus
Oat groats	Iron, magnesium, phosphorus
Orzo	Folacin, high-protein fiber, potassium, vitamin B$_6$, zinc
Brown rice	Folacin, iron, niacin, phosphorus, zinc
Quinoa	Folacin, iron, magnesium, phosphorus, potassium
Roasted buckwheat groats	B vitamins, copper, iron, magnesium
Rolled oats	Iron, magnesium, phosphorus
Saffron pasta	Folacin, high-protein fiber, potassium, vitamin B$_6$, zinc
Soy pasta	Folacin, high-protein fiber, potassium, vitamin B$_5$, zinc
Steel-cut oats	Iron, magnesium, phosphorus
Thin egg noodles	Folacim, high-protein fiber, potassium, vitamin B$_6$, zinc
Unhulled barley	Fiber, magnesium, phosphorus
Wehani rice	Folacin, iron, niacin, phosphorus, zinc
Wheat flakes	Folacin, iron, magnesium
Wheat pasta	Folacin, high-protein fiber, potassium, vitamin B$_6$, zinc
Wild pecan rice	Folacin, iron, niacin, phosphorus, zinc

Keep the Color Alive with Tea

Tea can stimulate digestion, cleanse the body, and give you lots of energy. These are all necessary treatments for every aging part of your body. What's more, there are 4,000 bioflavonoids found in different types of herbal and caffeinated teas. These bioflavonoids slow down your biological clock. Tea is also packed with polyphenols; the darker teas have much higher concentrations, which offer higher antioxidant values. I often combine two or three teas to get the most color and therefore the most benefit. For example, I brew a combination of red rooibos, blueberry, and green tea.

A Rainbow Brew of Tea
- Red: cranberry
- Orange: passion, ginger, orange spice, orange pekoe
- Yellow: chamomile, lemon
- Green: green tea
- Blue: blueberry tea
- Indigo: holiday spice tea
- Violet: raspberry

Blandness Is Killing Us: Spice It Up!

A diet high in simple carbohydrates—white flour, white salt, and processed food—is literally aging us. We are getting all the bulk without the nutrients, plus cravings. The key to a younger you is to incorporate more color onto your plate; color equals nutrients, antioxidants, and bioflavonoids.

Every little bit of color counts. For example, herbs and spices are packed with aging code–busting nutrients that can add color, flavor, and vitamins to many of your blandest dishes. Herbs and spices contain antioxidants and antibacterial factors to help maintain health. What's more, spicy foods boost your metabolism, so you'll burn calories quicker and more efficiently.

Incorporate these herbs and spices to get the healing power of the Rainbow Diet:

- The anti-inflammatory power of rosemary and basil
- The dementia-fighting power of cumin and sage
- The obesity-fighting power of cayenne and cinnamon

- The sugar-regulating powers of coriander and cinnamon
- The calming effects of lemongrass, nutmeg, bay leaves, and saffron
- The cancer-fighting power of turmeric
- The fungus-beating power of oregano
- The heart-pumping power of garlic, mustard seed, and chicory
- The skin-saving power of basil and thyme
- The immune-fighting power of turmeric, basil, thyme, saffron, and ginger
- The "blues"-busting power of coriander, rosemary, cayenne, and black pepper
- The blood-sugar-regulating power of allspice and cinnamon

Step 6: Antiaging Physical Exercise

Thirty minutes of exercise is all it takes to reverse aging and get younger. In their book *YOU: The Owner's Manual*, Drs. Michael Roizen and Mehmet Oz outline specific exercise regimens that are fun and easy to follow. They are also appropriate for all ages. This book is a great resource for that information. Take your AgePrint from the quiz in Chapter 2 into account, and discuss an exercise regimen with your doctor before you begin. Make sure to balance your exercise routine with aerobic, weight-bearing, and relaxation exercises, such as meditation.

Exercise Reverses All of Your Aging Codes

Dopamine	Combats obesity; improves blood sugar and balance
Acetylcholine	Improves memory, concentration, and overall cognition; increases blood flow to the brain
GABA	Relieves anxiety and stress; helps regulate breathing; reduces pain
Serotonin	Improves quality of sleep; combats depression

> ### Keys to Success: Exercise Raises the Fire with the Right Dopamine Program!
>
> Exercise increases dopamine, and dopamine increases your desire to exercise, which raises overall energy in the body. The more you exercise, the more your body thinks it's alive and the more you shut off the death codes.

The aging heart	Increases circulation throughout the body; lowers heart rate and blood pressure; increases pumping power of heart; dilates blood vessels
Low immune system	Reduces cortisol levels, strengthening the immune system and fighting cancer
Sexual dysfunction	Increases sexual stamina; increases blood flow to the sexual organs; increases production of sex hormones
Weak bones and muscles	Improves muscle strength and joint mobility; increases bone density; reduces risk of muscle injuries; improves muscle-fat ratio
Aging skin	Increases circulation to the skin; cleanses pores via perspiration

The Younger You Plan

All of antiaging medicine is based on the ideals of preventive treatment. Every disease has many stages and frequently what is called prevention is in reality early disease reversal.

Yet this doesn't mean throwing a bunch of darts at a target, hoping one of them will make the bull's-eye. Prevention is not about taking handfuls of vitamins, hoping that you'll feel better everywhere. So many preventive measures have been given a bad rap by the media because they are often overprescribed to a general population that doesn't need them. For example, you don't need to take prostate supplements unless you have a family history of prostate disease or if you have an enlarged prostate. If your AgePrint for andropause is normal, you don't need to treat it.

This book is not about fixing what's not broken; I do not believe in the "handful of vitamins" approach to "overall" better health. Instead, it's about taking the right supplements to reverse a pause you know you have because you took the AgePrint test. By the age of 30, there should be at least one or more parts of your body that are now 40. Most women have some menopause symptoms, whether it is drier skin, changes in concentration, or changes in sleep cycles. And even though other parts might be 20, you should focus on the part that is the oldest. Furthermore, by following up with your doctor, you might end up starting on a low dose of progesterone at 40 years old to counter the first stages of perimenopause, which is also helping to prevent later bone density loss.

Then you will follow a targeted effort in which we will repair this oldest part. Early disease repair involves sticking to the Rainbow Diet, evaluating your mental and emotional states, recognizing positive and negative personal relationships, following an exercise plan, and retaking your AgePrint test on the yearly basis.

Even with all these fixes, you will see other parts getting old that you will have to fix. We will continue to get chronologically older, but we don't have to live like old people. We won't be able to delay menopause, but we will be able to optimally control and reverse your symptoms.

2 + 2 = 5

Every time you fix one pause and one set of aging code, particularly in the brain, you are reversing your entire AgePrint. You've turned back the clock. Once you fix two or three pauses, the results are even more astonishing. As Dostoevsky said, 2 + 2 = 4 is nice, but 2 + 2 = 5 is more interesting. For example, I once had a patient, Joan, who came in complaining of a recent loss in the ability to achieve orgasms. I found that she was experiencing the early stages of menopause as well as somatopause. I was able to improve Joan's estrogen levels to deal with her menopause and improve DHEA and growth hormone levels. Soon Joan reported that her orgasms returned, and she was sleeping better. Better still, her memory and attention had improved.

The Rainbow Diet Cuts Your Appetite

Rainbow foods are nutrient dense with fewer empty calories than processed food. Brightly colored fruits, vegetables, grains, herbal teas, and spices are what make you feel satisfied and less likely to binge later.

By fixing her menopause and somatopause, I was able to provide a great lift on her brain-processing speed, attention, mood, and ultimately sleep. Two plus two actually then starts to multiply exponentially and synergistically. Joan's mobility improved, as did her endurance, coordination, and confidence. All of a sudden, her blood pressure started to drop as she began to lose weight.

Antioxidant Breakthrough

Though you probably haven't tasted one, wolfberries have the highest antioxidant value known to man. Oxygen radical absorption capacity (ORAC), a test that quantifies the antioxidant capacities of foods, measures wolfberries at a value of 25,000, whereas blueberries (the second-highest antioxidant food) are a mere 2,400! Wolfberry juice is available at select natural food stores and, of course, via the Internet.

You can achieve lasting, total health. The next step is to begin the Younger You Plan by finding out your unique AgePrint. Then start making small changes by incorporating treatment options one at a time.

2

The AgePrint Quiz

Knowing the age of every part of your body will help you choose the right health path. You need to prioritize based on your oldest parts.

You Are a Chain: Let's Find the Weakest Link

By the time we are 50, most of us will have gone through at least one, if not several, pauses. By age 40, we will begin to experience the ramifications of at least one pause sending aging codes throughout the body. Even at age 30, partial pauses begin to have significant impact on our well-being, energy, and health. Virtually every medical condition has a 10- to 20-year antecedent—you don't just fall apart overnight. For example, if you have been overweight for 20 years, you can be certain that your heart is not optimally functioning; it's had to work two or three times harder than it normally would if you were of average weight. If your bones have always broken easily, you are developing osteoporosis. These are all considered to be personal weak links. So if you are 50 years old, you didn't get there without some of these weak links getting older first. Make no mistake; those old sections and weak links will suck you into getting older still.

Physicians were not trained to think of aging as the first stage of disease. Detection of pauses can be tricky, and the chance of picking up something like ovarian cancer via a regular physical exam is slim. For example, not long ago I met with 50-year-old Cameron B. and noticed immediately that he had a large neck for someone of his frame. I asked him if he had ever been treated for thyroid problems, and he told me that his previous doctors had tested him, but the results were negative. I was not satisfied with that answer, and I decided that an ultrasound was warranted. His scan detected a mass in his neck. I sent Cameron for more advanced testing, where it was found that he was in the early stages of thyroid cancer. A surgeon removed his thyroid and, luckily, Cameron is alive today. I'll never forget the endocrinologist who called me and asked, "How did you know to do an ultrasound? No matter how many times I feel his neck I cannot detect his cancer." I said to my fellow colleague jokingly, "Don't you know that your fingers along with a stethoscope will be hanging in a museum of ancient, archaic medical devices?" This is the age of computers. This is the electrical age. This is the brain age of a new wonderful younger you where electronic machines are the servants of our well-being.

That's why everyone in my office receives what I call a "Star Trek" physical. These advanced diagnostic tools provide me with the clues I need to develop the right treatments for each patient. This type of physical exam provides the best, most accurate information for any condition. For example, BEAM testing can help to detect Alzheimer's disease and memory loss even before symptoms present. Through BEAM technology we can uncover, diagnose, and treat the imbalances associated with Alzheimer's disease, depression, insomnia, and schizophrenia. A DEXA scan can detect the beginning stages of osteoporosis in individuals as young as 10. Ultrafast, CT and angiography, and PET scans can detect heart disease or lung cancers almost instantly.

Head-to-Toe Ultrasounds

Ultrasound is superior in every way to a physical exam. Physicians who do examinations of the human body miss things on a regular basis. Although an MRI may be better at finding multiple sclerosis and certain cancers, a CAT scan is better at finding lung tumors and bleeds in the brain. A PET scan may find tumors better. But no imaging technique is equal to the ultrasound in terms of its global general review.

Nothing covers more areas of the body and identifies more diseases than a head-to-toe ultrasound. Here's an example:

- **Transcranial ultrasound**'s abnormal findings (increased velocity of the blood flow) could be due to vascular spasm or blockage.
- **Carotid ultrasound** shows early changes in blood flow, intimal thickening, or advanced atherosclerotic disease (blockages).
- **Thyroid ultrasound** shows goiterous changes, enlarged thyroid, masses, nodules, calcifications, cysts, or atrophy even in patients with a normal physical exam (except for enlarged thyroid).
- **Echocardiogram** will reveal heart size (all four chambers), early or advanced valvular disease, ejection fraction, changes in wall motion as a sign of previous or current heart attack and heart failure, or early changes in heart appearance due to increased alcohol intake or increased blood pressure.
- **Breast ultrasound** is the best test to find breast cysts. It also shows nodules, masses, and calcifications at times in patients with a negative breast exam.
- **Abdominal ultrasound** shows an enlarged liver and spleen at times in patients with normal physical exams or in obese patients; it finds early changes of alcoholic hepatitis, fatty liver, gallstones, gallbladder wall thickening, liver cyst, hemangiomas, other benign tumors and cancer, calcifications, cysts/calcifications of pancreas, enlargement, or atherosclerotic changes in abdominal aorta.
- **Renal ultrasound** shows kidney stones, cysts, or tumors, often as an accidental finding in patients without complaints; fluid collection in kidneys (hydronephrosis); or enlargement or kidney atrophy.
- **Pelvic ultrasound** shows uterine enlargement, fibroids, changes in ovaries (increased size, cysts, tumors), prominent endometrium, cervical cysts, fluid collection due to advancing ovarian cancer, or increased bladder size and stones.

- **Prostate ultrasound** shows size of prostate, its nodules, calcifications, mass, bladder size and function, or presence of residual urine in patients with enlarged prostate and at times in patients with normal DRE.
- **Scrotal ultrasound** shows size of testicles and epididymis, presence of varicocele, spermatocele, calcifications, or tumors at times not found on physical exam.

The AgePrint

Even with all of the latest technologies, every experienced doctor must first rely on patient information to assess physical conditions. You can accurately determine your organ pauses and aging codes as well as the age of each of your systems by creating your AgePrint. This simple quiz will help you determine not only which pause(s) might be affecting your health, but what stage they have reached. The results from the quiz assign an approximate age for every organ and system of the body.

Blood work as well as additional testing performed at a doctor's office can easily confirm your findings and is recommended once you have made your initial determinations. While this book is an important first step, I urge you to seek the care of a physician in terms of making conclusive decisions about your health.

Ignorance Will *Not* Be Bliss in 25 Years

Make sure you do an AgePrint every year. Call it your other checkup. You may have to check some parts of your body more frequently than others if, for example, you know that you have diabetes or another chronic condition. Having a better sense of the body causes people to work on their health, whether they have issues with glucose levels or bone density. In the words of Maya Angelou, "Once you knew better, you did better."

The AgePrint Quiz: Know Your Real Age at Every Part

By completing this simple questionnaire, you are on your way to identifying your personal core markers of aging. Are you at risk for obesity, chronic fatigue syndrome, or an addiction to food, cigarettes, or alcohol? Will you develop an anxiety disorder or Alzheimer's disease? Will you get depressed or have sleep problems? Is your heart losing pumping power, or is valve damage occurring? Are you developing cancer or autoimmune disease? Will you lose your libido or develop a big belly from loss of testosterone? Will you get osteoporosis or lose your memory from menopause? Will your skin start to wrinkle, or will you start to lose your hair before you are ready? By assessing your health today, your AgePrint will help you determine, and reverse, your pauses for a younger future.

AgePrinting Identifies If You Were Born Old

Your DNA may have preprogrammed you to have osteoporosis. That is why AgePrinting of all the organs is most useful when done at an early age, so you can work with your DNA and get younger. For example, if the proper treatments are implemented before osteoporosis sets in, we can prevent osteopause from ever occurring, reversing the fact that your bones were born old or with a predestination to be old.

Instructions

This quiz should not take more than 15 to 20 minutes but requires concentration. Try to take this quiz in one sitting. Find a time and a place that is as stress free as possible, away from distractions, noise, or other activities. Check your physical state. Postpone taking the quiz if you feel particularly out of sorts or if you're not well rested or well fed.

Each of the following questions can be answered as either true or false. Try not to think too long on any one question, but answer with regard to how you feel most or all of the time. There are no right answers to this assessment. Remember, we all have weak links, and we are all experiencing one pause or another.

If you want real insight into your overall health, answer the questions truthfully. It would be more astounding to find out that you are not experiencing any pauses than if you found out that you were. Some of the questions pertain to specific diagnoses you might have had. Make sure to check your medical records, ask your physician, or check the Internet if any terms are unfamiliar to you.

Scoring

Give yourself 1 point for every true response. Then total your points at the end of each section. Add a 0 to your total score: this is your AgePrint for that biological system. For example, if your score in the first section is 3, your AgePrint for brain power is 30. If your AgePrint is younger than your chronological age, you're in good shape. If your pause age is older than your real age, you need to carefully consider treatment. The earlier you treat each of your failing age pauses, the better.

The section with the highest points will be your oldest part, which should be addressed first. After you've seen results by following a particular treatment regimen described in this book, take the test again to see what other areas of your health can be improved. You may see that when one set of aging codes is adjusted, other areas of your overall health may benefit as well.

Group 1: The AgePrint of Your Brain
Electropause: The Pausing of Your Brain's Electrical Chemistry

Dopamine: Brain Firepower
1. I have gained more than 20 pounds since I was 20 years old. T/F
2. I am a smoker. T/F

3. I know I need to exercise, but I don't have the energy
   to do it. T/F
4. I overeat when I am stressed. T/F
5. I have problems staying focused at home or at work. T/F
6. I can never seem to get enough sleep. T/F
7. I need to have at least one cup of coffee to jump-start me
   in the morning. T/F
8. I have no sex drive. T/F
9. I have been diagnosed with heart disease. T/F
10. I drink more than three alcoholic beverages per week. T/F

Number of true responses: _____ ; add 0 to number = dopamine
age code: _____

(See Chapter 3.)

Acetylcholine: Brain Cognition

1. My friends have told me that I'm becoming
   absentminded. T/F
2. I have experienced hair loss. T/F
3. My ability to remember faces has decreased. T/F
4. I need to write down even the simplest lists, directions,
   or instructions. T/F
5. My ability to recall numbers has decreased. T/F
6. My memory has decreased. T/F
7. My management skills have decreased. T/F
8. I don't feel like my brain is working well. T/F
9. Alzheimer's and/or dementia runs in my family. T/F
10. I often forget where I put important things, like keys or
    prescription medications. T/F

Number of true responses: _____ ; add 0 to number = acetylcholine
age code: _____

(See Chapter 4.)

GABA: Brain Stability

1.	I often feel heart palpitations.	T/F
2.	As I get older, my patience is diminishing.	T/F
3.	My muscles feel tenser than ever before.	T/F
4.	I frequently have back pain.	T/F
5.	I am constantly on edge.	T/F
6.	I have high blood pressure.	T/F
7.	I tend to worry more than I used to.	T/F
8.	I get angry at the smallest incidents.	T/F
9.	I sometimes experience seizures.	T/F
10.	I have mood swings.	T/F

Number of true responses: _____; add 0 to number = GABA age code: _____

(See Chapter 5.)

Serotonin: Brain Serenity

1.	I find it harder to stay asleep at night.	T/F
2.	I'm never very hungry, although sometimes I find myself eating more than I should.	T/F
3.	I don't do the activities I used to enjoy.	T/F
4.	I used to be a risk taker, but now I have trouble making decisions.	T/F
5.	I find myself thinking about the same things over and over again.	T/F
6.	I feel that the world is passing me by.	T/F
7.	I can't handle crises.	T/F
8.	The smallest problems make me scream.	T/F
9.	I have frequent thoughts about suicide.	T/F
10.	As a young adult, I was told I was moody.	T/F

Number of true responses: _____; add 0 to number = serotonin age code: _____

(See Chapter 6.)

Group 2: The Overworked Cardiovascular System

Cardiopause: The Slowing and Aging of the Heart

1. I have swollen legs. T/F
2. I experience shortness of breath when I exercise. T/F
3. I often experience light-headedness. T/F
4. I have been told that I have a heart murmur. T/F
5. I have difficulty breathing when lying down. T/F
6. I have a rapid heartbeat. T/F
7. I am always tired during the day. T/F
8. I have a cough that does not go away. T/F
9. I have experienced pain, discomfort, heaviness,
   and pressure in my chest. T/F
10. My lips are often a bluish color. T/F

Number of true responses: _____ ; add 0 to number = cardiopause age code: _____

(See Chapter 7.)

Vasculopause: The Aging of the Peripheral Vascular System

1. I have had blood clots. T/F
2. I have cold hands and feet. T/F
3. I see more veins on my legs than I used to. T/F
4. My ankles, on occasion, swell. T/F
5. I have had ulcers on my lower legs. T/F
6. I have dry, thin, flaky skin. T/F
7. My nails are soft and brittle. T/F
8. The skin on my lower legs has turned to a darker or
   reddish shade. T/F
9. I have lost hair on my lower legs. T/F
10. I experience pain in my calves when I walk. T/F

Number of true responses: _____ ; add 0 to number = vasculopause age code: _____

(See Chapter 8.)

Group 3: Modulating Systems

Thyropause: A Weakening Metabolism and Associated Conditions

1. I have an enlarged neck.   T/F
2. I feel weak and fatigued most of the time.   T/F
3. I have a greater sensitivity to cold.   T/F
4. I have delayed reflexes.   T/F
5. I have been told that I am anemic.   T/F
6. I have a slow heartbeat.   T/F
7. My metabolism has slowed with age.   T/F
8. (For women) My periods are heavier than they used to be.   T/F
9. I am often constipated.   T/F
10. I am often hoarse.   T/F

Number of true responses: _____; add 0 to number = thyropause age code: _____

(See Chapter 9.)

Immunopause: Aging of the Immune System

1. I have noticed more warts or cysts on my body.   T/F
2. Cuts or bruises seem to take longer to heal.   T/F
3. My blood works shows a deficiency in T cells.   T/F
4. I have a persistent cough that won't go away.   T/F
5. I have had frequent ear or sinus infections.   T/F
6. I have bloating or fullness in my abdomen that isn't
   related to food.   T/F
7. I have seen blood in my urine.   T/F
8. I have had pain in my hips, spine, or ribs.   T/F
9. I often need to regulate my bowels with laxatives.   T/F

Number of true responses: _____; add 0 to number = immunopause age code: _____

(See Chapter 10.)

Group 4: Aging Sexuality

Menopause: For Women Only

1. My nails are weaker and chip or split more often.   T/F
2. My vagina is dryer than it used to be.   T/F
3. I lose lots of hair each week, and it feels more brittle than before.   T/F
4. My breasts have begun to sag.   T/F
5. I have hot flashes during the day.   T/F
6. I rarely feel like having sex.   T/F
7. My doctor has prescribed estrogen, progesterone, testosterone, or DHEA supplements. Subtract 1 point if these substances are natural.   T/F
8. I am experiencing the beginning stages of osteoporosis or height loss.   T/F
9. I can't remember details as well as I used to.   T/F
10. I have begun to have night sweats.   T/F

Number of true responses: _____; add 0 to number = menopause age code: _____

(See Chapter 11.)

Andropause: For Men Only

1. When I have sex, it takes me a long time to achieve an orgasm.   T/F
2. I carry my excess weight directly on my abdomen.   T/F
3. I have diminished sex drive.   T/F
4. I have thin arms and legs.   T/F
5. I have noticed that my ejaculate is diminished.   T/F
6. I do not need to shave as often as when I was younger.   T/F
7. I have lost hair on my body.   T/F
8. I notice that my neck is getting wider and broader.   T/F
9. My doctor has told me my testosterone level is diminished.   T/F

Number of true responses: _____ ; add 0 to number = andropause age code: _____

(See Chapter 12.)

Group 5: Musculoskeletal Aging

Osteopause: The Aging of the Bones and Loss of Bone Density

1.	I experience pain in my hips and knees.	T/F
2.	I have been diagnosed with osteopenia or osteoporosis.	T/F
3.	I have lost inches off my height over the years (take your height measurements now to find out).	T/F
4.	I have broken a bone in the past.	T/F
5.	I have a history of either curved spine or hunchback and/or curved posture in my family.	T/F
6.	I have weighed less than 110 pounds as an adult.	T/F
7.	I have abused recreational steroids in the past.	T/F
8.	(For women) I have missed my period for more than a year. (For men) I think about having sex fewer than two times a week.	T/F
9.	I have suffered from an eating disorder that caused me to lose an excessive amount of weight.	T/F
10.	I have fair skin and light eyes.	T/F

Number of true responses: _____ ; add 0 to number = osteopause age code: _____

(See Chapter 13.)

Parathyropause: The Brain-Bone Calcium Connection

1.	My eyebrows are thinning.	T/F
2.	I feel anxious more frequently.	T/F
3.	I have blurry vision.	T/F
4.	I have been told that I have cataracts in my eyes.	T/F
5.	I fall often.	T/F

6. I feel sluggish most of the time. T/F
7. I have been told that my personality has changed. T/F
8. My muscles twitch at times. T/F
9. I often have yeast or candida infections. T/F
10. My doctor has told me that my reflexes have diminished. T/F

Number of true responses: _____; add 0 to number =
parathyropause age code: _____
(See Chapter 13.)

Somatopause: Aging of Muscles and Loss of Muscle Mass

1. I have started to get wrinkles. T/F
2. My hair and nails are not growing as fast as they used to. T/F
3. My friends have far fewer gray hairs than I have. T/F
4. My skin is thinning. T/F
5. I am not as tall as I used to be. T/F
6. I am not as agile as I used to be. T/F
7. I am not as strong as I used to be. T/F
8. I have problems opening jars or carrying heavy loads. T/F
9. I have gained body fat, especially around my waistline. T/F
10. I have been told that my cholesterol is high. T/F

Number of true responses: _____; add 0 to number = somatopause
age code: _____
(See Chapter 14.)

Group 6: Changes to the Skin

Dermatopause: Aging of the Skin and Loss of Collagen and Structure

1. My skin is beginning to sag. T/F
2. I have many wrinkles. T/F
3. My skin does not appear as supple as it used to. T/F

4. I have age spots, skin discolorations, spider veins, or
   red spots.   T/F
5. I have external cysts, lumps, or bumps.   T/F
6. My skin has lost its glow.   T/F
7. I have been diagnosed with skin cancer.   T/F
8. The skin under my neck is noticeably sagging.   T/F
9. I have jowls.   T/F
10. I have spent much of my life in the sun without proper
    protection.   T/F

Number of true responses: _____; add 0 to number = dermatopause age code: _____

(See Chapter 15.)

Your Personal AgePrint

Record your age code scores in the following chart. You are creating your own AgePrint, which is as individual as you are. After six months of following the advice in this book, take the test again and see if any of your age codes have changed. Mark your worst age codes (highest numbers) for each of the intervals, and note if these change as well. By following the suggestions outlined in the rest of the book, you will be able to chart the dramatic improvements you'll see and feel in every aspect of your health.

If any one of your age codes is more than 20 years older than your actual age range, consider yourself in a severe health category and make an appointment to see your physician. If your electropause age in any of the first four categories is 90 or more, no matter what your true age, you are in a health crisis. See your doctor and a corresponding specialist immediately.

Going Forward

The remainder of the book will focus on each of the pauses. You will learn when they are most likely to occur and what the most common

AgePrint Worksheet

	Initial Age Code	6 Months Later	9 Months Later	One Year Later	18 Months Later
Dopamine					
Acetylcholine					
GABA					
Serotonin					
Cardiopause					
Vasculopause					
Thyropause					
Immunopause					
Menopause					
Andropause					
Osteopause					
Parathyropause					
Somatopause					
Dermatopause					

symptoms or related conditions are. You'll also learn about the necessary testing and all modalities of treatment.

The fix occurs in both the brain and body. Not only do your electrical signals need to be alive and firing appropriately, but your body needs to be in tip-top shape as well. That's the definition of reversing aging: learning the tools to enable your brain and body to function optimally even as you advance in age.

Keeping Your Brain Alive Slows Down the Pauses

Damaging your brain through illness in the body will speed up the pauses. For example, testosterone deficiency can be found in stressed men as early as age 20 or 30. Men can go into andropause between 40 and 80 depending on their brain health. While menopause is genetically programmed, the wide range of onset and progression depends on brain status. When brain stress is high, women can go into premature menopause.

Skip Ahead to Your Oldest Part

Once you have mastered controlling your brain's speed and power, you can then tackle the pauses. Read through the chapter that correlates to your primary pause. Then read through your next highest age code, until you have balanced each of them. Along the way, record your progress in the chart and congratulate yourself on the changes you'll be making toward a younger you!

Multiple Miniature Pauses

Old age can mean needing a set of repairs, and you may have to take the test frequently to uncover how each organ is doing. There are many other organs in the body not discussed in this book. To find out if your gastrointestinal system is aging or if your sensory system is weakening, go to our website (pathmed.com) and take the full AgePrint quiz. Here is a table of the other pauses not discussed in this book.

Pause	Decline in	Age	Aging Code Measurement	Reversal Formulas
Psychopause	Personality, attention, IQ, memory, and mood	50–60	Symptom checklists of major personality or psychiatric problems	Brain chemistry, neuro-feedback, and exercises for the mind
Pinealpause	Sleep depth, REM sleep cycle where repair occurs	5–10	Melatonin blood and urinary levels	Supplemental melatonin and tryptophan precursor therapy
Pituitarypause	Hormone and glandular health	After 50	LH/FSH blood levels	Hormone replacement
Sensorypause	Hearing, sight, smell, touch, and taste	After 50	Decreases in each of the five senses	Hormones, zinc, niacin, bilberry
Pulmonopause	Lung elasticity and compliance	40	Decreased score of lung function test	NAC, DHEA
Gastropause	Nutrient absorption; gastric acidity; absorption of calcium, folate, niacin, and vitamins B_1, B_2, and B_{12}	30	Blood levels of amino acids, fatty acids, vitamins, minerals, and trace elements	Nutrients
Adrenopause	DHEA	20	DHEA/DHEAS cortisol levels	Hormone replacement
Nephropause	Kidney function	40–50	Erythropoietin and creatinine levels	Hormone replacement and low-protein diet
Insulopause	Glucose tolerance and growth hormone levels	40	Obesity and increased glucose levels	Hormone and dietary changes
Uropause	Bladder control and infection resistance	40–50	Pelvic ultrasound, PSA levels, and urinalysis	Hormonal treatments and use of prostate-based nutrients
Genopause	DNA, base pair health	20	Purine degradation products	Antioxidants

PART 2

Your Brain Is the Key to a Younger You

3

Dopamine: Improving Brain Firepower

Brainpower is the fire that keeps your mind alive, awake, alert, and aware. However, when your brain is not producing enough dopamine, brainpower diminishes and you spiral down into a low-energy state. Without the brainpower that dopamine provides, you'll notice that your body begins to slow down in every imaginable way. At first, you might feel fatigue, look pale, or even experience light-headedness. Then more complicated symptoms arrive, including a decreased libido, sexual dysfunction, weight gain, and difficulty performing the most routine tasks. You may also experience a decreased level of energy for physical activity or even self-destructive thoughts.

Feeling tired all day is often too much to bear. Fatigue is a serious medical problem and a huge age accelerator. We seem to know this inherently because when we feel tired, we tend to respond; to compensate for a loss of energy, we unknowingly find ourselves self-medicating with food. Your brain and body begin to crave the energy they lack, and you become attracted to foods that will offer a similar energy rush, namely sugary foods, simple carbohydrates, and caffeine. Before you know it, you've gained weight and are literally addicted to these junk foods; without them, you'll feel the symptoms of withdrawal. And each time you turn to them, you'll need larger quantities to keep your energy and dopamine levels high. You may never overdose on comfort foods the way you can on cocaine, but the results of a food addiction are equally dangerous. Obesity, after all, is the number-one age accelerator.

Fatigue Is an Age Accelerator

The fact is a simple one: as you age, you will feel tired. Your dopamine production slows, your metabolism decreases, and you lose energy. Feeding your energy need with food only slows you down more. When fatigue is combined with illness and general aging, you have a recipe for disaster.

The good news is that we can restore your energy so you won't feel as tired. For example, Richard S., a 58-year-old male, came to me complaining of constant daytime fatigue. He was 5'10" and weighed 220 pounds. He described having shortness of breath, sexual dysfunction, and a lack of energy that was decreasing his quality of life. His body mass index (BMI), a score that is the ratio of weight to height, put him in the obese range. Yet, in a very short time he was able to get his body fat down to 12 percent by following the guidelines I've outlined in this book. Within a few months, Richard's fatigue had greatly diminished.

YOUNGER YOU FACT: Obesity Patients Get Bad
Medical Care

Physicians continue to get obesity all wrong. Worse, they don't treat heavy patients the same way they treat those who are fit. A recent survey of physician attitudes showed that they often characterize heavier patients negatively and—without looking at their dopamine levels—blame them for their lack of self-control. We know that obesity is not about lack of control but a serious brain metabolic disorder that can be treated and reversed, so that you can get the best possible medical care in the future.

My original research and a national conference done in conjunction with Kenneth Blum, Ph.D.; Nora Volkow, M.D. (the current head of the National Institute of Drug Abuse); and Ernie Noble, M.D. Ph.D. (former head of the National Institute of Alcohol Abuse) linked obesity to a loss of brain voltage and dopamine-affected genes.

Being overweight sends a code out to every part of the body, indicating that it is time to age. This code will strike at your weakest link, perhaps, for example, s triggering the development of cancer in your liver, which has been consumed with fat. Or your arteries might become clogged from fat, leading to a heart attack. As a result of the fat cells accumulating in your body with obesity, some signals will be sent out as your health starts to deteriorate. You might develop anxiety, depression, a heart condition, or insomnia; whatever the symptom, obesity could well be the cause.

Childhood Obesity: The New Epidemic

The Centers for Disease Control reported that 28 percent of high school kids and 33 percent of low-income children in New York State between the ages of two and five are overweight or at risk. The number of prescriptions for children with diabetes has doubled in just the past four years.

The Dangers of Low Dopamine Levels

Low dopamine levels affect every pause in your body. This is one of the most powerful age accelerators, sending a code to the rest of the systems in your body that it's time to stop functioning. Lack of dopamine can cause a cascade of poor health in every part of your body. The following pauses may be triggered by conditions that result from a dopamine deficiency:

• **Cardiopause:** The aging heart affects the rhythm of your heart by disrupting its electrical signals. The weight gain and fatigue that result because of a lack of dopamine raises your blood pressure, causing strain on the heart as it has to work harder than it used to. What's more, poor food choices because of this lack of dopamine can lead to fatigue, high cholesterol, and high blood pressure, further affecting the vascular system by clogging blood vessels all over your body, leading to plaque and blockages, and stroke.

• **Immunopause:** The immune system is like the sanitation engineers of the body, going around and cleaning up the garbage that makes you sick. When it's compromised by excess weight caused by a lack of dopamine, it loses the ability to do this job properly. This is where all the "-itis" diseases start: sinusitis, arthritis, dermatitis, to name a few. Once all the "-itises" cast their spell, the bones, muscles, joints, and skin all decline in a secondary cascade reaction. The excess fat interferes with the immune system's ability to fight viruses and bacteria and to recognize and regulate our own cell overgrowth. Our bodies are constantly making precancerous cells that we have to control as we try to grow and repair. Obesity also accelerates every form of cancer in every organ, be it your brain, bladder, prostate, ovaries, colon, lungs, or thyroid.

• **Menopause:** A lack of dopamine might actually accelerate the onset of menopause so that heavier women may begin menopause earlier. Remember, hormonal loss is a major age accelerator, so early menopause would begin a second cascade of spiraling health as well as the more recognizable symptoms and conditions. For example, you may experience either hair loss or increased hair growth, often in unsightly spots, particularly the face. Excessive weight gain, fatigue, disturbed sleep cycles, depression, anxiety, and addiction—all a result of a dopamine deficiency—can each cause a loss of sexual interest and feelings of low self-worth. Early menopause may also occur in women who are too thin.

• **Andropause:** For men, obesity resulting from a lack of dopamine can make detecting prostate cancer more difficult and results in a faster loss of genital size, sexual dysfunctions of all types, and loss of libido. Do you need a better reason to "just say no" to beer and chips on game day?

- **Osteopause:** Fat seeps into your bones during the development of osteoporosis, replacing normal bone. As a result of obesity, your bone structure thickens, making it all the more difficult to lose weight. Your skeletal structure was not meant to hold excess weight, and without a proper level of dopamine, you'll feel the pain this burden causes on your back, knees, and hips, accelerating arthritis.

- **Dermatopause:** An increased size literally stretches your skin, damaging its texture. As anyone who has gained and lost weight knows, stretch marks are a constant reminder of your once larger size. Couple obesity with smoking, and dry skin and even psoriasis often show the world that your dopamine voltage is off. You can easily spend $30,000 in plastic surgery with face-lifts, brow-lifts, butt-lifts, and so forth when you only need to increase the levels of dopamine when you are younger to avoid much of the physical look of aging.

Staying Youthful Means Staying Thin

Just controlling your weight takes 10 to 15 years off your AgePrint. A Twinkie might satisfy your sweet tooth, but it can't give you precious years with your loved ones.

Aging Leads to Obesity

Just as lower brain energy affects the rest of the body, the rest of the aging body affects brain energy. Before you start any diet regimen, get a full checkup to see if there are other possible contributing factors to your weight gain. Medications, including some that are prescribed for depression and epilepsy, can increase appetite, so be sure to ask your physician if your weight gain is a side effect from any medication you may be taking.

The first place to start is with your AgePrint. Compare your oldest part to the following, and see if there is a connection.

- **Cardiopause/vasculopause:** Changes in blood flow affect the brain, which results in a reduced metabolic rate.
- **The immune system:** The loss of immunity causes increased infection, which challenges the brain and results in brain trauma. Once the brain is injured, it craves carbohydrates. While you are experiencing these cravings, it is difficult to manage food selections properly. The loss of thyroid hormone can also alter your metabolic rate.
- **Male aging sexuality:** The loss of testosterone results first in abdominal obesity and then in total body obesity as muscle turns to fat.
- **Female aging sexuality:** The loss of estrogen, progesterone, and testosterone results in roughly 10 pounds of weight gain per decade beginning at about age 30.
- **Muscular skeletal aging:** The loss of growth hormone results in a decreased ability of the body to convert fat to muscle, the loss of muscle and bone, and the loss of physical strength. The loss of control of the parathyroid hormone bursting results in an increase of parathyroid hormone throughout the body and a loss in calcitonin, which can affect bone density, which can alter food selection. Remember, frail bones, frail brain, frail body, and frail life. When we are in a malnourished state, we crave unhealthy, calorie-dense foods such as french fries, potato chips, sweets, and pasta. Changes in bone density also impact overall health and emotional stress; when we become frail and feeble, we lose motivation for a healthy lifestyle and begin to make bad food choices.

Cleanse the Liver with a Low-Fat Diet

Obesity leads to liver disease. The buildup of fat cells impairs the liver's ability to properly cleanse the body of toxins, increasing your risk for infection and illness.

Metabolic Syndrome: Toxic Waist!

A common illness related to obesity is metabolic syndrome—a cluster of symptoms including impaired insulin sensitivity, hypertension, dyslipidemia, and a large waist size. It's amazing how the medical community talks about metabolic syndrome without connecting it to the aging body. Once you unlock the power of the AgePrint, you will understand that metabolic syndrome is a brain chemical disorder of dopamine.

A recent study found that when overweight patients with metabolic syndrome were put on diets similar to the one we recommend, the results were remarkable. These diets were designed to give participants 500 fewer calories than their daily caloric need while increasing consumption of fruits, vegetables, low-fat dairy products, and whole grains and reducing consumption of red meat, sweets, and refined grains. During the study, the participants had higher HDL ("good") cholesterol, lower triglycerides, lower blood pressure, greater weight loss, and more improved fasting glucose than those not on the diet.

Dining Together to Health

Schedule a regular dinner time for your family, and learn to cook quick, healthy meals. This way you can control what everyone is eating as well as spend valuable time together.

Phyllis's Story

My patient, Phyllis, was 52 years old when she began to notice her body morphing and aging. As for many women who begin menopause, everything seemed to change overnight. At first she developed many of the common symptoms her friends were experiencing, including hot flashes, thinning hair, and mood swings. Most troubling, however, was that within two years she gained 80 pounds. To Phyllis, this was almost incomprehensible; she was an active, athletic woman, as well as a professional dancer and health spa owner. She hadn't changed her diet or stopped her exercise routine. Her increased size was affecting her physical health and her emotional well-being. For the first time, her marriage was on the brink of disaster because she was constantly tired, worried, depressed, and irritable.

For the next 13 years Phyllis struggled with her weight, but she was never able to lose more than 10 pounds. Each doctor she went to told her that she was "fine." All she needed to do was "eat less, exercise more," but this mantra was not only wearing thin but also not yielding results. Phyllis estimated that she spent close to $50,000 attempting to solve her problem: trying expensive diets, seeing specialists, making environmental changes to her home, and changing her lifestyle completely. All money down the drain.

I met Phyllis when she was age 65. She had reached the point where she was resigned about her weight and had actually come to see me because her memory was slipping. Through comprehensive testing, I was able to determine that Phyllis was literally not the person she used to be. Her short-term memory was definitely going, and her body was completely out of balance. Her dopamine levels were so low that she was in serious danger of having a heart attack.

Keys to Weight-Loss Success

Knowing your BMI should become the fifth vital sign taken on any given checkup. Any successful weight-loss regimen has to include dietary modification and caloric restriction and a minimum of 150 minutes of exercise over three to seven days. The dopamine program outlines all the necessary nutrients and Rainbow foods to enhance a doctor-specified weight-loss program.

More drastic measures include weight-loss surgery and medication, but these are reserved only for people who do not respond to other therapies.

I treated Phyllis with a variety of prescription medications, nutrients, and bioidentical hormones. Over the first six weeks, Phyllis dropped 20 pounds effortlessly. Within the next year, she lost a total of 90 pounds. Now her dopamine levels are back where they should be. Her energy is high, her memory is sharp, and her relationship with her husband has tremendously improved. She looks and feels like a younger, more beautiful woman. In fact, another physician she regularly sees told her that she has the mind, body, and blood work of a 35-year-old woman. Not only did she get back the 13 unhealthy years she lost, she is able to enjoy her adult life all over again.

The Younger You Plan for Losing Weight

My multimodal approach for weight loss, based on managing the levels of dopamine, works. Whether you need to lose 10 or 100 pounds, you have the ability to take charge of your life—and your dopamine levels—to get to a more beautiful you. The dopamine regimen outlined here is a good start, because once your dopamine is controlled, you might find that your excess weight begins to drop.

For example, 50-year-old Karl F. is 6′2″ and came to me weighing 305 pounds. Besides being grossly overweight, Karl complained of decreased memory, depression, anxiety, insomnia, decreased libido, loss of muscle mass, back pain, and hypertension. Upon assessment, he had 36.48 percent body fat, attention disturbances, an enlarged heart, abnormal liver and thyroid, kidney damage, and a decreased growth hormone level.

I immediately started treating Karl with nutrient combinations that would increase his dopamine while addressing his memory and sleep issues. A medication regimen of Klonopin, Tenuate, Vasotec, and Cardizem controlled and reversed his health issues. A short seven months later he was 90 pounds lighter and his body fat dropped to 26.28 percent. All of his medical symptoms improved drastically; his blood pressure continues to be controlled, and his liver tests are now normal. Karl is amazed at the transition and feels younger now than he has in years.

Take Action: Get Back Your Energy for a Younger You

The good news is that this death code is easy to break; increase your dopamine levels and watch your overall health improve. By fixing your dopamine along with your aging code, you'll begin to see great results; 2 + 2 really will equal 5!

The quiz in Chapter 2 will frequently show you if you are losing dopamine. Alternately, a P300, the positive brain wave test that is part of the BEAM test that measures brain power, will yield similar results. You can choose a variety of ways to fix this problem, through either prescription medications, bioidentical hormones, or nutrients, supplements, and diet. Your choice can be guided by your deficiency. If your AgePrint for brainpower was more than 20, you can address it with nutrition and lifestyle changes. If your score was between 40 and 60, you will need to address your personal reversal with hormones. At levels greater than 60, you will need medications to reverse your brain age to a more normal state.

Decode your predisposition to obesity by getting these blood tests.

Blood Levels	Function
Fasting glucose	Measures level of sugar in blood (diabetes)
Hemoglobin A1c	Serves as three-month marker of diabetes control
Insulin level	Measures level of insulin
Urinalysis	Checks for ketones or protein, which could be signs of diabetes
Hormone levels: estrogen, testosterone, gh, TSH	Many of these hormone level measurements apply to many other pauses as well

Prescription Medications That Increase Your Brain Juice

Obesity can be treated through brain chemistry manipulation, altering appetite. Ask your doctor about these medications and the effects they may have for you. There are many drugs that are designed to reverse

Metabolic Testing May Provide the Answers You're Looking For

Metabolic testing identifies your unique target caloric zones so you can lose weight. It is a quick and painless test that can be provided in your doctor's office. It identifies your resting metabolic rate and gives suggestions as to how many calories your body really needs and how many calories your body could burn during exercise. With this information you will be able to target a weight-loss plan that will work. You will be given a range to eat the maximum amount possible and still lose weight.

dopamine deficiencies that impact the entire body's energy system. Each of the following drugs will increase your overall firepower and address a specific condition. Some medications have better results depending on the user. If you try one for a month and it's not working, discuss with your doctor the option of prescribing a different medication.

Attention deficit disorder: Ritalin, Clonidine, Adderall
Obesity: Tenuate, Ionamin, Fastin, Prelu
Cocaine abuse: Parlodel, Desipramine
Fatigue: Effexor, Desipramine
Hypertension: Tenex, Clonidine
Narcolepsy: Provigil, Dexedrine
Parkinson's disease: Tasmar, Eldepryl
Tobacco abuse: Wellbutrin
Treatment-resistant depression: Adderall, Dexedrine, Ritalin
Depression: Parnate, Nardil

There are people who self-medicate. They try to give themselves a dopamine boost by abusing cocaine, nicotine, methamphetamine, or other nonregulated stimulants. These all have serious side effects and cause great destruction to lives.

Hormones Help Break the Obesity Aging Code

As we get older, dieting will almost always get harder. This is because we're losing our brainpower that controls hormone production, and hormones play a critical role in weight control. One prominent hormone is insulin, which helps the body turn food into fuel. Insulin is created in the pancreas along with glucagon and somatostatin, two other hormones that aid in digestion and support our metabolism. Incretin is a bioidentical form of glucagon stimulation for the pancreas and blood sugar reversal. Growth hormone or insulin-like growth factor 1 will accomplish the goals of somatostatin. In the end both hormones have amazing effects on weight loss (as much as 10 to 15 pounds a year), with improvement in metabolism, appetite reduction, increase in muscle mass, and better blood sugar regulation.

Choosing the Right Hormones for Weight Loss

Lower levels of the sex hormones estrogen, progesterone, and testosterone all contribute to weight gain, so boosting them would reverse the trend. Cortisol is considered the body's primary stress hormone. Chronic stress is thought to create higher than average levels of cortisol, which would increase our appetites and food cravings. Lowering this hormone would be the key to treating this imbalance. Taking DHEA supplements is the way to lower cortisol. DHEA is our natural cortisol, which prevents our body from running on overdrive. Boosting growth hormone production may help the battle against fat accumulation, particularly in the belly.

Hormones Help Control Addiction

The loss of brainpower and subsequent food addiction is your obesity code; your brain is sending signals to choose junk foods to feed your energy needs. Meanwhile, your body's metabolism slows, meaning you process all this extra food at a slower rate, leading to more weight gain

Leptin Controls Dopamine Levels

The hormone leptin is also important for beating obesity. Leptin is secreted by the fat tissue in our bodies and regulates our appetite. The more leptin present, the less hungry we are. It may be possible that our appetite was established in our brains just after birth and may then be set for the rest of our lives. The amount of leptin in our systems in those first few weeks of life is controlled by genetics, not by what we are fed.

and fatigue. Over time, you might start looking for other ways to boost your energy, substituting other addictions for food including cigarettes, recreational drugs (such as cocaine or crystal meth), or prescription medications.

CODE BREAKER: Breaking Through with CCK

The hormone cholecystokinin (CCK) has recently been tagged as a new breakthrough treatment for controlling obesity. CCK, a hormone secreted in the small intestine, plays a key role in digestion and has been found to help control obesity by raising your dopamine. Three forms of natural treatment that absorb better than the synthetic version have been developed by my colleague Dr. Marc Rosenberg.

One of my wealthiest patients flew in from abroad, begging me to help him get off marijuana. He told me that after years of abuse, pot was ruining his life and his marriage. I prescribed to him tryptophan and inositol. He was able to completely stop smoking within two weeks and continues to be drug free three years later. Other added benefits that resulted when he kicked the habit were that he lost weight and his blood pressure dropped, which was no surprise. Once his dopamine was restored, his metabolism shot up and his health rebounded. Take a look at the following table and discuss these hormonal treatments with your doctor.

Hormonal Treatment	Primary Effects	Suggested Dosage per Day
Testosterone (transdermal cream)	Diminished sex drive	Consult your doctor
Estrogen (Estradiol)	Poor skin, hair, teeth, circulation	0.5–1.5 mg
Dehydroepian-drosterone (DHEA)	Fatigue	25–200 mg
Thyroid	Low mood	¼ grain–3 grains
Human growth hormone (HGH) (repairs the body)	Loss of bone mass or muscle tone	15–30 mg
Erythropoietin (increases oxygenation)	Reduces anemia because of failed kidney function	50–100 u/kg, 3 times per week
Calcitonin	Bone loss	200 IU
Insulin, Incretin (restores blood sugar and can result in weight loss)	Blood sugar	Varies on individual
Somatostatin (currently being studied as a treatment for weight loss in both adults and children)	Stimulates metabolism	0.04–0.08 mg/kg
Cholecystokinin (CCK) (currently being experimentally administered in capsule and micronized forms for the treatment of weight loss)	Stimulates digestive tract	0.1 mL/kg

Natural Treatments That Win the Fat Battle

While increasing your levels of dopamine is essential, several nutrient supplements can reduce total body fat and create a lean body when combined with the proper diet and exercise program.

- **Conjugated linoleic acid (CLA)** facilitates weight loss and reduces the amount of additional fat cells from being deposited in existing body fat.
- Preliminary studies suggest that **garcinia cambogia (HCA)** may reduce the conversion of carbohydrates into stored fat by inhibiting certain enzyme processes, as well as suppressing appetite and inducing weight loss.
- The precursor to the neurotransmitter serotonin, **5-hydroxytryptophan (5-HTP)** has been shown to reduce appetite and to promote weight loss.
- **Phenylalanine**, a precursor to adrenaline, alleviates obesity by stimulating the body's brown adipose tissue to "burn up" regular adipose tissue. It also helps to release cholecystokinin (CCK), a hormone that increases your sensation of fullness.
- **7-KETO** is a bioidentical hormone related to dehydroepiandrosterone (DHEA) and may also work to promote weight loss.
- **Essential fatty acids (EFA)**, such as gamma-linolenic acid (GLA), facilitate weight loss.
- **Fish oils** facilitate loss of fat, raise serotonin, and decrease appetite.
- **Vitamin D** and magnesium control metabolic syndromes and help you lose weight.
- Increasing **calcium** metabolism results in better fat metabolism and helps speed up weight loss.

Boost your brain power with natural supplements that create internal energy.

Natural Treatment	Primary Effects	Suggested Dosage per Day
Tyrosine	Regulates mood	2 g
Phenylalanine	Helps fatigue and is a natural pain reliever	500–2,000 mg
L-dopa	For treatment of Parkinson's disease	100–500 mg
Rhodiola rosea	An herb that fights depression and fatigue	75–375 mg
Thiamine	B vitamin that helps the body convert carbs to glucose; helps with addictions	50–500 mg
Chromium	Fights fatigue	500–1,000 mcg
Folic acid	Enhances dopamine transmission	1–2 g
Ginkgo biloba	Enhances blood flow and glucose utilization, which enhances dopamine	No RDA
Yohimbine	Enhances sex drive	5.4 mg
Methionine	Enhances production of dopamine and adrenaline	60 mg
Guarana	Works like caffeine and helps fight fatigue and raises ATP	100–500 mg

Change Your Weight by Changing Your AgePrint

Being low in dopamine on the AgePrint quiz means that no matter what you do to change your life, you can't make a permanent change in your weight unless you change your brain chemistry. No diet will save you without brain energy. No fitness regimen can sustain you forever. You must be able to change your brain chemistry and increase the energy, voltage, and speed of the brain code.

Craving Caffeine?

Coffee does provide a jump start that low-dopamine individuals crave, especially when tired. It can also help the aging pancreas and greatly reduces the risk of diabetes. But like everything else, it's only good for you in moderation. Top off with no more than two to four cups per day (300 milligrams is enough, depending on the size of your cup).

Teas, sodas, and chocolate are equally dangerous. Make sure to check with your doctor about your caffeine consumption, especially if you know that you have specific health problems. It's also important to know the ratio of how much water you're drinking as compared to your caffeine intake; caffeine is such a powerful stimulant that it burns up your body's water supply. If you're not also drinking lots of water, you might find that you are becoming dehydrated.

Keys to Success: Choose Your Caffeine Wisely. These caffeine choices are healthiest because they are also high in nutrients and antioxidants. Fresh-brewed tea and loose tea leaves have far more nutrients than tea bags or bottled teas.

Green tea

Oolong tea

"Energy" flavored vitamin water
(often contains guarana; a source
of natural caffeine)

White tea

Rooibos tea

Get Over Being Tired

Catherine was 46 years old when I diagnosed her with chronic fatigue syndrome. She instantly knew that her diagnosis was correct. Catherine did not have the energy to pull herself off her living room couch, no matter how hard she tried. It was hard for me to imagine when Catherine told me that she used to be a very active woman. But lately, she could muster the ability to get up only when she had to use the bathroom. Catherine lost her appetite and was unknowingly starving herself by the time she was able to come into my office to seek help.

I told Catherine that even though she was 46 years old, her brain was behaving as if it were 80. Catherine and I are now working together to get her brain age balanced with her chronological age. I'm already seeing signs that we are on the right track, and Catherine has begun to resume her old life. Her energy has been restored, and every day she is able to do a bit more. She gratefully tells me every time I see her that I was able to give her back her life.

Sleep Your Excess Weight Away

Because sleep deprivation contributes to fatigue, you must get yourself and your dopamine back on track. Getting seven hours a night is critical for weight loss. One study showed that people who get four hours of sleep per night were 73 percent more likely to be obese than those who slept seven to nine hours.

Rainbow Diet to Break the Obesity Aging Code

The Rainbow Diet breaks the obesity code by creating a complete eating plan that is low in sodium and high in fiber. It's high in protein and low in fat and includes lots of colorful fruits and vegetables. Eating nutrient-dense, rather than calorie-dense, foods is the key to maintaining weight loss and a balanced brain chemistry.

Choosing Rainbow foods will help you conquer your cravings. For example, drinking vegetable juice, eating a dark green salad, or having a warm bowl of vegetable soup about 20 minutes before lunch or dinner can help you cut your calorie intake by as much as 30 percent. These treats are so filling that you won't need to eat much more.

Rainbow Fibers: The Whole Truth About Whole Grains

Fiber is an important tool for weight loss. Fiber is like a scrub brush for your digestion, scouring your system until it is sparkling clean. It cleans out your colon, controls your blood sugar, pulls fat from your arteries, raises your "good" HDL cholesterol, and detoxifies your body. What's more, it's bulky; fiber fills you up so you eat less. High-fiber foods such as oatmeal, brown rice, and broccoli can also absorb excess estrogen compounds, which are produced during menstruation. It can be used as a powerful appetite suppressant when you are experiencing PMS cravings. The recommended dosage of daily fiber is 40 to 45 grams every day.

Season Your Brain

Herbs and spices can be digested easily and can boost your metabolism, getting your dopamine up and running again because they are nutrient dense. A stronger metabolism helps you burn calories more efficiently, so that you will lose weight. Choose from all the great seasonings of the world: cinnamon from Vietnam, basil from Thailand, cilantro from Mexico, turmeric from India. The hotter the better, except if you are suffering from gastroesophageal reflux disease (GERD).

The following herbs, spices, and flavorful foods are code breakers that beat obesity:

Flaxseed	Onion
Garlic	Stevia
Green tea	Yarrow
Mustard seed	

CODE BREAKER: The Rainbow Plate Rule

Choose a combination of three foods for each meal. Each item should come from a different food group: one must be a protein, and the other two should be different colors.

Leptin-Producing, Appetite-Suppressing Super Foods

Eat one complete serving of each of these foods to boost your leptin production. For the most bang for the buck, broccoli is clearly the best dopamine-enhancing food:

Apples	Salmon
Broccoli	Pomegranate juice
Carrots	Spinach
Egg whites	Unsalted almonds

Rainbow Diet Energy-Boosting Meal Plan

An energy-boosting eating plan needs to be high in protein so you feel satisfied and will not binge on the carbohydrates you crave. Foods high in calcium and vitamin D are other effective obesity busters. The following sample menus show how to choose energy-boosting foods.

Breakfast Options

- Two soft-boiled or poached eggs with spinach and garlic
- Omelet with roasted turkey and fresh radishes
- Sardines with mixed lettuce
- ½ cup plain yogurt with mixed berries, almonds, and walnuts

Lunch Options

- 4–6 ounces of sardines with multicolored vegetable salad; add 1–2 tablespoons of olive oil with balsamic vinegar and some seasonings
- Tuna sandwich on whole-wheat bread with lettuce, tomatoes, and onions
- Oven-baked salmon on a garden salad with olive oil and vinegar with a few whole-wheat or rice crackers

Dinner Options

- 1 cup lamb stew with ½ cup brown rice, grilled asparagus, carrots, and onions
- Beet and apple salad with 2 ounces of goat cheese and balsamic vinegar
- 4–6 ounces of grilled chicken breast, steamed snow peas with red beans and corn
- 4–6 ounces of lean steak or veal with steamed green beans, toasted almonds, and cranberries

Dessert and Snack Options

- 2 ounces of cottage cheese with grapes
- Raw carrots
- Green apple with 2 tablespoons of almonds
- Rice or whole-wheat crackers with guacamole dip

Add Yogurt to Your Rainbow

The Rainbow Diet requires eating a cup of yogurt a day to improve your bowel health, immune system, and digestion; reduce overall inflammation; and decrease "bad" LDL cholesterol.

Body Fat Counts!

The number on the scale is important to track, but to stay healthy, you also need to know your total body fat percentage. Normal body fat percentage for men should be 8 to 18 percent and for women 16 to 25 percent.

For example, Sybil, an executive for a major fashion label based in New York City, decided to give herself a present and came to my office for a complete evaluation. At 5'7" and 175 pounds, Sybil did not look like one of the more extreme weight-control cases I had seen come through my doors. However, her initial body fat measured in at an unhealthy 34 percent. She began eating only Rainbow Diet foods and started an exercise regimen. I prescribed tyrosine, phenylalanine, and human growth hormone (HGH) to enhance her diet and exercise program. One year later, at 137 pounds and 19 percent body fat, she was sexy and strong, and her self-esteem has never been higher.

Body fat can be measured with a caliper, an instrument most internists can keep in a drawer. Another method is called a DEXA scan, which is an ultrasensitive x-ray. Ask your doctor where you can have this test performed. Kelly D., a 35-year-old woman, went from 34 to 24 percent body fat in her arm by following my regimen. Losing that much body fat in an arm is considered almost a miracle.

Forget Small, Frequent Meals

You have to learn to budget your calories. Studies have shown that cutting calories by as much as 40 percent may help you live a longer life. Another key to success is eating large breakfasts and dinners, with little else in between. This strategy flies in the face of diet gurus who have promoted eating small, frequent meals all day to curb hunger. But studies now show that eating several small meals is not necessarily better than eating larger, less frequent meals.

Keep Drinking Water

A large percentage of your body makeup is water, and we need to keep supplying it with more to stay healthy and young. Water continuously flushes your digestive system, moving food particles along at a rapid rate, leading to weight loss. And if you're busy drinking your eight glasses of water all day, you won't have the desire to add the higher-calorie beverages such as sodas or juices.

Diets Won't Cure Everything

Although a healthy diet is important, it may not decrease your risk for some diseases, such as heart disease and some cancers. According to a recent study, reducing fat consumption after menopause offers most women little, if any, protection against breast cancer or several other diseases. The research shows that there are no significant differences in rates of colorectal cancer, heart disease, or stroke between groups of women who followed a low-fat diet and those who didn't. Some information gained from the study suggests that women who previously ate an "unhealthy" diet and then switched to a low-fat "healthier" diet did have the most to gain. This group may have been more protected against breast tumors than those on continuous unhealthy diets. Aging is a cause of cancer, so a low-fat diet can be helpful.

Can't Afford Not to Buy Fresh Veggies and Fruits

The myth that one "can't afford" to eat healthfully is merely an excuse and, quite simply, untrue. According to the *Journal of the American Dietetic Association*, a survey of 637 foods by a nutrient-to-price ratio compared with a calorie-to-price ratio, showed fruits and vegetables did significantly better than other classes of foods, proving that you will always get more nutritional bang for your buck with plain raspberries than with the raspberry cheesecake. When you think of all the money you will save on the quadruple bypass surgery you won't need in 25 years, you can't afford *not* to buy that extra kale.

Now that we've discussed the energy of the brain, we will move on to improving brain speed. The combination of increasing brain speed and brainpower leads to total cognitive or thinking efficiency of the brain. $E = mc^2$, as Einstein says. The raw output and energy of any brain is the voltage $\times$ speed^2. Truly, the best aspect of a younger you is a live-wire brain.

4

Acetylcholine: The Key to a Smarter You

Mona was 82 years old when she came into my office. When she came through my door, I thought I was looking at a ghost. Mona was in a wheelchair and drooling on herself. She was unable to speak and had no concept of who she was or who was with her, even though she was accompanied by her own daughter. Even without performing a complete AgePrint, I knew that her brain speed had completely diminished and the age of her brain was higher than that of a 100-year-old. Acetylcholine is the primary chemical messenger that creates a younger, faster brain.

I first thought that treating Mona's dementia would be an almost impossible task. However, I was determined to make some improvement and secretly hoped her daughter would go through our dementia-prevention program because I felt that the best way I could help the mother was by treating the daughter as well. Mona was not a lost cause. I immediately placed her on a total dementia-reversing program consisting of several natural hormones: human growth hormone (HGH), natural estrogen, dehydroepiandrosterone (DHEA), calcitonin, and parathyroid. Equally important in her treatment plan were nutrients, including choline, huperzine A, deanol, acetylcarnitine, phosphatidyl serine, lipoic acid, fish oil, glycerol phosphocholine (GPC), manganese, conjugated linoleic acid (CLA), and ginkgo biloba. Exelon, a medication often used to treat symptoms of dementia, was used to complement these natural treatments.

Remarkably, within two months and with very few changes to her prescribed regimen, Mona actually began to speak and communicate reasonably with her family. Her first words to me were, "Thank you, Dr. Braverman." I was stunned. I had never before witnessed such a remarkable turnaround with end-stage dementia.

As we progressed with her care, her AgePrint decreased from 100 to 90, and although I would not consider hers a complete reversal of dementia, I was more than happy to witness a partial reversal. A slow brain is a very aging code. Over time, Mona was able to share her thoughts and memories with her children; she was once again living what most would consider a happy life because her children were not in pain over her condition, and she was able to communicate with them.

Bad Thinking, Bad Health

With the advent of cloning, stem cell repair, advanced pharmaceuticals, and new imaging techniques, it is conceivable that many of us will be able to extend our lives to age 120. Why, then, has study after study shown that nearly 50 percent of us will be senile and barely functioning by the time we reach 85? Because as we age, our brain speed slows down, and we lose brain cognition. The consequences include both mental decline and a deteriorating body. So a loss of brain speed is not only an issue of "losing your mind," but it relates to your total survival.

Break the Aging Code: Don't Drop the Balls of Memory

Losing brain cognition is directly related to a loss of the neurotransmitter acetylcholine, which regulates our ability to process sensory input and access stored information; essentially, it's about remembering. An acetylcholine deficiency can occur in two ways. You are either not creating enough of this powerful neurotransmitter and your brain and body begin to dry out, or your brain is speeding so quickly that you are literally burning it up. So when you don't have enough acetylcholine, you'll begin to slow physically and emotionally and you'll lose your brain cognition skills. You will not be able to recognize when you are hungry, sad, or in pain. You will not be able to take care of your everyday needs or communicate these needs to others.

Lower levels of acetylcholine can lead to myriad symptoms:

Cognitive Changes
- New forgetfulness
- Trouble understanding spoken and written language
- Difficulty finding the right words before speaking
- Forgetting common facts
- Disorientation
- Attention difficulties
- Impulsivity
- Inconsistency

Psychiatric Symptoms
- Withdrawal
- Apathy
- Depression
- Anxiety
- Fearfulness
- Paranoia
- Hallucinations

Personality Changes
- Agitation
- Disinterest
- Social withdrawal

- Excessive and inappropriate flirtatiousness
- Easy frustration
- Explosive spells

Problematic Behaviors
- Wandering
- Noisiness
- Restlessness
- Falling when getting out of bed at night
- Insomnia

Changes in Daily Life
- Difficulty driving
- Getting lost
- Neglecting self-care
- Neglecting household chores
- Difficulty handling money
- Making simple mistakes at work
- Trouble with shopping

Are You Really Losing Your Mind?

If you or anyone you know is experiencing these symptoms, see your doctor immediately for a mental status exam. Cognitive decline is a disease, and just like any other disease process, the earlier you catch it the easier and more effectively you can reverse it.

Losing Cognition Is One of the Primary Age Accelerators

The loss of acetylcholine can be even more devastating than a loss of dopamine. Losing your brain speed is one of the most aggressive age accelerators, quickly spiraling down to cognitive decline, dementia, and often into Alzheimer's disease. Worldwide studies of older adults document a 15 to 25 percent occurrence of serious mental disorders later in life directly related to cognitive decline and a loss of acetylcholine. Alzheimer's disease and related dementias will affect approximately 10 percent of the population over the age of 65 and as many as 40 percent of those older than age 85. These numbers show that you or someone you will be taking care of will suffer from dementia.

The Body Dries Out as Brain Speed Declines

When your mind begins to deteriorate, the rest of your health breaks down as well. In this case, the brain, which is depleted of acetylcholine, sends a death code to the organs and hormone-producing glands of the body that it is losing or has run out of this vital neurotransmitter. This loss directly affects the other pauses.

- Osteopause: arthritis, atrophying muscles and bones (osteoporosis)
- Menopause: decline in sexual activity due to vaginal dryness
- Andropause: erectile dysfunction
- Vasculopause: diabetes and eye disorders
- Cardiopause: elevated cholesterol
- Somatopause: multiple sclerosis related to loss of growth hormone, which also affects memory, neuromuscular quickness, and strength

Conversely, the presence of these same medical illnesses can damage cognition and have all been linked to the progression of dementia. Is this another part of the riddle? A bad chicken-and-egg joke? No! It just goes to show how clearly the mind and body are linked. These medical conditions can be present 10 to 20 years before you begin to experience their mental components. You now have been forewarned. These symptoms will come if you don't pay attention to the pauses and your AgePrint.

When the Body Goes, the Brain Goes (and Vice Versa)

A recent study was performed to determine whether improvements in metabolic control of blood sugar and insulin could help overcome the poor thinking associated with diabetes. The results show that cognitive improvement—particularly through raising the levels of acetylcholine—was achievable with pharmacological interventions targeting levels of sugar in the body. Bottom line: our thought processes improve when our blood sugar levels are maintained. By improving your brain cognition, you will succeed at stopping the aging pattern of your brain!

Trust the Ancients

The great philosopher and physician Galen of Pergamum practiced medicine throughout the ancient world around the year 150. Even back then, he understood the age accelerators and the role they play in health and death. He used to say that everyone eventually dries out. He didn't know that he was talking about acetylcholine, and he didn't have access to the tools to prevent this drying from occurring. But we do!

Choose Longevity by Changing Your Lifestyle

The brain will naturally produce less acetylcholine as we age. Some people are born with old brains; they have always had low brain speed and are much more at risk for developing dementia and at an early age. We also unconsciously mess with our brain speed by the way we choose to live. The following are lifestyle choices we make or conditions that we suffer from that are burning up our brain:

- Poor working conditions
- Alcoholism

- Depression
- Drugs or addiction
- Lack of intellectual activities
- Lack of sleep
- Lack of social activities
- Nicotine
- Poor diet
- Retirement
- Sedentary lifestyle
- Exposure to toxins or mold

Each nerve is wrapped in insulation called myelin, which is made of a type of choline (acetylcholine). As illness sets in, the insulation breaks and then the brain burns, especially as we age. We dehydrate and can't put the fire out.

The Younger You Will Avoid the Seven Stages of Cognitive Decline

There are seven stages of cognitive decline that occur—often because of a lack of acetylcholine—prior to reaching full-blown dementia or Alzheimer's disease.

Stage 1: Loss of Brain Processing Speed

Every idea you express or judgment that you make should take between 0.3 and 1 second. Because of a lack of acetylcholine, the majority of us begin to lose about 10 milliseconds (msec) per decade from age 20 on.

If you feel that you are already losing your brain speed, you need to take immediate action to find out exactly how fast you think. The AgePrint quiz in Chapter 2 serves as a fairly accurate diagnosis. Following that, diagnostic testing in a doctor's office should be done to determine actual brain speed.

Your brain speed peaks at 300 milliseconds plus your age if your brain is in good health. For example, an ideal brain speed of a 20-year-old is

320 milliseconds. This will change not only with age but when there are dysfunctions or abnormalities such as memory loss, depression, or other psychiatric issues, including thought disorders.

The following are typical brain processing speeds at various ages:

Chronological Age	Brain Speed	Definition
20	280–320 msec	Vibrant cognitive state
30	300–330 msec	Normal
40	330–340 msec	Beginning stages of cognitive decline; slight changes in memory, attention, and learning ability
50–80	340–370 msec	Increased loss of cognitive functioning and you will experience noticeable changes in memory and attention
90–100	370–410 msec	Severe cognitive deficiency and significant dementia

Stage 2: Lapses in Memory and Forgetfulness

Experiencing memory lapses is not an inevitable consequence of aging and is often the result of a loss of acetylcholine. These lapses are concrete indications of brain chemical deficiencies and *can* be reversed. If you experience any problems with your memory, don't ignore them.

Memory Testing Is the EKG of the Head and a Core to the Brain Code. Memory tests often convey results that are often not well articulated. For example, I once had a patient whose memory test scores were so at odds that I doubted my test. Carly, a 60-year-old woman, came to me complaining of memory problems, so I had her take a variety of memory tests. Her verbal memory score placed her in the superior range. During testing, Carly was able to recall vast amounts of information. However, she scored extremely poorly on the visual memory portion of the test; she was unable to recall or describe pictures, faces, or numbers that she had recently seen. Since visual memory is processed in the right hemisphere of the brain and verbal memory in the left, it is conceivable that one side of her brain was functioning much better than the other. The good news for Carly was that her issues were completely reversible. Once she followed her new memory regimen of natural testosterone and supplements of the nutrient zinc, which boosted her acetylcholine levels, her visual memory improved greatly.

Stage 3: Loss of Attention

Attention problems are generally thought to be associated with children, but these problems not only continue into the adult years for affected children but also can first reveal themselves as people age. Our computer testing predicts attention deficits, as well as driving safety and the likelihood of accidents. If you've been forgetful lately, keep shifting from one activity to another, seem especially accident-prone, can't think clearly, feel abruptly either hyperactive or apathetic, or find it difficult to get along with family, friends, and colleagues, the problem may be with your attention and acetylcholine levels.

Women and Dementia

Women develop dementia more frequently than men because of earlier hormonal loss.

Stage 4: Changes in Personality and Temperament

It should be no surprise that your personality and temperament are also regulated by your current levels of dopamine, acetylcholine, GABA, and serotonin, the four primary neurotransmitters. These neurotransmitters draw all their life from your brain's electricity. After all, life is light and therefore the true life of the body is the brain's electrical code.

Depending on your levels of each of these biochemicals, you may be more introverted than extroverted, intuitive instead of practical, a logical or rash decision maker, or organized or freewheeling. Your unique brain chemistry dictates certain facets of your personality, so none of these traits is better than another.

However, if you always thought of yourself as one personality type, and you find that you are thinking or feeling more like another, you may be losing brain speed. A drastic overall personality change can be a stage of early dementia, which is probably a result of lowered acetylcholine levels. These personality imbalances can also be corrected, especially if you can catch them early.

A Young Healthy Brain Is Always a Good Thing

The brain's outer mantle (or cortex) gets thicker during childhood and starts to thin during the teen years. However, it has been noted that children of superior intelligence often have one thing in common: their cortex reaches its thickest stage a couple of years later than other children. While no one is exactly sure why this happens, the delay may occur because children with higher intelligence are "younger" than their peers. Because they are processing more complex information while their brain is continuing to grow and thicken, it may inadvertently have an antiaging effect.

Stage 5: I'm Not as Smart as I Used to Be

Your IQ is not just how smart you are; it quantifies different aspects of how you function in the everyday world. There are four main categories of intelligence; each starts during school age (3 to 10 years old) but peaks, matures, and weakens in different ways throughout our lives. It's quite common that you can be highly developed in one area and deficient in another. A noticeable decline in any of these four areas of intelligence would be considered as "cognitive decline" and is a definitive hallmark that you are losing brain speed.

- **Abstract or traditional IQ (voltage/dopamine):** Writer Marya Mannes best sums up abstract intelligence as "the ability to control emotions by the application of reason." Abstract IQ is defined by your ability to master schoolwork, including arithmetic, spelling, reading, and writing. You might think of someone who scores high in this area as being the typical genius, but he or she could be a complete mess in other areas.

- **Creative IQ (speed/acetylcholine):** F. Scott Fitzgerald believed that intelligence was the ability to hold two opposing ideas in the mind at the same time and still retain the ability to function. To me, this expresses the creative process: to be able to think outside the box, to incorporate other people's ideas and change your world view. Individuals with high creative IQs are usually very empathetic.

- **Emotional IQ (symmetry/GABA):** First brought to public awareness by author Daniel Goleman, emotional IQ can best be summed up by psychologist Robert Steinberg's quote, "the capacity for self-management." It also includes the ability to be sensitive to others and to sustain long-term relationships.

- **Common sense or perceptive IQ (synchrony/serotonin):** Philosopher George Santayana put it best by saying that common sense is "a quickness in seeing things as they are."

Stage 6: Mild Thinking Impairment, No Dementia

Mild cognitive impairment typically begins after age 30 and is a transition stage between the cognitive changes of normal aging and the more serious problems associated with Alzheimer's disease. You may notice you forget things more often, misplace things, or repeat actions you didn't remember that you have already done. However, reasoning skills and the ability to perform daily activities are still intact at this stage, so you might not realize that your brain has lost speed. If you notice any of the symptoms, this stage is a critical time to get checked out by a physician.

Stage 7: Dementia: The Ultimate Acetylcholine Age Accelerator

Dementia is defined as the clinical condition in which loss of memory and cognition become severe enough to hamper social and occupational functions. Full-blown dementia affects more than four million people over the age of 65, with 40 to 75 percent of them over the age of 85. Dementia can begin at any age, although it usually afflicts the elderly. You can break the Alzheimer's disease code with modern medicine and nutrition, as long as you begin treatment at the earliest possible stages.

Dementia not only affects your ability to remember, but it affects your judgment, abstract thinking, personality, and mood, and it clouds your orientation to time and place. Here's a set of scenarios so that you can clearly see the difference between normal aging and Stages 6 and 7 of dementia:

Dementia Code	Stage 2: Forgetfulness	Stage 6: Mild Cognitive Impairment	Stage 7: Severe Cognitive Impairment
Impairment of short- and long-term memory	"Now, what did I come into the kitchen to fetch?"	"How do I make my family's favorite pound cake?"	"I burnt my hand making my pound cake because I forgot to use a pot holder when I was taking the cake out of the oven."
Language problems (aphasia)	"What's the word that I'm looking for?"	"I use that thing for my mouth," [instead of saying "toothbrush"].	"What is the word for that furry animal that barks?"

Dementia Code	Stage 2: Forgetfulness	Stage 6: Mild Cognitive Impairment	Stage 7: Severe Cognitive Impairment
Motor-skill problems despite intact physical capacity (apraxia)	"I'm always dropping my keys."	"I can't get my key into the front door."	"I can't remember how to open the front door."
Impaired judgment	"I can't remember why I bought a second food processor."	"Why did I wear four layers of clothing when it's 60 degrees outside?"	"I can't remember who will get my inheritance."
Impairment in abstract thinking	"I've really got to keep better records; balancing this stupid checkbook is too hard."	"Balancing my checkbook takes twice as long as it used to."	"How do I even use all these numbers?"
Failure to recognize or identify familiar objects despite intact sensory function (agnosia)	"I misplaced my car keys again."	"I often wander around parking lots because I can't remember where I parked."	"Why are my keys in the watering can?"
Personality changes	"I'm not as outgoing as I used to be."	"My wife can't handle my mood swings."	"People are out to get me."

Decoding Alzheimer's Disease—the Primary Forming of Dementia

Have you noticed changes like these in someone you know?

- Forgets things more often
- Has problems doing familiar things
- Puts things in strange places
- Forgets common words or uses wrong words
- Has frequent problems with complicated tasks
- Has a major change in personality (confused, suspicious, or afraid)

- Is confused about where he or she is (or what time of day it is)
- Has lost interest in doing things (or loses interest quickly if not encouraged)
- Has sudden change in mood or behavior
- Does things that don't seem to make sense

Take Action: How to Improve Your Brain Cognition

Just as you are only as young as your oldest part, your ability to learn and grow is only as healthy as its weakest part. We all need to focus on improving our weak areas. For example, a tennis player might have a great forehand, but to consistently win he needs to have a good backhand as well. Knowing your brain's AgePrint and being cognizant of the areas of weakness is the key to breaking the brain code.

The following are the best ways to test for declining brain speed:

- The AgePrint quiz is a quick and easy start toward understanding how your brain is functioning.
- BEAM testing accurately measures brain speed. BEAM is one of many forms of computerized electrical measurements of the brain that measure brain speed, voltage, rhythm, and synchrony. It includes visual and auditory thinking stress tests of the brain. It also includes a computerized or quantitative electroencephalography (EEG) that can determine whether people in their 60s and 70s will develop dementia in the next 10 years.
- MRI scans can detect brain atrophy in the brain as well as hemangiomas, tumors, as well as the development of multiple sclerosis.
- CT scans detect bleeding and brain atrophy.
- PET scans show loss of metabolism in dementia and damage from radiation treatments of the brain.

Sal Broke the Alzheimer's Code

Sal J. is already living younger because of early detection. Though it wasn't yet noticeable to his family and friends, Sal realized at age 54 that he was forgetting things. I explained to Sal that we needed to identify his brain's age and determine if he had already lost brain processing speed. After he took this noninvasive test, I was able to establish his brain age at 68. Sal was right: his mental functioning was beginning to slow down.

After following his personalized Younger You Plan, which included mental exercises, a change in diet, and supplementation with nutrients and natural hormones, Sal was able to reverse his brain age, which now measures in at 32. Sal's thinking is clearer than it has been in years, and his scores on his memory and attention tests put him at a cognitive peak for a man his age. Sal is a prime example of how early detection for dementia can add years to your life.

Boost Your Brain Speed for a Fuller Future

The most effective way to break the acetylcholine code is for you to increase your acetylcholine and improve your brain cognition. A multimodal approach, which includes medications, hormones, nutrient supplements, and specific dietary suggestions, increases the power of your brain.

You can choose a variety of methods to increase your brain cognition, either through prescription medications, bioidentical hormones, or with nutrients, supplements, or diet. Your choice can be guided by your deficiency. If your acetylcholine age code was between 20 and 40 years older than your chronological age, you can start by changing your diet and supplementing with nutrients. If you scored between 40 and 60 years older than your chronological age, you might want to add bioidentical hormones and possibly medication. If your age code was 60 to 80 years older than your chronological age, it requires a combination of all these treatments at higher dosages.

Effective Code-Breaking Medicines

Many drugs that can stop further memory loss and improve your brain's overall function, including cardiovascular drugs, are already on the market. These medications treat patients by boosting the strength of their

Your Blood Pressure May Not Improve, but Your Brain Just May

For six years, scientists observed a group of 3,300 people over the age of 65 who were on various medications to reduce blood pressure. They found that by taking any kind of blood pressure medicine, these study participants decreased their chances of getting Alzheimer's disease by 36 percent. Subjects who were taking diuretics showed the greatest reduction, up to a 74 percent decrease in some cases. Surprisingly, these strong results were achieved whether or not the medicine had any effect on their blood pressure. If you are battling high blood pressure, you still may not be able to eat as much cake as you want, but at least you'll remember what color the frosting was.

existing brain signals. While these drugs can reverse symptoms, they do not cure the disease. Worse, an improvement in cognition and ability to conduct day-to-day activities may not last.

Gene therapy and vaccinations against dementia regularly appear in the media, but they are only in the very earliest experimental stages and are unlikely to be available for human testing for many years. Preventive measures, beginning with knowing your AgePrint, are still your best defense.

The following medicines can reverse brain cognition problems:

Conventional Treatment	Typical Recommended Dose
Donepezil	5–10 mg
Neostigmine bromide	15–30 mg
Tacrine	40–160 mg
Rivastigmine	3–12 mg
Razadyne	8–24 mg
Statin drugs	5–80 mg

Natural Hormones for Improving Brain Cognition

Hormone supplementation has been prescribed by doctors as a preventive treatment against the development of dementia, regardless of whether or not these hormones appear to be deficient. If your overall AgePrint reveals that you are indeed deficient in any of these hormones, protecting yourself from memory loss and dementia is another reason to enhance that particular code breaker. For example, a recent Columbia University study on postmenopausal women showed that boosting estrogen levels can delay the onset of Alzheimer's disease by as much as 20 years.

Remember: depletion equals dementia, so consider taking these acetylcholine-boosting hormones.

Hormonal Treatment	Suggested Dosage per Day (unless otherwise indicated)
HGH	5–90 mg per month
Vasopressin	5–60 units
DHEA	5–200 mg
Calcitonin	200 IU
Parathyroid	20–40 mcg

Nutrients That Unlock the Power of the Brain Code

Many nutrients have been proven to improve brain speed. Some of the research regarding certain nutrients is stronger than others, but we've provided you with a complete list here. One of the easiest ways for you to boost your acetylcholine is by supplementing your diet. When your acetylcholine is deficient, your body needs more of its building blocks. Choline begins as vitamin B and is converted through digestion to acetylcholine. Another goal of an acetylcholine diet is to boost your lecithin, an enzyme that the body uses to synthesize choline. Consider these natural treatments.

Nutritional Treatment	Suggested Dosage per Day
Choline	200–3,000 mg
Deanol Dimethylaminoethanol (DMAE), Deanol	100–3,000 mg
Acetylcarnitine	500–5,000 mg
Phosphatidyl serine	100–300 mg
Lipoic acid	25–1,000 mg
Fish oils (omega-3)	500–3,000 mg
Glycerol phosphocholine (GPC)	125–1,000 mg
Manganese	2–10 mg
Conjugated linoleic acid (CLA)	1–6 g
Piracetam (derivative of GABA)	2,000–4,800 mg

Herbal Treatment	Suggested Dosage per Day
Huperzine A	50–400 mcg
Vinpocetine	5–20 mg
Ginkgo biloba	50–300 mg
Bacopa monnieri	100–400 mg
Gotu kola	500–1,000 mg

A Rainbow Diet to Remember

When your brain sends the signal that it's drying up, you begin to crave fat and fatty foods, which deliver an instant choline boost. Yet we all know what happens when we eat too much fat. You'll need to be vigilant and feed your needs by choosing good fats over bad fats. Substitute the following high-fat foods for low-fat ones whenever possible, and break the fat code while boosting your brain speed.

Use the following list to help you trim the fat from your diet:

High-Fat Food	Lower-Fat Option
Whole or condensed milk	Skim milk, buttermilk, nonfat powdered milk
Bacon	Canadian bacon

Bologna, frankfurter, sausage	Chicken or turkey, lean, thinly sliced
Avocado	Cucumber, zucchini, lettuce
Creamy or high-fat cheeses	Low-fat cheese, cottage cheese
Ice cream	Ice milk, frozen low-fat yogurt
Hot fudge sundae	Frozen yogurt or ice milk with sliced or crushed fruit
Ground beef/fatty meats	Lean meats with all fat trimmed
Sour cream	Low-fat yogurt, imitation sour cream
Regular salad dressing	Reduced-calorie salad dressing, vinegar, lemon juice
Cream	Skim milk
Fried eggs	Poached, boiled, or baked eggs
Marbled meats	Fish

Herbs and Spices That Improve Brain Cognition

If the sight of a lemonade stand takes you back to yesteryear, go ahead and buy a cup (as long as it's sugar free)—it could help you continue to remember the old days way into the future. Lemon balm, an herb used commonly in tea, has recently been studied as a possible treatment for Alzheimer's disease. Lemon balm is an antioxidant that stimulates acetylcholine receptors, and it also works as a mild sedative.

Turmeric—which I call the spice of life—is a great acetylcholine-related spice. Turmeric and cumin have been proven to help unclog

Boost Your Memory Power with Asparagus

Asparagus has been shown to block the production of acetylcholinesterase, the enzyme that destroys acetylcholine. Make this delicious green vegetable a part of your Rainbow Diet to help keep your acetylcholine high and your memory sharp.

amyloid, which is a waxy substance that blocks the highways of the brain when conditions like Alzheimer's disease are present. Without this amyloid, your thinking is much clearer. The following is a complete list of other herbs and spices that improve your brain speed:

- Basil
- Black pepper
- Lemon rosemary
- Sage
- Turmeric
- Mint
- Salvia

Boost your brain speed with these menu suggestions:

Breakfast Options
- 1 cup low-fat yogurt topped with strawberries, blueberries, ⅛ cup granola, and 1 teaspoon of cinnamon
- Whole-wheat or wheat-free waffle with ½ teaspoon of peanut butter
- Two soft-boiled eggs covered in 1 teaspoon olive oil and balsamic vinegar mixed with cumin, garlic pepper, and basil

Lunch Options
- Caesar salad with 2 ounces of Parmesan cheese (skip croutons) topped with 4 ounces grilled salmon
- Bowl of chicken soup with one slice of whole-wheat toast
- Multicolored vegetable tofu salad with olive oil and vinegar
- Smoked salmon sandwich with low-fat cream cheese, lettuce, tomatoes, and onions on whole-wheat bread.

Dinner Options
- Stir-fry of cauliflower and carrots served over ½ cup brown rice
- Grilled vegetable mix with fava beans, couscous, and 2 slices of lean beef or veal

- 4 ounces grilled chicken with cabbage salad with raisins and broccoli

Desserts and Snack Options
- ¼ cup roasted soy nuts
- One hard-boiled egg with carrots
- Celery with 1 tablespoon peanut butter
- 8 ounces of grape juice or ½ cup grape sorbet
- 8 ounces low-fat latte sprinkled with cinnamon

CODE BREAKER: Fish Is Brain Food

Fish is a direct source of omega-3 fatty acids, shown to be essential for cognitive development and normal brain functioning. Fish consumption has long been associated with lowering the risk of dementia and stroke. Recent studies have suggested that consumption of one omega-3 fatty acid in particular, docosahexaenoic acid (DHA), is important for memory performance. Next time, pick up some salmon at the supermarket before you can't remember to do it anymore.

Brain Sharpening

The phrase, "use it or lose it" is the world's biggest understatement when it is applied to cognition. Just as you need to exercise to keep your body fit, your brain needs a workout as well. Brain sharpening can be as simple as reading, writing, doing crossword puzzles, socializing, going to lectures, listening to sermons, playing video games, or participating in other hobbies that keep your brain thinking. A study that was published in the *New England Journal of Medicine* found that among leisure activities, reading, playing board games, playing musical instruments, and dancing were among the best for keeping your brain young and supple.

By being mentally active, you're on your way to keeping your younger brain. For example, if you are right-handed, a great brain challenge is to learn to use utensils and write with your left hand. Right- and left-brain balance can improve brain speed.

Pump Up Your Body, Pump Up Your Brain

Physical exercise can also help prevent memory loss. Exercise and mental sharpening are linked; by exercising your body you are also sharpening your brain. Even moderate exercise, such as taking a brisk walk for 30 minutes or more, increases blood flow to the brain, thus keeping brain cells strong and efficient. Adults who exercise at least three times a week have a 30 to 40 percent lower risk of developing dementia later in life than those who do not exercise. So go out for that run and then tackle the *New York Times* crossword puzzle—it's like your brain is bench-pressing 200 pounds!

If you find that boring, the Bible or any great book such as Tolstoy's *War and Peace* can be a great puzzle of complexity and paradox to exercise your brain.

5

GABA: Controlling the Anxiety/Pain Pendulum to Create a Younger You

A healthy brain rhythm handles diverse processes—what we see, hear, and think as well as our total behavior—in a calm, even stable fashion. The brain rhythm is primarily controlled by the biochemical gamma-aminobutyric acid (GABA). GABA has a calming, stabilizing, organizing effect over the brain, keeping all of the other biochemicals in check. When the brain ticks unevenly, so does the entire rhythm cycle of the body. GABA controls the brain's rhythm so that we function, both physically and mentally, at a steady pace. By monitoring your internal rhythm, GABA directly affects your personality and determines how you handle life's stresses.

Similar to a pendulum, your brain can fluctuate from highs to lows as it produces more or less GABA. When you have an abundance of GABA, your life takes on a Zenlike quality; your mind is at peace, and your body is at its peak. When you've depleted your GABA, the pendulum swings all the way over to the other side, and you may experience anxiety and/or chronic pain. As it swings back and forth, hovering over the "normal" middle ground, your body may feel not quite right, and you may have moderate to severe mood swings.

GABA Accelerates Aging Everywhere

As your brain experiences larger and more frequent swings from the anxiety pendulum, whether it is from aging, stress, drug or alcohol abuse, or just burned-out GABA, you have engaged in the GABA death code. Beyond cortisol release, a GABA loss directly affects all pauses, including the heart, the immune system, sexual functioning, as well as the bones, muscles, and skin.

- GABA deficiency leads to choppy signals from the brain to the heart, which can lead to cardiac arrhythmias and heart attacks.
- Anger and anxiety, caused by low GABA levels, are two of the strongest predictors of high blood pressure.
- Lack of internal calm can lead to digestive problems, including reflux, heartburn, diarrhea, irritable bowel syndrome, or constipation.
- Low GABA leads to pain in your bones, muscles, and joints, such as chronic back pain.
- A constant state of tension and anxiety can lead to a loss of sexual interest as well as sexual dysfunction.

Typical symptoms of low levels of GABA include:

- Restlessness
- Feeling on edge
- Being easily fatigued
- Difficulty concentrating or mind going blank
- Irritability
- Muscle tension
- Rapid heartbeat
- Shortness of breath
- Sweaty, clammy hands
- Cold extremities
- High startle response

- Feelings of panic
- Excessive worry
- Attention deficit disorder (ADD)
- Mood swings
- Headaches
- Sleep problems
- Out-of-body feelings
- Obsessive compulsive disorder (OCD)

Cortisol Stress Is GABA's First Death Code to Your Brain Rhythm and the Health of Your Body

When the pendulum stays on the side of GABA deficiency, our constant anxiety sends a death code to the rest of the body by way of excess cortisol. Cortisol is a damaging hormone produced by the adrenal glands when the body is under stress, or even as it ages. It counteracts all your other "good" hormones, increasing your pain, anxiety, and mood swings. These aging codes cause the brain to deteriorate even more.

When cortisol is secreted, it causes a breakdown of muscle protein, leading to the release of amino acids into the bloodstream. These amino acids are then used by the liver to synthesize glucose for energy. This process raises the blood sugar level so the brain will have more glucose for energy. At the same time the other tissues of the body decrease their use of glucose as fuel. This contributes to loss of muscle tissue because lean tissue is being converted into glucose. Chronic elevated cortisol also causes a decrease in insulin sensitivity and an increase in appetite, which is why so many of us eat when we are anxious or under stress.

The constant release of cortisol is followed by a cascade of physical symptoms, including increased stomach acid, headaches, and heart palpitations. It accelerates aging throughout the brain, diminishing other hormone secretions, and physically ages the bones, skin, and other vital organs. Cortisol directly affects the pauses like this:

- Accelerated heart rate, heart disease, and stroke, leading to cardiopause
- Memory disturbance, leading to electropause
- Increased appetite and obesity, leading to dopamine biopause
- Depression, triggering serotonin biopause
- Chronic yeast infections, instigating menopause
- Decrease in bone mass and increased risk of osteoporosis, leading to osteopause
- Cancer, triggering immunopause

Keeping Cortisol in Check

The best way to prevent cortisol from creating havoc is by learning how to stay calm during particularly stressful periods of life. Researchers have found that massage therapy can lower cortisol levels. Whether it be with massage, yoga, or reading, getting relaxation time into your life will keep your cortisol, and your stress levels, down.

Break the Stress Code with Rhythm-Stabilizing Bioidentical Hormones

Two recent studies, one using pregnenolone and the other using dehydroepiandrosterone (DHEA), showed that natural steroids can help regulated mood in patients with anxiety. The key here is to balance the hormones that are being overproduced with ones that need supplementation. Remember, choose bioidentical hormones for fewer side effects and better results.

Hormonal Treatment	Suggested Dosage per Day
Progesterone	100–200 mg
Pregnenolone	10–25 mg
DHEA	25–200 mg

CODE BREAKER: Prozac Nation No More

Anxiety can also be controlled with nutritional supplementation and proper diet. You'll save a bundle on medication, too, giving you one less thing to worry about.

The Anxiety Code Distorts Your Normal Personality

Anxiety is the primary GABA age accelerator. As we age and produce less GABA, the brain's power and speed are generated in bursts rather than a smooth, even flow. This is called an arrhythmia, and it can upset your system in a variety of ways, none more pronounced than your personality and emotional well-being. Even the calmest people will begin to feel anxious, nervous, or irritable. You may find that you start worrying about things that you never usually think about. Or, you may become completely stressed at home or at work, when before you were able to handle the daily grind in a much more reasonable fashion.

CODE BREAKER: Am I Anxious?

One in four Americans experiences frequent anxiety. In fact, more than 50 million people experience this loss of brain stability, manifesting in continuous and often unsuccessful psychotherapy. Therapy often does not work, because the real problem behind anxiety is never addressed: brain chemistry.

It's Not in Your Head: Anxiety Can Create Real Physical Pain

As the body responds to the choppy messages of the varying levels of GABA in your brain, you will begin to feel pain in areas of your body that used to be healthy. Pain is a complex and often subjective phenomena. You may become pestered by mild annoyances, such as dull aches or muscle cramps. These pains often strike at your weakest link; if you always have a sensitive stomach, it may be due to a GABA imbalance instead of a digestive disorder. Or pain may occur even when there is no physical justification. This is called somatization disorder. For example, recent studies involving individuals who have asthma found that psychological stress can worsen asthma symptoms.

The same anxiety that makes you emotionally uptight and nervous can take a physical toll. When we are tense, we unconsciously clench our bodies. When you keep your shoulders raised to your earlobes all day long, eventually you are going to feel pain. Worry and anxiety impair function on all levels and lead to serious illness. If you are worrying instead of meditating and praying, if you are worrying and not having sex or exercising, then you're done for. Live your life, treat your anxiety, and know that 90 percent of what we worry about never comes to pass (and that's a conservative estimate). The real power of prayer, meditation, and exercise is in balancing the rhythm.

Anxiety Increases Your Metabolism

I once had a patient, Tom L., who couldn't gain weight (believe me, it really does happen). Tom was 5'10" and weighed 125 pounds. He went to every doctor and had every body scan available because he was convinced that he was dying of stomach cancer. When he came to see me, I ordered the one test no one had considered: a brain map. Instantly, it was clear that Tom had seizurelike activity in his brain, a typical GABA deficiency. The underlying issue for his slender build was directly related to his brain rhythm. The solution would be to manage his anxiety and see if he could gain weight. I prescribed Neurontin (an anticonvulsant and GABA agent) with 10 milligrams of Pamelor (an antidepressant that boosts serotonin), and incredibly Tom gained 40 pounds in six months. His brain chemical anxiety and depression could not be helped with psychotherapy, because he had a brain chemical sprain.

Mood Swings Will Make You Old

The constant pendulum swing caused by fluctuations of GABA in your brain takes its toll on your mind as well as your brain and body. This fluctuation is both mentally challenging and physically exhausting and can lead to a rapid cascade toward psychological impairments even to the point of bipolar disorder or manic depression. Before this drastic decline, you must learn to keep your emotions in check, which is a very difficult endeavor.

Mood swings can also be caused by living with chronic pain or disease; very few of us are actually pleasant to be around when we are not feeling well. When pain increases, you will be irritable. One gastroenterologist once joked with me about the real reason why they call digestive disorders irritable bowel syndrome: the personality becomes irritable as well as the colon. If you know anyone with this condition, you know that he wasn't kidding!

Keys to Success: Treating Illness with Calmness

Arthritis pain improves dramatically if you treat the mood disorders associated with it. You will also have a much better chance of reversing the disease itself when you are more relaxed during treatment. In fact, this theory holds true for most diseases; calm down first and you'll find your symptoms will resolve quicker and easier.

Head traumas, infections, and endocrine problems can all destabilize the brain's chemical messages, so you end up burning out your GABA from this direction and experiencing mood swings. The good news is that when your health is restored, your personality will shift back to a more relaxed state.

Take Action: Test for Anxiety Before It Makes You Old

Decreases in brain rhythm are real and quantifiable. The quiz in Chapter 2 will show you if you are losing brain stability. In addition, your doctor can perform a few tests that test your GABA levels.

There are two psychological profiling tests, including Axis I (for more severe thought disorders, depression, blues, or anxiety) and Axis II (for the less severe personality "quirks" of life), that can test directly for the effects of constant stress and anxiety. The Millon Clinical Multiaxial Inventory (MCMI-III), developed by Dr. Theodore Millon, created a whole new science of psychiatric diagnosis. It is another well-validated and reliable questionnaire-based assessment that can be administered in your doctor's office. From this test we learn the worst we can be when we are most stressed.

A test that you can do on your own is the Myers-Briggs Type Indicator (MBTI), one of the most widely used and reliable personality type indicators. Most of the time we live somewhat in between. Knowing both the alpha and the omega helps us live the best we can.

A New Meaning to the Term *Burnout*: Chronically Out of Rhythm

GABA will diminish eventually, but you may be unconsciously draining your brain with these lifestyle choices:

- Overuse of cell phones and exposure to other electromagnetic fields
- Frequent exposure to loud noises
- Lack of sleep
- Constantly being on the go
- Obesity
- Poor diet
- Sedentary lifestyle
- Living and/or working in a toxic environment

The joys of creativity and expressing yourself can give some relief to your brain. The brain, mind, and body can sometimes feel like a Rubik's Cube. Exploring outside of that rhythm can be refreshing.

CODE BREAKER: All Shook Up

Don't laugh when you hear the commercials for "restless leg syndrome." Ekbom's syndrome is a very real and annoying GABA condition where sufferers are unable to sleep at night and need to vigorously move in an attempt to relieve themselves of dull aches that creep up and down their legs. Keep in mind, though, that not all restless leg disorders are GABA related. In fact, virtually every disease is really just a cluster of symptoms, and any number of brain codes can be out of rhythm at different percentages.

It's no surprise that so many people are burned out. Americans, for example, take the least amount of time off of almost any industrialized nation in the world and it's literally killing us. People who seldom take time out are more likely to be stressed and unhappy, and sick. In a recent survey, 1,500 women were asked how often they took a vacation. Twenty percent said it had been six years or more! So get out of town, take a vacation, and see all of your stress issues resolve.

If you can't physically get away right this second, try going outside and getting some fresh air and exercise. Remember the ABCs of exercise and you'll be reaping the benefits in no time:

- A is for *active*, such as jogging, swimming, or dancing.
- B is for *brisk*; you have to break a sweat.
- C is for *consistent*; just a little every day or every other day goes a long way.

Stress Doesn't Always Come from GABA Loss

It's true; life happens, and it isn't always pretty. When you have to deal with stress, you are actually burning up your GABA as well. Sometimes, stressful situations are obvious, and other times, you might not even realize what you're stressed about. For example, retirement is an age accelerator because of related stress. It might not look stressful, but the transition from working to being at home and "taking it easy" can be stress producing. Here are some more classic causes of stress:

- Breakup with a boyfriend or girlfriend
- Separation or divorce
- Trouble with a sibling
- Taking on too many obligations
- Conflict or arguments
- Change in financial status
- Serious illness or injury of a family member
- Death of a loved one
- Negative thoughts and feelings

Stress Leads to Drug and Alcohol Addiction

Those experiencing any type of stress without an action plan for dealing with it are more likely to abuse drugs and alcohol. High-stressed individuals are twice as likely to smoke, drink excessively, and use illegal drugs.

Is there such a thing as "good stress?" Yes! Stress for short periods can invigorate the mind and body; remember how good you feel after a really intense workout? Your thinking is clearer, you feel good about yourself, and you look forward to the next day at the gym. It's the long battles with stress that will kill you.

One secret to a younger you is then not to strive toward a stress-free life, avoiding confrontation or challenges. Instead, you need to find the right balance where you are pushed just enough to keep things fresh and exciting without compromising your mental or physical health.

When Low Levels of GABA Can Trigger Chronic Pain

The proper evaluation of pain is often difficult when a doctor relies only on subjectivity. Our measurements of brain rhythm, extensive markers of subtle inflammation and pain, and nerve conduction studies can easily identify all sources of true body pain as opposed to "brain pain," which is different. It may seem real to the individual, but it does not have any true physical cause. Unfortunately, this factor is often overlooked by many physicians, and many Americans become hooked on narcotic pain medications. GABA agents are remarkable painkillers. However, as a doctor, my goal is to identify not only the cause of the pain but how much physical discomfort each patient is experiencing. Most of my patients with mood problems tend to unconsciously overemphasize their pain. Therefore, extensive testing must be done until the root of the problem is found.

Calm the Brain and Ease the Pain

A younger brain is a calm brain. A healthier you relies on a younger brain. When you lose your GABA, your brain can no longer send its signals smoothly and effortlessly to the rest of the body. The good news is that this death code is easy to break; increase your GABA levels and watch your overall health improve. By fixing your GABA along with your primary pause, you'll begin to see even greater results. What's more, you'll be more relaxed and able to face new challenges.

You can choose a variety of ways to increase your GABA, either through prescription medications, bioidentical hormones, or nutrients, supplements, or diet. Your choice can be guided by your deficiency. If your AgePrint for brain stability was more than 20 years more than your chronological age, you can address it with nutrition and lifestyle changes. If your score was between 40 and 60 years more than your

Progesterone Is a Woman's Natural Valium

Loss of progesterone in women as they age results in a higher rate of GABA deficiencies. Progesterone can be considered as a relaxing agent for the anxiety pendulum.

chronological age, you will need to address your personal reversal with hormones. At levels greater than 60 years more than your chronological age, you will need medications to reverse your brain age to a more normal state. This approach is not one size fits all, however. Some people respond to more traditional drug regimens while others respond to other therapies; it is a decision best left to you and your doctor.

A Younger You May Require Medication for Pain Relief

When you see your doctor for chronic pain, he may be quick to prescribe narcotics such as codeine and OxyContin. While these are reasonable choices for the short term, they are dangerous, addictive drugs. With every dose you take, your body develops a tolerance to the drug, leading you to need more and more medication to mask your pain.

The term *narcotic* is derived from the Greek word for *stupor*, and that's literally what these medications do to your body and brain. Aside from extreme drowsiness, confusion, attention and memory problems, and nausea and constipation, narcotic pain medications cause a host of other problems and can begin their own pause cascade:

- Use of narcotics can depress the function of the immune system, which increases incidence of infections, and enhances of tumor growth, causing atrophy of the spleen and thymus gland, all of which could lead to immunopause.
- Ongoing narcotic use causes low energy, which could trigger dopamine biopause.
- Some pain medications can decrease brain speed, leading to acetylcholine biopause.
- Narcotics can cause hypersensitive skin, triggering dermatopause.

If your doctor makes this kind of recommendation, ask about other pain-relieving options. Today, there are four million OxyContin addicts out there who are medicating the wrong problem, and you don't need to be one of them. Instead of fixing their brain first, they are mistakenly fixing their body. Although the body should not be ignored, in this case, taking OxyContin is like coloring your hair with magic markers; you haven't solved the real problem and are in fact creating a new one to boot.

CODE BREAKER: Don't Join the Fan Club
Addiction is not just a problem for rock stars and Hollywood celebrities. Hundreds die every year as a result of misusing painkillers, particularly Darvocet, one of the most commonly prescribed conventional pain medications. Painkillers slow your brain speed, putting you at risk for serious mistakes and accidents.

You Can Be Pain Free Without Becoming Addicted

Now that you understand the intricate relationship between anxiety and pain, it should be no surprise that the same medications that resolve panic attacks are also equally effective at treating your aches and pains. For example, many of my multiple sclerosis patients relieve their pain and spasticity with anxiety medications such as Klonopin. Some of my patients with osteoarthritis are shocked that much of their condition was due to anxiety, and when they are treated with anxiety medication, their pain and discomfort disappear.

Many GABA agents are successful at treating other "unrelated" disorders, such as irritable bowel syndrome, stiff joints, muscle pain, and back pain, because when you take a GABA agent, it relaxes your system and gives it a chance to heal. But you know that there is no such thing as unrelated symptoms. The whole brain and body are connected in sickness and in health.

Most anxiety medications fall into two main groups: azaspirones and benzodiazepines; the former may have fewer side effects than the latter. The most commonly prescribed azapirone is BuSpar. Benzodiazepines are also used to treat panic disorders and social phobia. These traditional medications include Ativan, Dalmane, Klonopin, Librium, Restoril, Serax, Tranxene, Valium, and Xanax.

The following are anxiety and pain medications that do not have addictive side effects.

Conventional Treatment	Suggested Dosage per Day
Ambien	5–10 mg
Ativan	0.5–10 mg
BuSpar	20–30 mg
Calan	120–480 mg
Depakote	250–2,000 mg
Dilantin	200–600 mg
Gabitril	4–56 mg
Klonopin	0.25–4 mg
Lamictal	50–400 mg
Mysoline	100–750 mg
Phenobarbital	15–120 mg
Restoril	7.5–30 mg
Serax	40–120 mg
Tamoxifen (secondary effect)	20–40 mg
Topamax	25–200 mg
Tranxene	15–60 mg
Valium	4–40 mg
Xanax	0.25–4 mg

Off-Label Medications Used for Pain Management, Anxiety, and Mood Symptoms

If you are living with extreme pain that is limiting your daily functioning, you have many options other than dangerous narcotics. Often medications that were developed for one purpose can be used for another. These medication groups are often prescribed for anxiety, pain management, and mood symptoms even though they are not "anxiety" medications. However, don't raid your medicine cabinet and self-medicate without direct orders from your doctor. Often, the prescribed amount for one set of symptoms will be different from another. Also, do *not* resort to the use of illegal drugs. I've had many patients who are upstanding citizens, successful Wall Street bankers, lawyers, and so forth who have tested positive for PCP, cocaine, opiates, steroids, or marijuana. So many Americans are still puffing away on a joint a day, driving their mind into a distorted relief of their rhythm disorder. Marijuana and alcohol are the most commonly abused drugs for GABA imbalances. Cocaine, Ecstasy, and amphetamines are the most commonly abused drugs for dopamine-deficient individuals. PCP, angel dust, and mushrooms are the most commonly abused drugs for acetylcholine deficient individuals.

Talk with your doctors about using these alternatives:

• **Antihistamines:** These mild sedatives can be useful to calm sporadic anxiety. Some commonly used antihistamines can be found over the counter, including Benadryl, or you can ask for prescription Atarax.

• **Beta blockers:** These cardiac drugs counteract the effect of adrenaline and alleviate certain anxiety symptoms such as shaking, palpitations, and sweating. Commonly used beta blockers are Inderal and Tenormin.

• **Antidepressants:** Mainly SSRIs and tricyclic antidepressants have an analgesic effect and have all shown promising results in the treatment of chronic pain. They work because chronic pain causes depression and depression causes pain. The most commonly prescribed medication for anxiety and pain is Elavil.

Amy B. Stopped Her Brain's Pain Code

Amy B. had been experiencing severe and debilitating localized headaches for almost a year before coming to see me. She described them as incapacitating, which was frustrating because they most often

Pain Management You Can Be Happy About

Classically, antidepressants were used to relieve aching pain and anticonvulsants were typically used for shooting pain conditions. More recently, physicians use antidepressants as a first line for both types of pain because of greater success and fewer side effects. Best of all, the pain-relieving effect of antidepressants usually occurs within a week.

occurred in the middle of the day. Being a pediatrician, Amy had access to the latest high-tech screening tests at the hospital where she worked. She had already undergone a CT scan, an MRI of the head, and excessive blood testing, all of which showed no issues. Instead, Amy was convinced that she had a cancerous tumor that doctors were unable to find.

Move Over, Tylenol—There's a New, Natural Pain Reliever

It seems the future of pain relief just got a lot less painful. A regimen of gabapentin (100 to 3,000 milligrams per day) plus your daily cup of coffee (or the equivalent to 0.025 grams of caffeine) has been found to be the most effective treatment for an array of painful conditions. In 115 out of 142 patients, with conditions ranging from migraines to pain following surgery, this combination beat many prescription drug options for pain relief. One patient in the study had been suffering from painful spasms because of multiple sclerosis; he was able to find relief from these attacks within two days after starting on gabapentin. Three other patients saw a return of their chronic abdominal pain after stopping treatment with gabapentin, only to have the symptoms disappear again when they got back on it.

When I assessed her psychological status, I saw that she suffered from generalized anxiety disorder. When Amy and I talked, it was clear that she was experiencing these "incapacitating" headaches during her most stressful times of the day, when she was overwhelmed with seeing patients. I put Amy on a treatment regimen of natural supplements including tryptophan and a very low dose of Klonopin. Within one week, her headaches disappeared.

Here are some natural pain and stress busters:

Natural Treatment	Suggested Dosage per Day
Inositol	100–10,000 mcg
Kava	200–700 mg
Vitamin B$_3$	50–3,000 mg
Branched-chain amino acids	5–20 g
Gabapentin (Neurontin)	100–3,000 mg
Taurine	500–10,000 mg
Glycine	500–5,000 mg
Magnesium	300–1,000 mg
Theanine	100–500 mg
Tryptophan	500–2,000 mg
Phenylalanine	500–2,000 mg
Saint-John's-wort	Consult your doctor

CODE BREAKER: Parkinson's, PMS, and Phenylalanine

Phenylalanine is an amino acid found in abundance in high-protein foods (meat, cottage cheese, and wheat germ, to name a few); its use in the treatment of premenstrual syndrome (PMS) and Parkinson's disease has been found to enhance other pain-relieving holistic treatments such as acupuncture.

Shirley Calmed Down and Got Younger

Shirley, a 50-year-old woman, came to see me at the urging of her daughter. It was clear to me that, like many women, Shirley was more accustomed to tending to everyone else's needs before she took care of herself. Yet she quickly recited a litany of health issues such as anxiety, sleep problems, chest pain, shortness of breath, fatigue, allergies, high cholesterol, dry hair, and dry skin. Her body fat was an unhealthy 41 percent. Anyone could see that Shirley was a mental and physical wreck, and I knew that her problems stemmed from a brain chemical imbalance. I did her AgePrint and was not surprised to find that Shirley's GABA was deficient: her AgePrint for brain calm was more than 75.

I started Shirley on a precise regimen of GABA agents, which would calm her anxiety-producing brain activity down and rev her metabolism up to lose weight. Taking the GABA agents relaxed her enough so that she could focus during the day and sleep well at night, which in turn enabled her to be a compliant patient. She started her GABA Rainbow Diet and supplemented with nutrients including fish oils and niacin, compounds that sharpened her intellect and memory while lowering her cholesterol. She took glucosamine for her joints, while dehy-droepiandrosterone (DHEA) improved her mobility and general quality of life. After working the program for just one year, she felt more mentally stable and dropped to an astounding 18 percent body fat.

CODE BREAKER: Cottage Cheese—Good for What Hurts You

Cottage cheese contains one whole gram of methionine per serving. Methionine, an essential amino acid, can be a useful adjunct therapy for Parkinson's disease because it stimulates production of the pain-relieving L-dopa. Larger doses of methionine may be effective in treating osteoarthritis and other kinds of chronic pain. Furthermore, taking methionine can help relieve the anxiety that comes with acutely stressful situations when taken in conjunction with tyrosine. While I'm not supporting that you eat your way out of stress and anxiety, a little low-fat cottage cheese can go a long way!

A Rainbow Diet for a Younger, Calmer Brain

Choose a variety of foods that contain code-breaking GABA nutrients that are high in vitamin B. The following lists some of the foods that are high in glutamine, the amino acid that is a precursor to GABA. Bananas, broccoli, and brown rice are all packed with inositol, another B-complex vitamin that boosts GABA production. If your brain age in this category was higher than 20 more than your chronological age, try to incorporate at least two of these foods into your meal plan every day.

- Almonds
- Banana
- Beef liver
- Broccoli
- Brown rice
- Grapefruit
- Halibut
- Lentils
- Oats
- Oranges
- Potatoes
- Rice bran
- Spinach
- Walnuts
- Whole grains

Rainbow Diet Stability-Enhancing Meal Ideas

The following sample menus show how to choose brain-calming foods. Stay away from simple carbohydrates, which calm the mind and body only temporarily and have an addictive nature. Pass on the junk food, simple sugars, white flours, and wheat products, and focus on lots of protein (especially organ meats), citrus fruits, and plenty of colorful veggies.

Breakfast Options
- 1 cup whole-grain granola with bananas, cantaloupe cubes, oranges, and almonds
- Raspberry herbal tea
- 1 cup mixed fruit with plain yogurt with 1 whole-wheat waffle

- 8-ounce smoothie made with mixed berries and yogurt
- 8 ounces soy or rice milk with ½ cup bran cereal

Lunch Options
- 4 ounces grilled liver and multicolored salad dressed with olive oil and vinegar
- Mixed greens and citrus fruit salad
- 1 cup lentil soup with 1 slice of rye toast
- Veggie burger with ½ cup jasmine rice
- Mixed grilled vegetable salad

Dinner Options
- 4 to 6 ounces grilled halibut with ½ cup brown rice with cinnamon
- Apple, raisin, and walnut salad with goat cheese and a splash of balsamic vinegar
- 4-ounce grilled turkey breast with mushrooms with steamed potato salad mixed with scallions, radishes, and carrots in a light sour cream
- 4 ounces baked chicken with sweet potatoes and a cup of beet and onion salad

Desserts and Snack Options
- 1 cup fresh fruit salad sprinkled with cinnamon
- 1 whole-grain bar
- ½ cup banana puree and a touch of cocoa powder
- ¼ cup mixed nuts and raisins

The following herbs, spices, or foods stop the anxiety pendulum:

- Cilantro
- Cinnamon
- Cloves
- Lemon
- Lemongrass

- Licorice root
- Marjoram
- Passionflower
- Peach seed
- Peppermint leaves
- Saffron
- Turmeric

CODE BREAKER: Feeling Edgy? Try a Fig Newton

Whole-grain breads and cereals, figs, spinach, and kale all contain magnesium—great for calming down nervousness and irritability.

Cranial Electrical Stimulation (CES)

Cranial electrical stimulation (CES) is a gentle, therapeutic, FDA-approved procedure that can be done in the privacy of your own home. Using a battery-powered electronic device, CES can help control anxiety, depression, and insomnia. CES helps balance our brain waves by altering the abnormal electrical connections that develop with age. CES is safe and noninvasive, is nonaddictive, has no pharmaceutical side effects, and can be used daily. Positive results may be experienced immediately, though for some, it can take up to three or four weeks before results occur.

For more than 10 years I have seen how CES can relieve hypertension, headache, and pain. The CES device is particularly effective for men who are tense and have anxiety-prone health imbalances. You can use it for up to 30 minutes a day while you watch TV, read in bed, or enjoy any other quiet activity. For lasting benefits, treatment should be continued at regular intervals. Obtaining a CES device requires a prescription from a physician. The FDA has approved CES use for anxiety, depression, and insomnia.

The following are the positive effects of CES:

- Enhanced cognition
- Reduced anxiety

- Reduced depression
- Reduced insomnia
- Reduced withdrawal symptoms
- Improved brain waves
- Enhanced neurotransmitter functions
- Relapse preventions
- Prevention of substance abuse in high-risk individuals

Stella Got Her Groove Back with CES

Stella was a 47-year-old woman who had migraine headaches for more than 13 years. They occurred about twice a month but had become more frequent as she noticed that she was beginning to experience the signs and symptoms of menopause. A neurologist had given her feverfew and a variety of medications, including Elavil, Cafergot, Reglan, Meclomen, Corgard, Calan, Blocadren, Vistaril, Norgesic, and Anaprox. None of these drugs offered her relief.

When I met Stella, I did her AgePrint. Her brain age was 60, almost 15 years older than her real age. I immediately put her on the seizure medication Depakote. Her results were good, and a few months later I started Stella on the CES device and was able to reduce her Depakote prescription almost immediately. After using the CES device for about two months, she began to lower the Depakote further. A year later, Stella can control her migraines with the CES device and only requires her medication on rare occurrences. What's more, her AgePrint is down to 39; Stella got back eight years of her life, and she is in better shape entering menopause than she was before it occurred.

Get Younger and Get Rid of Your Stress, Anxiety, and Chronic Pain

Most of us reach for Tylenol or Advil in times of acute pain. But there are other alternatives with better side effects. Try some of these ideas before you reach into your medicine cabinet.

- **A good night's sleep:** Studies show that people are able to cut back on Tylenol use when they have gotten a good night sleep. Sleep is one of the best code breakers, and it's free!

- **Exercise and yoga:** Both are stress and anxiety reducers, whether you like it slow and concentrated or hot and sweaty.

- **Meditation:** Calm the mind and the body will follow. I've sent many a patient for classical meditation training, and they all come back reporting significant improvement.

- **Alternative therapies:** The power of touch is undeniable, especially in the hands of a professional massage therapist. Acupuncture, physiotherapy, and manipulation are all holistic remedies that should be considered to relieve stress and chronic pain.

- **Peer support:** There are many peer support groups that bring people with similar conditions together to discuss health issues and attend events in the community. Getting out and socializing will do wonders for your emotional and physical state.

- **Taking a break from stressful situations:** Activities such as listening to music, talking to a friend, drawing, writing, or spending time with a pet can reduce stress.

- **Staying away from caffeine:** This includes coffee, tea, soda, and chocolate. Caffeine's stimulating properties increase feelings of anxiety and agitation.

- **Learning to be more assertive:** For example, express your feelings in a polite, firm, and not overly aggressive or passive way. You'll soon see that life is a lot less stressful when you can ask for what you truly want.

Don't Let Chronic Pain Make You Old

When we start to limit our activities and behavior because we are in pain, we can get into even more health trouble. It is far too easy to become sedentary. Then, when you try to perform the mildest activities, you are burdened by even more pain.

With the exception of broken limbs, ruptured vertebrae, disk problems, or torn muscles, keep moving. It will be your lifesaver. Remember, emotions affect pain and pain affects emotions. Maybe you get anxious, irritable, or frustrated when you are in pain. Or you might even become severely depressed. These emotions will only make the pain more intense. Keeping active will help you feel more emotionally stable and physically limber, and ultimately younger.

6

Serotonin: Happiness and Rest Break the Aging Code

Through his famous character Snoopy, Charles Schultz best posed the statement, "Happiness is . . ." We all get to fill in the blank for ourselves. It may be wealth, power, a sense of peace, a nice car, a beautiful soul mate, a loving family, or a warm puppy! To my mind, happiness is your set point. When we talk about happiness, we mean our state of mind based on our expectations: our approach to life, plus the conditions of how we live, plus how we choose to spend our time. If we have a positive attitude, enjoy where we live, and find our daily lives compelling, then we've achieved happiness. We then compare every day to this set point, and from there we can tell if we are euphoric or even depressed.

One of the hard truths of growing up, and certainly of growing older, is that it's not so easy to be happy. Some personality types are never happy. Perfectionists, for example, are never satisfied and are always reaching for more. Free-spirited types live in the moment, so they quickly become happy but lose their contentment with their lack of commitment. The egocentric narcissists never get enough of what they want. The histrionic, or dramatic, never get enough attention. Happiness is about spending our free time in a way that is valuable and meaningful. Happiness is about being in sync and about having serenity. Serotonin is "serenitytone" and is the core stage of being happy. Without it, calmness and stability can't be had.

Happiness Begins in the Brain

Like every other aspect of the mental and physical health we've been discussing, happiness begins in the brain. Serotonin is the key to the brain's happiness. When your serotonin is high, you experience a great mood during the day and restful sleep at night. When it's low, you will be depressed, unable to get enough sleep, and your mind spins out of control toward unusual fears and phobias; most of the time we are somewhere in the middle.

Serotonin manages the biochemical messages leaving the brain. It creates the electricity for sight and rest and also controls your cravings. If your brain is out of sync, the left and right sides of your brain will be off balance, and your brain's ability to recharge itself is compromised. A serotonin loss creates a disconnect between the brain's left side's rationality and the right side's creativity. When this happens, you simply cannot think clearly; you might feel overtired, unhappy, emotionally out of control, and unable to get restful sleep.

A loss of serotonin sends a signal from the brain to the rest of the body to stop optimally functioning. It has three major age accelerators: depression, phobias or fears, and sleep disorders. Each one can set off different pauses. Conversely, keeping our serotonin levels up will reverse these specific problems as well.

Depression

Randy C. was a 64-year-old man who had been suffering from severe depression for most of his adult life. For the past 40 years, he had been diagnosed with organic affective syndrome. When he came to see me, he recounted a painful history of symptoms: depression, memory problems, dizziness, stomach trouble, fatigue, sexual problems, difficulty concentrating, anxiety, loss of appetite, tremors, paranoia, abnormal fears, obsessive thoughts, racing thoughts, insomnia, fear of people, antisocial feelings, and a constant nagging feeling of regret. On top of a crippling addiction to Valium, Randy had tried no fewer than 11 different antidepressants. Yet even with medication, he was never able to get past his depression, and now that he was close to retirement he found that he had nothing to look forward to. His suicidal thoughts were the last straw that brought him into my office to seek help.

Randy's physical exam showed low testosterone levels, elevated cholesterol, and hypoglycemia. His AgePrint for his internal systems was consistently 70, so his body seemed to be aging consistently. However, his AgePrint for brain serenity was 90. Simply put, Randy had a biochemical imbalance, a loss of serotonin production that no medical or hormonal treatment could completely restore. He only slightly improved on a regimen of methionine, phenylalanine, tyrosine, tryptophan, multivitamins and antioxidants, garlic, magnesium, calcium, and fish oil.

At this point I started treating some of his other pauses occurring in his body, concentrating on his next weakest link or oldest part, his aging sexuality. Interestingly, within six months his andropause age (which we'll discuss in Chapter 12) went down to 50. Randy was pleased to share that for the first time in years, he was involved in a romantic, sexual relationship that was bringing true happiness into his life.

Out of Sync on Both Sides of the Brain

Serotonin keeps the right and left brain in balance; the creative side of our brain balances with the organized side of our brain. No matter what the source of our blues; we become out of sync because of a serotonin imbalance.

A lack of serotonin will often cause depression and trigger the onset of other pauses. A lack of serotonin will:

- Accelerate calcification, leading to osteopause
- Lower your sex drive, triggering menopause and andropause
- Lower your testosterone, leading to andropause
- Lower your estrogen and progesterone, triggering menopause
- Weaken your immune system, leading to immunopause
- Accelerate skin aging or wrinkles and frown lines, triggering dermatopause

- Contribute to obesity and low metabolism, leading to dopamine biopause
- Harden and cause blocks to your arteries and capillaries, instigating diabetes and vasculopause

---

The Cardiopause Connection

Depression can hurt your heart and your brain rhythm by causing premature ventricular contractions, a type of cardiac arrhythmia or irregular heartbeat.

Double Depression

Many patients are chronically blue and have exhausting fatigue. The most common form of depression is dysthymia, characterized by a chronic feeling of low mood or "the blues." If you guessed that they must be low in both serotonin and dopamine, you are correct. If you suffer from these two symptoms, see your doctor immediately. She may prescribe a medical stimulant to pull you out of your biochemical rut and then place you on a more natural regimen, which may include diet and lifestyle changes.

Is Feeling Blue Not for You?

When both right (creative, emotional, extroverted, intuitive) and left (thinking, organizing, introverted) sides of the brain are abnormal, you begin to get serious forms of depression because both regions of the brain are out of sync. Resetting the levels of serotonin in your body can really help. Take a look at the signs and symptoms here to see if you are experiencing some form of depression:

- Constant fatigue
- Frequent crying
- Decreased desire for sex

- Decreased or increased physical activity
- Difficulty getting out of bed in the morning
- Difficulty getting through routine tasks
- Difficulty in concentrating
- Difficulty paying attention
- Diminished relationships with friends and loved ones
- Recurrent bouts of feeling like a failure
- Inexplicable sadness
- Generalized dissatisfaction with life
- Hopelessness
- Insomnia and early morning awakening
- Irritability
- Desire to be left alone
- Lack energy
- Lack of confidence
- Lack of motivation
- Episodes of lashing out at loved ones
- Loss of appetite
- Loss of memory
- Mood changes
- Nightmares
- Preference for lying in bed all day over going to any social function
- Strange fears
- Thoughts of suicide, self-destruction, or death
- Trouble making decisions
- Unexplained aches and pains
- Withdrawal from once pleasurable activities

Gripped by Fear and Scared to Death

A lack of serotonin and living in fear are amazing age accelerators. If you are constantly fearful, you are unconsciously reinventing the world around you, generating unnecessary stresses that will rapidly age you far beyond your chronological years. What's more, when you are in a state of fear, you are not relaxing and you're not sleeping, two signs of serotonin trouble. With these two deficiencies combined, you will quickly become a mental and physical wreck.

Fear, and the subsequent lack of serotonin, may:

- Accelerate heart rate; fear can cause a blood clot and/or stroke, leading to cardiopause/vasculopause
- Create sexual dysfunction, triggering menopause or andropause
- Disable erectile function, instigating andropause
- Accelerate inflammation and cancer, leading to immunopause
- Damage your thyroid gland, leading to thyropause

Fear of Disease Means You Are Out of Sync

Fear prevents you from living the Younger You life and lowers your serotonin levels. I've met so many patients who walk into my office saying, "I put off coming in because I was afraid of your test. I didn't want to know what could be wrong." They were afraid of being fixed and instead ended up being afraid that they waited too long. Their serotonin levels were clearly down, resulting in anxiety and fear. Being in sync and having the correct amount of serotonin leads to faith that you can live with the realities of life that good and bad things happen to us all.

Obsessive Compulsive Disorder

One distinct form of irrational phobias is obsessive compulsive disorder (OCD). This is characterized by repetitive behavior that is meant to alleviate the fear, such as constantly washing hands or creating unnecessary routines, such as checking for bugs before going to sleep. OCD can severely affect daily life and the ability to care for oneself. Often, the numbers of repetitive behaviors and routines build, so that those afflicted with OCD find it increasingly difficult to leave their homes. These patients also understand that their compulsion is illogical, are ashamed of the behavior, and want to change. Some examples of OCD are

- Fear of germs, sticky substances, or dirt
- Fear of harming self or others

- Fear of doing something embarrassing
- Hoarding or collecting
- Excess concern with what is right and wrong

OCD is not a factor of an aging mind but is an extremely effective age accelerator. Eighty percent of OCD cases occur by the age of 35. Research has shown that these patients typically hide their symptoms and avoid treatment for as much as seven years! The average age of occurrence falls somewhere between 20 and 25, and fewer than 5 percent of patients experience onset after the age of 40. However, as OCD begins to control more and more of a person's life, the rest of the person's health will rapidly fade.

Meg Lost Her Serenity and Lost Her Health. Meg V. was 30 years old when she was diagnosed with OCD. Meg was filling her day with so many unnecessary routines and unexplainable fears that she could no longer keep up with the habitual health tasks we all take for granted. For example, one of her routines was that she would have to check the stove hundreds of times to make sure it was off, especially if she planned to leave the house. This checking routine often started early in the morning and kept her so busy she never had time to brush her teeth. Eventually she had a mouthful of cavities and root canal problems.

Her primary care physician wanted her to see a psychiatrist and be placed on Prozac. Her mother, Wendy, brought her to see me instead. Wendy wanted to find out if there was a nutritional protocol that Meg could try before she placed her daughter on an antidepressant. Because nutrients supply the raw material needed by brain chemicals, there is certainly a natural protocol I often recommend. Several SSRIs have proven to be effective in mitigating OCD symptoms, and while medication might be necessary to provide initial symptom relief, I don't recommend it for the long term.

After a full physical and AgePrint, I concurred with Meg's previous diagnosis: she definitely exhibited the signs and symptoms of OCD. What's more, her serotonin levels were low, and her AgePrint for brain serenity was 50. I suggested to her mother than we place Meg on bioidentical hormones, supplements, and dietary nutrients that could all positively affect Meg's serotonin levels. With carefully monitored hormone replacement therapy, I felt that Meg's condition would improve. I also suggested that Meg try to exercise daily as well as learn how to meditate. These two known stress-busters would also help calm her mind.

Six months later I received a phone call. Wendy was exuberant. The protocol had worked, and Meg never took a single antidepressant. Her OCD was brought under control, and Meg could finally take care of herself again.

Serenity = Sleep

One of the easiest ways to become a younger you is to get back to a schedule of restful sleep. Abundant sleep is like happiness: it takes us to a peaceful place where we restore our mind and body. When we wake up from a good nap or a long sleep, we are ready and eager to face the day.

Serotonin levels manage our sleep, cycling in and out of each stage of consciousness until we are in deep sleep. While we're sleeping, serotonin can help regenerate almost any part of the body. What's more, our mind resets or, more accurately, reboots. Our brain is electric, mak-

A Nightcap Is a Bad Choice for a Good Night's Sleep

Alcohol and carbohydrates, a typical nighttime mix, are often used as a form of self-medication for anxiety and depression. Some believe that alcohol relaxes you so that you will get a better night's sleep, but don't fall into this trap. Instead use exercise, meditation, yoga, or prayer. Even small doses of alcohol can reduce the quality and the length of your sleep. Alcohol suppresses deep sleep, causing sleep fragmentation and contributing to sleep apnea, a sleep disorder where breathing stops briefly but frequently all night long.

ing each of us a living circuit. We short-circuit when we don't go to sleep or "shut down."

If you have a serotonin deficiency, your delta sleep waves are actually more elevated during the day, blocking your alertness, creativity, and playfulness. Your brain waves are showing the wrong levels of balance. You are also not sleeping well. Poor sleep can manifest itself in different ways. You may have difficulty falling asleep at night, or you might be plagued with night terrors or nightmares. You may wake up frequently to go to the bathroom, or you may never get to sleep at all, tossing and worrying all night long.

Sleep Restores Serotonin

Getting better, more restful sleep is an antidote to fear. Once the brain's synchrony has been restored, your brain can reboot, keeping your nighttime thought patterns where they belong: at night! Second, being happy and not taking life so seriously is another antidote to fear; if we can enjoy ourselves, we won't let our fears destroy us.

The Sleep Cascade. When you do not sleep in a deep state, all your fears, phobias, obsessions, compulsions, and blues all become exacerbated, which results in a cascade of the whole body going out of sync.

If you have a serotonin deficiency, you may feel sleepy during the day, affecting your alertness, creativity, and playfulness. You are also not sleeping well at night. Poor sleep can manifest itself in different ways. You may have difficulty falling asleep at night, or you might wake in the middle of the night and be unable to go back to sleep. You might be plagued with night terrors or nightmares. You may wake up frequently to go to the bathroom, or you may never get to sleep at all, tossing and worrying all night long.

When Sleep Doesn't Come

The mind and body will not recover from losing so much sleep—it's probably an indication that your serotonin levels are low. Losing sleep is a major age accelerator, affecting all of the other pauses, as well as adding to your depression and fears. The lack of sleep may:

- Accelerate inflammation, weaken your immune system, which often leads to cancer and immunopause
- Cause mood swings, leading to GABA biopause
- Contribute to decreased libido, premature ejaculation in men, and lack of orgasm, triggering andropause or menopause
- Accelerates and contributes to diabetes or its earliest form, metabolic syndrome
- Contribute to bone loss, leading to osteopause
- Cause skin dehydration and inflammation, instigating dermatopause
- Contribute to arrhythmias and elevations in blood pressure, leading to cardiopause
- Cause diminished circulation in your hands and feet, triggering vasculopause
- Cause decline in memory, attention, and cognition, instigating electropause
- Lead to addiction, leading to dopamine biopause
- Cause depression and irrational fears, triggering serotonin biopause

It Takes Seven Hours to Boost Your Serotonin Levels

My patient, Sam W., recently called me. He was a very successful medical specialist and was continually on the go. As we were catching up, he wasted no time in reporting that he was up for the last 20 hours, a routine I thought we broke years ago. He wasn't complaining; in fact, Sam was bragging about how much paperwork he was getting done in the early morning hours. I had to set him straight.

I reminded Sam that not getting enough sleep is an age accelerator. His mother had dementia, and she couldn't sleep. Just because Sam was smart doesn't mean he won't get dementia. The lesson to learn from

CODE BREAKER: What's Your Sleep Debt?

Sleep debt is defined as getting fewer than 49 hours of sleep per week, the amount you need to keep your serotonin levels in check. That's an average of seven hours a night. If you are sleeping less than this, you are beginning to accelerate your aging code.

this example is to make sure that you get seven hours of restful sleep every night. By doing so, you are likely to live a long time.

Position Yourself for a Good Night's Sleep, and Boost Your Serotonin Levels

- Try to go to bed at the same time each night.
- Set up a nighttime routine that does not involve television or working on the computer immediately before bed. For example, listen to relaxing music in the darkness of your bedroom.
- Finish dinner at least three hours before you go to bed.
- Sleep in a cool, dark room that is only used for "bedroom" activities.
- Lavender-scented candles, aromatherapy oil, or night cream relaxes the mind before bed.
- Do not drink caffeinated beverages or alcohol, and do not smoke cigarettes before bed.
- Get into bed when you are sleepy; don't fall asleep on the couch.
- Avoid naps in the late afternoon or early evening.

Remember that boosting your serotonin by getting enough sleep is like taking a vacation. Allowing your brain to resynchronize itself gives

YOUNGER YOU FACT: Sleep Enhances Creativity and Brain Speed

Your ability to learn motor skills increases when you've had a good night's sleep. While your serotonin is balanced, your dopamine and acetylcholine can advance, leading to new deep thoughts and artistic skills.

it a feeling of rejuvenation. Your brain will thank you, and you will save thousands of dollars if you forfeit that vacation.

It's Easy to Boost Serotonin

It's easy to boost your serotonin and balance your brain. A multimodal approach including medications, hormones, nutrient supplements, and specific dietary suggestions will help you break the death code of depression, fear, and sleep disorders that may already be evident by your AgePrint.

You can choose a variety of ways to return your brain's balance, either through prescription medications, bioidentical hormones, or nutrients, supplements, and diet. Your choice can be guided by your deficiency. If your AgePrint for brain serenity was more than 20 years older than your chronological age, you can address it with nutrition and lifestyle changes. If your score was between 40 and 60 years more than your chronological age, you will need to address your personal reversal with hormones. At levels greater than 60 years more than your chronological age, you will possibly need medications to reverse your brain age to a more normal state.

Depression is no different from any other physical ailment and it can be treated. If you are constantly feeling blue or in a funk, share your feelings with a family member or close friend. Depression not only is related to a loss of serotonin, but it's also in your DNA. That means that someone else in your family may also be dealing with this disease. No matter what, don't hold your feelings inside; you're not helping yourself or saving your family from embarrassment by not being honest and seeking treatment.

Professional counseling can be an effective supplement to a health program that includes antidepressant medications in treating depression, phobias, and sleep disorders; in my experience, cognitive and behavioral psychotherapy yield the best results. What's more, you will need to see a counselor who can prescribe medication, if necessary. Most physicians will agree with me that often antidepressant treatment is necessary for all types of depression and is the fastest, most effective way to improve the brain serenity aging code.

Take Action: Early Detection Is Key

By taking the AgePrint quiz in Chapter 2, you've already taken the first step toward better health. The blood test for determining serotonin levels is called a serum serotonin level test, also known as 5-hydroxytryptamine (5-HT). If you are concerned about obsessive compulsive disorder (OCD), you can take the Yale-Brown Obsessive-Compulsive Scale (YBOCS) test online at various OCD websites. If you are concerned about sleep apnea, you might want to consider participating in a sleep study. If you have sinus disease, allergies, asthma, or have been told that you snore, I would recommend having this study done.

Medications That Break the Serenity Code

Antidepressants come in many varieties. Selective serotonin reuptake inhibitors (SSRIs) are the medications of choice because they have the fewest side effects and are less sedating than older antidepressants. The side effects of SSRIs include dry mouth, nausea, and sexual dysfunction and are usually tolerable. SSRIs work by allowing the body to make

Sexual Side Effects of Antidepressants

Whether you are a man or woman, your sex life does not have to suffer when you treat your depression. There are many other antidepressants that do not have sex-related side effects, including Remeron, Wellbutrin, Serzone, and Lexapro. Talk to your doctor about switching to one of these treatments. And read Part 5 on sexual aging for more natural treatments for improving your sex life.

the best use of the reduced amounts of serotonin that it has, allowing it to linger in the brain longer. Eventually, it will help naturally increase the levels of serotonin, creating a younger brain. Any of the SSRIs are also good for sleep disorders and are also used to combat OCD. Make sure that your prescribing physician is aware of all the medications you are currently taking before you begin an antidepressant program. There is a great concern about drug-to-drug interactions, especially for older patients.

Serotonin loss is serious, so talk to your doctor about taking these medications:

Conventional Treatment	Suggested Dosage per Day	Use
Carbamazepine (Tegretol)	400–1,200 mg	Unstable personality, manic depression
Paroxetine (Paxil)	10–60 mg	Social phobia
Sertraline (Zoloft)	25–200 mg	Generalized anxiety
Ondansetron (Zofran)	4–16 mg	Nausea
Trazodone (Desyrel)	100–400 mg	Sleep problems
Ergoloid mesylates (Hydergine)	3–12 mg	Memory loss
Venlafaxine (Effexor)	37.5–375 mg	Mixed depression, blues
Triptans	Varies	Headaches
Fluvoxamine (Luvox)	25–300 mg	OCD
Clomipramine (Anafranil)	25–250 mg	OCD
Sibutramine (Meridia)	5–15 mg	Weight loss

Break the Aging Code with Depression-Busting, Bioidentical Hormones

A younger, balanced you may require that you increase your hormone levels. For treating serotonin deficiencies, one of the most powerful hormones is human growth hormone (HGH), which is naturally made in the pituitary gland. Your levels of HGH peak during adolescence, but after age 21, the HGH levels already fall by 14 percent per decade. That means by the time we're 50, most of us are either partially or completely deficient in HGH.

However, this decline can be completely reversed through bioidentical hormone supplementation. By increasing your growth hormone, not only will you find that you are less blue, but you will sleep like a baby, letting your brain and body fully repair overnight and be ready for the next day. It is also linked to helping memory retention, sharper vision, and enhanced cognitive performance.

So remember, depletion equals depression, so take these serotonin-boosting hormones:

Hormonal Treatment	Suggested Dosage per Day
Progesterone	100–300 mg
HGH	5–30 mg
Pregnenolone	10–25 mg

Get Happy with Supplements and Nutrients

Natural supplements offer a side effect–free alternative to sleep medications. They are gentle on the mind and body and may offer the relief you need to get a good night's sleep. Many amino acids can improve mood and depression. For example, tryptophan is the amino-acid precursor to serotonin. L-tryptophan is available as an over-the-counter supplement and is often found in many megavitamin formulations.

Consider trying these natural serenity boosters:

Natural Treatment	Suggested Dosage per Day
Melatonin	0.3–10 mg
Tryptophan	500–2,000 mg
Vitamin B_6	10–50 mg
Fish oils (EPA/DHA)	500–3,000 mg
Magnesium	300–1,000 mg
Vitamin B_3/niacinamide	500–1,000 mg

CODE BREAKER: Take Two Melatonin, Call Me in the Morning

Melatonin, an important hormonal supplement for sleep, may also decrease your risk of Alzheimer's disease.

The Serotonin-Boosting Diet

The levels of serotonin in your body can be boosted through dietary choices, especially by choosing foods that are high in tryptophan. You might already know that turkey is full of tryptophan, which is one reason why we feel so tired after eating a big Thanksgiving meal. Watch out for the junk food and carbohydrates you might crave to keep your energy up; ultimately, they will only slow you down with excess weight.

Your serotonin can be supported all day long with the following menu selections:

Breakfast Options
- ½ cup oatmeal with blueberries and bananas
- ½ cup rice bran cereal with ½ cup skim milk
- 4 ounces smoked or baked salmon with tomatoes
- 1 cup low-fat yogurt with wheat germ
- Two hard-boiled or poached eggs
- ½ cup cottage cheese with fresh fruit

Lunch Options
- Sandwich meats, including turkey or roast beef with whole-wheat crackers
- Sandwich made with 4 ounces chicken breast and slice of Swiss cheese on whole-grain bread
- Avocado and beet salad
- Tofu and broccoli stir-fry over brown rice

Dinner Options
- 4 ounces sliced oven-roasted turkey breast with baked beans
- One-half Cornish hen and a baked potato
- 4 ounces broiled bluefish with steamed broccoli

Desserts and Snack Options
- Guacamole with veggies for dipping
- 1 cup yogurt parfait with mixed nuts and berries
- Swiss cheese on whole-wheat crackers
- ¼ cup mixed nuts
- ¼ cup sunflower seeds and raisin mix

The following herbs and spices can help boost your level of serotonin:

- Basil combats stress.
- Black pepper aids in digestion and has been shown to help sinusitis and epilepsy.
- Borage calms inflammation.
- Cayenne pepper helps pain, headaches, neuropathy, and rheumatoid pain.
- Cumin aids in digestion and helps carpal tunnel syndrome.
- Nutmeg helps gastrointestinal problems and has psychotropic properties.
- Peppermint helps tension and fatigue.
- Rosemary relaxes muscles.
- Sage helps relieve fear, anxiety, paranoia, and delusions.
- Thyme controls spasms, helps respiratory problems, and fights fungal infections.
- Turmeric is a natural body cleanser and helps protect the liver.

CODE BREAKER: Choose These Rainbow Foods When You're Feeling Blue
- Trout, herring, eggs, sea vegetables, soybean products, and kelp are high in vitamin B_{12}, which boosts your mood.
- Egg yolks, soybeans, and whole grains contain biotin. A biotin deficiency is correlated with low mood.

Dealing with Food Temptations
Some people cannot bring themselves to eat when they are depressed or overtired. Others will overeat, self-medicating their fatigue with junk

food, simple carbohydrates, and fatty "comfort foods." While Ronald McDonald may be whispering your name when you are depressed, you do not have to heed the call.

You can best avoid food-related pitfalls by not allowing your brain to get low in the first place. However, we aren't always on top of our health. For those days, here's a few ways to work around food traps:

1. **Don't fall for "fat-free foods":** Quite frankly, these so-called healthy alternatives are some of the biggest marketing scams out there. If you take fat out of food, you have to put something back in so people will eat it. Replacements usually include sugar, preservatives, and chemicals that make these foods *higher* in *calories*, defeating the whole purpose. You're better off sticking with the occasional smaller portion of your favorite treat.

2. **Stay out of the company break room:** The ubiquitous boxes of cookies, doughnuts, and other fats litter counters of break rooms all across the United States. Make sure you eat a good breakfast before you get to the office, so you will be better able to resist snacking altogether.

3. **Satisfy your sweet tooth:** Try herbal tea with honey—it will smell sweet, satisfy your cravings, and up your intake of age-fighting antioxidants.

4. **Stay savvy when eating out:** No matter what cuisine you choose, drink plenty of liquids such as water, tea, or tomato juice, all of which are appetite suppressors, when you first arrive at a restaurant. Start with a soup course, push the breadbasket away, and pick menu items such grilled or steamed fish and vegetables. Have the waitstaff put half of your entrée in a to-go box before they plate your meal so you will keep the portion size in check.

5. **Plan ahead when eating on the road:** Travel with a stash of healthy snacks such as nuts or energy bars. Make sure to drink extra water on a plane—flying dries out your skin.

CODE BREAKER: Think Good Thoughts and You'll Be Younger

Extreme pessimism is associated with later development of dementia. Looking for the positive in everything you do is better for the brain than dwelling on excessive negative thinking. Keep this in mind when your life seems to be getting in the way of your happiness.

Out of the Brain, into the Body

A younger you relies on a completely balanced brain, where all four of the neurotransmitters are plentiful and working at their full potential: high power, tremendous speed, Zenlike calmness, and total balance. We've broken the brain's code and identified the great age accelerators: obesity, addiction, cognitive decline, anxiety, sleep disorders, and depression. By boosting your dopamine, acetylcholine, GABA, and serotonin through medications, hormones, nutrient supplements, and diet, you are taking the first important steps toward living happily, healthfully, and 15 years younger.

We now can move forward and explore each of the body's pauses. Go back to the results of your AgePrint in Chapter 2, and locate your highest score. That will be your primary pause and the one that should be addressed first. For example, if your highest score was related to the aging heart, you need to address either your cardiopause or your vasculopause. If your highest score was for menopause, skip to that chapter, make the necessary changes, and then go back and take the test again. The AgePrint is so important because the biological clock controls more than your ability to procreate. It's ticking away on every illness. The earlier you can catch a health problem, the easier it is to reverse. Beating the clock means knowing your AgePrint.

But don't for one second think that we're done with the brain; remember, the brain is the master organ that controls the rest of the body. It controls its health and its pauses. You'll see that in each of the subsequent chapters, the pauses can be fixed by both taking care of that particular organ's needs and by taking care of your brain. You'll also see how each pause is interconnected; the reversal of one will likely lead to the reversal of another.

PART 3

The Overworked Cardiovascular System

7

Cardiopause: The Slowing and Aging of the Heart

Heart disease can—and probably will—kill you. In fact, it's more likely that you'll die of heart disease than any other medical complication, disease, accident, or terrorist attack. This year alone, an estimated 700,000 Americans will have a heart attack, while 500,000 will be having their second. But you don't have to be one of these people. Heart disease is often completely reversible and preventable. By taking care of your brain and your body, you will not be one of these statistics.

The collective condition known as "heart disease" refers to disorders of the heart as well as the 60,000-mile vascular highway system, the internal network of blood vessels through which the heart pushes blood. The two sides of this illness can be described simultaneously as cardiovascular disease. I like to differentiate between them as *cardiopause* (pertaining to the heart) and *vasculopause* (pertaining to the peripheral blood vessels). Both cardiopause and vasculopause are ultimate killers; they can be completely compromised by all of the brain's age accelerators and lead to death. However, if you catch your symptoms and treat them early enough, you can reverse these pauses, regain your health, and work your way back toward regaining a younger you.

CODE BREAKER: The Heart Is Not as Powerful as the Mind

Although it is critical to have a healthy heart, the brain and the nervous system truly control your health. The heart is beating at one cycle per second. When the brain is asleep, it is beating at four cycles per second. This means that the brain is more actively managing your body than the heart. Even when you are exercising and your heart rate is up to two or three cycles per second, it is still not as active as the brain when it is asleep.

Cardiopause Can Be Reversed

I have witnessed long-term improvement in heart failure patients—in some cases almost full reversals that last for years. These results are possible because we look at heart failure as a systemic issue. In other words, we treat the whole person, not just the pumping condition of the heart (although that's obviously a key element of our program). This treatment includes making healthy lifestyle changes as well as introducing nutrients and supplements designed to improve the heart's function and prevent future problems without the side effects of prescription drugs.

For example, Juan, a 55-year-old man, was already taking five prescription medications for his heart disease when he came to see me. Between his heart failure and the side effects of the drugs, he reported that he was feeling horrible all the time. He had episodes where he would pass out completely. His cardiologist told him that he had five years to live and recommended that he undergo surgery to receive an implantable cardioverter defibrillator (ICD). This device monitors your heartbeat and, if a dangerous heart rhythm occurs, delivers a powerful shock to "reset" the heart to a more normal rhythm.

I had a feeling that Juan's situation could be reversed without surgery. I had him take the AgePrint quiz and started him on a new regimen of heart medications. It took small steps, but eventually Juan began to feel better and younger.

It's now more than 10 years since it was first recommended that Juan have surgery. He never had the heart surgery, and he no longer needs a galaxy of prescription medications. Better yet, he's now able to work in his yard for hours at a time, he can take his daughter and granddaughter to Europe for monthlong vacations, and he feels better than he has for years. Recently, we reevaluated his AgePrint, and his cardiopause was down to 50 from age 75. Juan got 15 years younger in 10 years, which is not bad for a man who had been told to make plans for his funeral.

When Cardiopause Strikes, the Heart Reacts

These are the likely scenarios of cardiopause:

• **Coronary artery blockages transpire.** This is measured as plaques developing from cholesterol, triglycerides, and calcium. I have seen as much as 95 percent blockage reversed on many of my patients.

• **Valve damage occurs.** This swelling and inflammation or calcification of the heart can be significantly reduced.

• **Heart chambers become enlarged.** This is due to valve damage, high blood pressure, and alcohol abuse and can be completely reversed.

• **Pumping action of the heart decreases.** This is measured as ejection fraction. My program can correct pumping action from as low as 15 percent to return to 50 percent efficiency. The ideal is 65 percent.

Ejection Fraction: Your Heart's Aging Code

The most common measure used to monitor heart failure is ejection fraction (EF). This number indicates how much blood your heart pumps out with every beat. An ejection fraction of 55 to 75 percent (65 percent is ideal) is considered normal. Heart failure patients typically eject only 10 to 40 percent of the blood in their heart.

EF is the dominant marker of the age of the heart. Compare these numbers with your AgePrint to see what kind of damage has already occurred. The change in EF is primarily due to hypertension and heart disease, both of which increase in likelihood with age.

EF	AgePrint	Results
10 percent	100	Certain death
20 percent	90	Average survival 2–4 years
30 percent	80	
40 percent	70	
50 percent	60	Beginning of heart failure
60 percent	50	Normal
70 percent	40	

The Five Biggest Risk Factors of Cardiopause

1. Family history of heart disease
2. Smoking
3. Hypertension
4. Diabetes
5. High cholesterol, called dyslipidemias (low HDL, high LDL)

Cardiopause refers to the weakening of the heart code that is delivered through the coronary arteries, the major highways that bring blood to the heart. When these arteries become clogged, their size decreases, making it difficult for blood to pass back into the heart and toward the rest of the body. Arteries become clogged because of inflammation or from plaque buildup.

Blockages: I Hear You Knocking, but You Can't Come In

Plaque is created from cholesterol, the substance that we've all heard of but still can't wrap our minds around. There are two types of cholesterol, but knowing which is "bad" and which is "good" can be confusing. Both types of cholesterol are comprised of a waxy, fatlike substance that is actually necessary for your overall health. It is an essential component of every cell and is required by the body to perform certain functions, such as helping the liver manufacture bile, helping the body digest fats, and acting as a building block for certain hormones. Cholesterol also coats and lubricates the body, helping the smooth flow of blood. It is usually produced in the liver, but if the body requires more than the liver can produce, it will create its own cholesterol from the foods we eat. However, if more cholesterol is produced than the body can process and use, it becomes deposited inside the walls of blood vessels. When this happens, cholesterol begins to turn from a helpful necessity to a harmful substance.

Cholesterol is the precursor to all your sex hormones, such as estrogen, testosterone, DHEA, and progesterone. An increase in cholesterol is simply part of the aging process, just the same as losing our testicles, ovaries, or adrenal functions. Therefore, when we treat aging with natural hormones, not only do we treat our aging sexuality, we are helping our heart.

Here's the confusing part: there are two types of cholesterol. The "bad" LDL cholesterol comes directly from the liver and is delivered to the cells of the body. If overproduced, it will line the arterial walls. The "good" HDL cholesterol is going the other way; blood transports this type from the arterial walls to the liver, where it is broken down and removed from the body.

What's more, there are triglycerides to consider. Triglycerides are a type of fat your body obtains from the foods you eat. When your body digests food, fats in the food change to triglycerides. Your body can also make more triglycerides in the liver from fat, carbohydrates, and protein. Triglycerides also clog the arteries and contribute to all forms of heart disease.

A younger you requires these numbers at all times:

- HDL cholesterol levels greater than 40
- LDL cholesterol levels lower than 130
- Total cholesterol level lower than 200
- Triglyceride level less than 150

Cholesterol Doesn't Tell the Whole Story

Every pause can cause heart disease. Knowing how much fat is circulating in your blood vessels is just an immediate marker. It's like checking your wallet to see how much cash you have; it's good information, but it has no bearing on what's in your bank account. The state of your cholesterol or triglycerides do have some predictive value, but you can't neglect the other aspects of your health that impact your heart.

Valve Damage: When the Doors to Your Heart Don't Close

The heart responds to the clogged arteries by swelling itself, just like a door frame during a humid summer. Now blood can't make its way into or out of the heart. The heart is unable to pump enough blood to adequately supply your body with oxygen, which strains the entire cardiovascular system, as well as the rest of the body; all those other organs need blood, and without it, they will not work.

Anytime you have a significant heart or related condition, you may require the attention of a cardiologist. But how do you know if you have heart disease or if you are at risk for developing it? The two most common markers for cardiopause are a positive family history for heart disease as well as leading a generally sedentary lifestyle. The majority of patients who die of a heart attack have few or no symptoms. That's why it's called a silent killer: it sneaks up on you.

However, you can be on the lookout for these signs and symptoms and make sure you see your doctor immediately if you are experiencing any of them:

- A sudden onset of sharp pain in an arm, a shoulder, the back, or the stomach
- Shortness of breath
- Chest pain
- Sudden dizzy spells
- Memory loss, confusion
- Anxiety, sweating

Tell Your Body, "Don't Go Breaking My Heart"

I once befriended a local politician. At 63 years old with what must have been a 50-inch waist, he was clearly suffering from obesity. He was short of breath, he looked ghostly, and I could tell that he was not drinking enough water. He had to have the AgePrint of an elderly individual. Not knowing what his medical care was like, I begged him to see me, but unfortunately I could not convince him. Instead, he tried to convince me to contribute to his political lobbying effort. I remember telling him I could not believe he cared about political issues when he didn't care about his own health. Only a year later I recognized his name in the obituaries.

Just as your heart affects the other organs of the body, the health of your entire body affects your heart. There's no time like the present to start breaking this death code. After age 40, many people experience up to a 20 percent decline in their maximum heart rate because the heart becomes less responsive to dopamine. However, by treating your heart and your brain well before you experience symptoms, you lower your risk of this aging code dramatically.

Let's first look at the connection between your heart and the brain's own age accelerators. Basically, when the brain breaks, the heart breaks. Now you have a broken heart and a broken brain. A lack of the following neurotransmitters can put you at risk for cardiopause:

- **Dopamine:** A lack of dopamine may lead to obesity, which accelerates all forms of heart disease because it causes your blood vessels to become clogged with fat. Addiction (food, alcohol, smoking, and cocaine) can all accelerate heart disease. (See Chapter 3 for more on dopamine.)

- **Acetylcholine:** A lack of acetylcholine can cause your brain and mind to deteriorate and heart disease can accelerate. Many individuals who have intact brain capacity but the advanced stages of heart disease will live longer than an individual who has deteriorated brain capacity and a heart condition. I also find that people who are losing their memory and attention also try to feed their brain with stimulants such as cigarettes and caffeine, both of which constrict the blood vessels. Or their failing cognition causes a mismanagement of diet, leading to obesity, which leads to heart disease. (See Chapter 4 for more on acetylcholine.)

- **GABA:** Anxiety and stress are well-known causes of heart disease. GABA deficiency typically begins as a loss of calm and a simultaneous increase in blood pressure. (See Chapter 5 for more on GABA.)

You Don't Need a Cardiologist to Tell You What Your Waist Already Knows

In assessing your heart attack risk, you could do a stress test, get blood work done, and spend a day with your friendly neighborhood cardiologist. In many cases, however, simply looking at the notches on your belt will tell you all you need to know. An increasing waistline is an equally reliable indicator of your risk for heart disease. Even if your blood tests are "normal," they cannot stay that way for long if you're lugging around a beer belly. If you have abdominal obesity, get a cardiac checkup.

- **Serotonin:** A lack of serotonin may lead to depression, which often disrupts sleep patterns. Too little or too much sleep might increase your risk of developing heart disease. What's more, coronary artery disease is often associated with depression. This combination can sharply increase your chances of having a potentially fatal heart attack. (See Chapter 6 for more on serotonin.)

Other Age Accelerators

Many of the other pauses also directly affect heart function. Just reading this list once again makes the point that our bodies really are interconnected:

- Somatopause: DHEA and growth hormone loss weakens the heart muscle.
- Andropause: Loss of testosterone weakens the heart's muscle.
- Menopause: Estrogen and progesterone loss causes stress on the heart.
- Thyropause: When the thyroid slows, heart disease increases.
- Parathyropause: When you lose height and start to develop osteoporosis, increasing changes in your bone, deposits calcium in your arteries, triggers changes in your heart.
- Immunopause: A weakened immune system makes you more vulnerable to infections of the heart and other heart-related conditions.
- Dopamine biopause: Being overweight contributes to high blood pressure and clogged arteries, thus heart attack and stroke.

Depression and Heart Disease: When Your Heart's Got the Blues

With depression and heart disease being the leading accelerators of death, is it any wonder that there is a strong connection between the

Women and Heart Disease

Women develop heart disease differently than men. As they enter into menopause, they often get dysthymia, or depression, which begins a horrendous cascade of inflammation that affects the vascular system. A major study of 28,000 women at Boston's Brigham and Women's Hospital provided conclusive evidence that painless inflammation of heart tissue is the main trigger of heart attacks—worse even than high cholesterol. Women with high levels of inflammation are twice as likely as those with high cholesterol to die from heart attacks and strokes. This inflammation can be easily measured with the C-reactive protein test, a test that measures proteins made by the body to fight injury and infection. I have been using this test, as well as numerous other tests that identify early heart disease stages, for 20 years.

two? Studies have shown that depression is more common among people with heart disease than those without. Small wonder when you know that depression has been linked to increased blood pressure and abnormal heart rhythms as well as chronically elevated stress hormone levels that increase your heart's workload. The complex interplay between these two conditions frequently allows for one or both to go undiagnosed by medical professionals and individuals, who often can't recognize their own symptoms.

Dysthymia, or "the blues," hurts your heart. Depression increases your likelihood of premature death, heart attack, and pump failure as well as other serious cardiovascular events such as stroke, blood clots, and infections that can damage your heart. You need to be mindful of your emotional state; when depression goes up, heart disease goes up.

Children with Heart Disease: You Can Be Born Old

Children can be born with damaged arteries and will enter their teen years without being properly diagnosed. Many teenagers in my practice have small holes in their hearts as well as other heart defects that are discovered. Or by the time they reach early adulthood, thickening of the arteries can occur just from eating fast food that is full of greasy, saturated fats. By the time these teens are 20, they will be old.

Breathe Easier—You're Preventing a Heart Attack

Besides their lungs, asthmatics also need to worry about their heart. A little-known fact is that asthmatics have higher rates of heart attacks. Asthma treatment shouldn't just involve inhalers; it should also involve using your head. By treating asthma through the brain and fixing the pauses that are contributing to it, you'll breathe easier and have less stress, better sleep, fewer allergies, better sinuses, and better moods, all of which can save you from a heart attack. A pulmonary function test can determine if you are suffering from mild asthma. Although this test is underused by doctors, it can greatly assist in the detecting of pulmonary and cardiac disorders.

Take Action: Healing a Broken Heart

The traditional approach to heart disease is to manage the symptoms of the condition while trying to improve the pumping action of the heart. It is not uncommon for heart disease patients to be prescribed as many as five medications. This usually means taking ACE inhibitors to decrease the workload of the heart and increase cardiac output; diuretics to help rid your body of excess fluid; digitalis, an herb known to increase the heart's pumping ability; blood thinners; and beta blockers to reduce the workload of the heart and lower blood pressure.

My approach is different: the Younger You Plan begins with early testing and designing a whole-person program that treats the pumping action of the heart as well as all of the associated problems. Pump failure itself is not always the cause of the death. Rather, you might die because of blood clots caused by the heart failure or stress from their condition that will provoke an arrhythmia, or heart rhythm irregularity. My goal is not just to fix your pump but to reverse your cardiopause to get to a younger you. This involves looking at not just the heart but the whole person and anticipating problems before they happen.

Should I Consider Cardiac Bypass Surgery?

In all my years of practice, I have never recommended a single patient for bypass surgery. This doesn't surprise me but will shock every other doctor in the country; bypass surgery is the most common major surgery in the United States. Every year, tens of thousands of patients get one, but not mine. The procedure is designed to increase your blood flow and prevent future heart attacks. However, I know better methods of prevention, including earlier, more accurate testing and preventive care. Even in the cases of relatively advanced heart disease, studies have shown that patients can stop and sometimes even reverse their disease through lifestyle changes and supplementation alone.

Bypass surgery is completely preventable if you follow the Younger You Plan. Discuss these ideas with your physician. If you take care of your heart now, not only will you live like you're 15 years younger, but you'll make those fancy cardiac surgeons start taking the subway to work.

The Importance of Early Testing

No matter what your AgePrint, you can never start a cardiovascular program soon enough. If your AgePrint is more than 20 years above your chronological age, you need to be seen by a physician at least once a year. Your condition should be carefully assessed with a complete battery of tests, including EKG, Thallium stress test, 24-hour continuous EKG, CT angiography, and a complete blood workup, including checking levels of C-reactive protein and interleukins, fibrinogen, homocysteine, cholesterol and other blood lipids, and atrial and B-type natriuretic peptides.

True or False: One Scan Can Detect Your Heart Disease

The answer is false. New studies show that stress tests are the worst of the tests and often fail to pick up heart disease indicators. Many people die after having normal results. Other tests are not faultless, either. A stress thallium test cannot detect coronary calcium buildup. An angiogram misses small vessels, and approximately 50 percent of the time doctors disagree on their reading.

The standard battery of tests for heart disease—an EKG, exercise stress test, and cholesterol (lipid) panel—fail to detect even advanced heart disease in 90 percent of people. Don't settle for a cardiologist who only uses these methods. Find one who will do the far more accurate "big three"—lipoprotein testing, CT heart scans, and an ankle-brachial index (ABI). Lipoprotein testing examines fat-carrying proteins in the blood, CT heart scans assess arterial wall calcium and total plaque buildup in your heart, and the ABI measures blood flow in your extremities. While no tests are foolproof, your odds of catching heart disease in the early stages and preventing death greatly improve; 95 to 98 percent of all heart disease can be detected with these tests.

You can have superior heart functioning but have a major blockage in your arteries or veins without you or your doctor even knowing it. Within a moment's notice these types of blockages can cause sudden death. Many people still need to do conventional stress testing because they have coronary calcium buildup. I strongly believe that computers can better identify the compromise of arterial or venous blood flow better than any physician can. The new CT angiography replaces most conventional coronary imaging techniques and helps us catch heart disease before it catches you.

Heart Healthy Tests	Description
CT angiogram/coronary artery calcium score	An x-ray that shows the blood vessels surrounding the heart to determine location and type of narrowing; can detect coronary calcification from atherosclerosis before symptoms develop; predicts coronary heart disease in your future; is used to detect calcium deposits found in atherosclerotic plaque in the coronary arteries

Heart Healthy Tests	Description
Echocardiogram/ ejection fraction	Determines pumping action of the heart; a sonogram of the heart that measures heart size and valve structure and function, including prolapse, regurgitation
Holter monitor	24-hour measure of heart rate; checks for abnormal heartbeats and rhythm
Cardiac PET scan	Examines health of coronary arteries and the heart muscle

The following are important blood tests that you should have:

Blood Levels	Function
Hormones That Affect EF	
Dehydroepiandrosterone (DHEA)	The major androgen produced by the adrenal glands
Brain natriuretic peptide (BNP)	Marker for congestive heart failure
Serum cortisol	High cortisol levels indicate that the body is stressed, which could lead to high blood pressure and other heart conditions
Lipid Tests	
Lipoprotein electrophoresis	Used to identify rare familial lipid disorders to anticipate problems in children
APO lipo, A1, B	The major protein of HDL and LDL; used to assess risk for heart disease
APOLIPO, A1/B ratio	The most sensitive test to assess risk of heart disease
Triglycerides	High levels are associated with peripheral vascular disease

Blood Levels	Function
Lipid Tests	
Cholesterol	Used to monitor and screen for hyperlipidemias
HDL cholesterol	Higher levels protect against atherosclerosis
LDL cholesterol	High levels increase risk for heart disease
Nutritional Tests	
Taurine, methionine, arginine, carnitine	Low nutritional levels are associated with heart disease
Toxins	
Homocysteine	Testing for lead, cadmium, aluminum, and mercury; high levels of homocysteine are associated with increased risk of blood clots in arteries and veins
Free erythrocyte protoporphyrin (FEP)	Helps determine cause of anemia; marker of lead poisoning
Lead	Measures level of lead in blood
SMAC	Chemistry test that measures electrolytes, proteins, kidney, and liver function
Complete blood count (CBC) with differential	Checks for anemia, infection, platelet count

Reverse Cardiopause with Life-Saving Medications

Sometimes, medications may be needed to help prevent or control coronary heart disease and to reduce the risk of a heart attack. Here are the most common and how they work:

- **ACE inhibitors** block the chemical that makes blood vessels narrow; they are used to help control high blood pressure and for a damaged heart muscle. They may be prescribed after a heart attack to help the heart pump blood better.

- **Beta blockers** slow the heart and make it beat with less contracting force, so blood pressure drops and the heart can work with ease. They are used for high blood pressure and chest pain, to treat and prevent arrhythmias, and to prevent a repeat heart attack. However, other medications provide better choices for primary prevention.

- **Diuretics** (water pills) decrease fluid in the body to lower blood pressure and treat edema.

- **Calcium channel blockers** relax blood vessels, lower high blood pressure, and reduce chest pain.

- **Blood thinners**, such as aspirin, help to reduce the risk of a heart attack and stroke. They also help to keep arteries open and is especially effective for those who have had a previous bypass surgery.

The bad news is that cholesterol and high blood pressure medications are age accelerators. While these medications will keep your cholesterol in check and may help prevent Alzheimer's disease, they reduce your sex drive, aging all of your major organs (heart, brain, lungs, and kidneys) and can shorten your life by more than 16 years, especially if you are more than 10 pounds overweight. While they play an important role in fixing your cardiopause and achieving age reversal, especially if your AgePrint is more than 40, they should be used in combination with other more natural treatments to minimize side effects.

You can choose a variety of ways to reverse your cardiopause, either through prescription medications, bioidentical hormones, or nutrients, supplements, and diet. Your choice can be guided by your deficiency. If your AgePrint for the aging heart was greater than 20 years more than your chronological age, you can address it with nutrition and lifestyle changes. If your score was between 40 and 60 years more than your chronological age, you will need to address your personal reversal with hormones. At levels greater than 60 years more than your chronological age, you will need medications to reverse your AgePrint to a more normal state.

Discuss with your doctor these cardiopause medications:

Conventional Treatment	Suggested Dosage per Day
ACE inhibitors, e.g., Vasotec, Lotensin, Capoten, Monopril	Vasotec: 2.5–40 mg
Calcium channel blockers, e.g., Verapamil, Norvasc, Cardizem, Plendil, Cardene	Verapamil: 120–480 mg
ACE receptor blockers, e.g., Cozaar, Atacand, Avapro, Micardis	Cozaar: 25–100 mg
Vasodilators, e.g., hydralazine, Loniten, NitroQuick, Nitro-Dur	Hydralazine: 40–300 mg
Beta blockers, e.g., Coreg, Inderal, Corgard, Lopressor, Tenormin	Coreg: 6.25–100 mg
Alpha blockers, e.g., Cardura, Minipress, Hytrin	Cardura: 1–16 mg

Bioidentical Hormones

Many heart patients benefit from hormone therapy, especially growth hormone and testosterone therapy. Together, these hormones strengthen the heart muscle, which will aid in heart contraction and improve the heart's pumping ability. DHEA may help protect men from atherosclerosis and cardiovascular disease. In a Japanese study, lower levels of DHEA were significantly correlated with higher values of carotid artery wall thickness scores.

Urinalysis Can Save Your Life

Minor leaks of protein in your urine (albuminuria) is an early indicator of stroke or heart attack.

A report from *JAMA* suggests that the hormone erythropoietin (EPO) may have a beneficial impact on chronic congestive heart failure. It helps prevent inflammation, and studies show it can prevent cell injury and maintain cell integrity. EPO may improve blood flow to ischemic cells that are starved for oxygen and nutrients because of arterial blockage, decreasing the amount of nerve damage.

So you can help bring your heart back to life with the following natural hormones:

Hormonal Treatment	Suggested Dosage per Day
Human growth hormone (HGH)	5–45 mg
Estrogen	1–2 mg
Testosterone	Men: 5 g of 1 percent (1–2 packets per day); women: 2.5–10 mg daily
Progesterone	100–300 mg
Pregnenolone	10–25 mg
DHEA	25–200 mg

Natural Supplements for a Younger Heart and a Younger You

To decrease the possibility of heart disease, I recommend a variety of supplements, including:

- Fish oil, to prevent blood clots
- Niacin, helps raise your "good" HDL cholesterol
- Taurine, to improve pumping action and reduce stress
- Inositol, to reduce stress, a major contributor to heart failure

- Melatonin, to promote sleep, which is often a problem for heart failure patients
- B-complex vitamins to reduce homocysteine
- Policosanol is a mixture of eight solid alcohols extracted from sugar cane that has a remarkable ability to both lower "bad" LDL cholesterol and increase "good" HDL cholesterol

Add these nutrients to help reverse the cardiac aging code. They are available over the counter in supplement form.

Natural Treatment	Suggested Dosage per Day
Coenzyme Q10 (CoQ10)	25–1,200 mg
Carnitine	500–5,000 mg
Hawthorn	200–1,000 mg
Magnesium	300–1,000 mg
Potassium	3,000–5,000 mg
Fish oils (EPA and DHA)	500–3,000 mg
Garlic	500–3,000 mg
Policosanol	5–20 mg
Vitamin B_6, B_{12}	B_6: 10–500 mg; B_{12}: 100–5,000 mcg
Folic acid	200–1,000 mcg
Betaine	500–5,000 mg
ISO flavonoids	200 mg
Taurine	500–10,000 mg
Tocotrienols (vitamin E)	50–200 mg
Niacin (vitamin B_3)	50–3,000 mg

A Rainbow Diet to Avoid Cardiopause

The Rainbow Diet is an important cornerstone of avoiding cardiopause. First, by eating a diet rich in fruits, vegetables, healthy whole grains, and lots of low-fat proteins, you may lose some of the weight that is contributing to your heart disease. Talk to your physician about combining this regimen with a low-calorie plan that will get you to achieve your weight-loss goals.

The Rainbow Diet also points you to foods that are low in sodium, which will naturally reduce internal swelling and water retention. I also replace high-risk foods that create cholesterol with low-risk foods break cholesterol and high blood pressure.

Top 10 Foods That Stimulate the Body to Make "Bad" LDL Cholesterol and Raise Triglycerides

1. Bacon
2. Butter
3. Cheese
4. Shellfish
5. Lard
6. Milk
7. Pork
8. Red meat
9. Cream
10. Fried foods

Consult the following list to help trim the fat:

Instead Of	Try
Bacon	Turkey bacon
Ground beef	Lean beef
Cream	Skim milk
Eggs	Egg whites
Ice cream	Sorbet or low-fat frozen yogurt
Sour cream	Nonfat yogurt
Potato chips	Rice crackers, soy crackers

Try the following Rainbow Diet meal options in order to lower your cholesterol:

Breakfast Options
- 1 cup fat-free low-fat plain yogurt with a handful of pumpkin seeds and fresh berries
- ½ cup oatmeal and 2 to 3 tablespoons of unsweetened soy or rice milk
- One-half grapefruit sprinkled with cinnamon and sugar substitute mix, served with one poached egg over lightly steamed spinach leaves
- Two scrambled egg whites with a slice of whole-wheat toast

Lunch Options
- 1 cup chicken soup served with whole-wheat pasta
- 1 cup vegetable soup served with one slice rye bread topped with low-fat cheese
- Salad greens mixed with garbanzo beans, corn, and walnuts, tossed in a light vinaigrette
- 4 to 6 ounces poached salmon with raw veggies

Dinner Options
- 4 to 6 ounces skinless chicken breast with ½ cup brown rice
- Caesar salad made with spinach, celery, and carrots, topped with one hard-boiled egg, low-fat feta cheese, sardines, or salmon tossed with a lemon, mustard, and olive oil dressing
- 1 cup whole-wheat pasta and meatballs (made from leanest ground beef), low-sodium marinara sauce
- 4 to 6 ounces broiled lean steak served with green beans and sliced almonds

Desserts and Snack Options
- ¼ cup unsalted mixed nuts
- Apple slices or other fresh fruits

- 1 tablespoon peanut butter on rice crackers
- ½ cup low-fat cottage cheese mixed with unsalted nuts and berries

The following herbs, spices, and aromatics help the heart stay healthy:

- Garlic
- Ginger
- Mustard seeds
- Rosemary
- Willow bark

Drink Tea for a Younger You

Second only to water, tea is the most-consumed beverage in the world. Our ancestors must have had some clue about tea's benefits; archaeological evidence credits the first use of tea more than 500,000 years ago, even though science has only started empirically proving tea's numerous health benefits in the past 20 years.

The three main types of tea (black, green, and oolong) all come from the same plant. The differences in color and taste result from the degree of fermentation the tea leaves undergo after harvesting. The fermentation, in turn, determines the type and amounts of flavonoids that are present in the final product. Tea is thought to be beneficial because the flavonoids in it have been shown to have powerful antioxidant properties.

By drinking tea, you stay younger and healthier. They combat the free radicals, or toxins that can alter the chemical structure of your cells, which affects your DNA. Without tea, your DNA starts to age, which means you do too.

As if keeping your cells younger weren't enough, the *American Journal of Epidemiology*'s report on tea consumption and cardiovascular disease reported that for every three cups of tea a person consumed in a day, there was a 26 to 66 percent reduction in the risk for stroke. Another 2003 study revealed that when combined with a diet low in saturated fat, taking a supplement of bioflavonoid-enriched green tea extract served to further lower "bad" cholesterol levels. Unlike other prescription drugs, which can have some unpleasant side effects, the green tea supplement was well tolerated. Catechins, one of the many flavonoids found in green tea, may help to prevent plaque buildup in the heart. A cup a day is cheaper than an angioplasty, folks, so keep on drinking the green stuff.

YOUNGER YOU FACT: Bioflavonoids

Bioflavonoids possess amazing medicinal powers, such as protecting against heart disease, improving circulation, and strengthening the walls of blood vessels. They are found in fruits, vegetables, herbs, spices, and teas.

It's the Red, Not the Wine

A new study from Greece shows that people with diseased arteries received the same benefits from a single glass of alcohol-free red wine as they received with a glass of the harder stuff. In other words, it's the red grape juice that's good for you, not the alcohol. What's more, eating red foods is an especially great way to ensure that your heart keeps pumping. Phytonutrients such as lycopene and anthocyanins are found in abundance in foods such as raspberries, cherries, tomatoes, and watermelon, and they reduce the risk of heart-related illnesses, including heart attacks.

Salt Is Not a Great Choice During Cardiopause

We know Emeril and Mario use it all the time, but salt is loaded with sodium that can raise your risk of high blood pressure. The only relative benefit of sea salt is some extra minerals.

Putting Eggs Back on Your Breakfast Plate

Eggs used to be off-limits because of their high cholesterol content. However, researchers have shown that eggs do not raise blood cholesterol levels by more than 2 percent. Rich in amino acids, eggs are almost a perfect protein, increasing your feeling of fullness so that you won't overeat. Compared to many other traditional breakfast options, such as pancakes, waffles, bagels, or toast, an egg or two is a far better choice for total nutrition and satiety.

A Younger You Releases Stress

Stress takes its toll on your heart, your brain, and your entire body. While we can't always walk away from the stresses in our homes, jobs, and families, we all need to find an outlet to get rid of some of the stress that builds during the day. I'm sure you've heard these suggestions before, but they work, so they bear repeating:

- Take a yoga class.
- Meditate for 20 minutes before you go to sleep.
- Find the power of prayer at home alone or among friends.
- Take up a relaxing activity that interests you, such as reading, sewing, or walking.
- Turn off the TV and walk away from the computer.

8

Vasculopause: Repairing the Highways and Side Streets of Your Body

Vasculopause usually begins around age 50. It is the second limb of heart disease and is equally as important to detect and reverse as cardiopause. Vasculopause refers to changes in your blood flow from the heart to the rest of the body. The vascular system carries oxygen-rich blood away from the heart through blood vessels, arteries, and tiny capillaries into the tissues, and back to the heart through the veins.

Blood pressure is a measure of force exerted by the blood against the walls of the arteries. It is simply a measure of how hard your heart has to work to circulate blood through your body. As the diameters of all the blood vessels narrow and the arterial walls stiffen from plaque buildup, there is 20 to 25 percent increase in your blood pressure. This is what high blood pressure—also known as hypertension—is all about.

The Brain's Still the Name of the Game

All of the brain biochemicals can impact blood flow throughout the entire body. Increased dopamine plus aerobic exercises can strengthen the vascular system; increased acetylcholine keeps blood vessels stretching and young. Anxiety and the loss of GABA are particularly destructive to blood vessels, because during a state of anxiety, your blood vessels tense up. Getting adequate rest is a significant treatment, as well as boosting your serotonin levels so that you can relax.

Hypertension: Stress and Hardening of the Arteries

Blood pressure is one of the two important measurements of heart disease, the other being cholesterol. An elevation in your blood pressure can lead to a heart attack, stroke, and other cardiovascular disorders including an aneurysm (a rupture of a blood vessel) or death.

High blood pressure is painless, symptomless, and often unexpected, although there is a high genetic component. It affects the middle-aged and elderly who are obese or heavy drinkers. It also affects women who are currently taking oral contraceptives or using recreational drugs. Fifty million Americans are walking around with hypertension every day, including three-fourths of all women over the age of 75. Next to old age and obesity, high blood pressure is the most potent predictor of death. Most surprising is that 10 million of these victims are taking medications that are either of questionable value or may even be exacerbating their illness.

Your blood pressure is measured as a fraction. The top number is the systolic number, which measures the rate that the heart is contracting, and the bottom number is the diastolic number, which measures the time the heart is relaxed. A reading equal or greater than 140/90 can have serious implications on your health.

Deborah's Hypertension Was No Hype

Deborah, a 55-year-old teacher with a five-year history of hypertension, was looking for new answers. Like so many others I see at my clinic, Deborah was not being treated correctly by her previous physician. At 159 pounds and 5'2", her blood pressure was 176/100, and her "bad" cholesterol was 250. These numbers showed me that her health was not being controlled by statin drugs and blood pressure medications. Instead, I had Deborah start a new protocol with supplements including fish oils, primrose oil, and my nutrient hypertension vitamin formula that includes niacin, safflower oil, and magnesium. Her triglyceride count fell from 639 to 166. After one month, her cholesterol fell from 250 to 225 while her "good" HDL levels remained stable. Her weight fell from 159 to 148 pounds, and she was able to discontinue her diuretic while maintaining a blood pressure of 140/78. To this day she continues to do extremely well, with excellent control over her blood pressure and continued lowering of her cholesterol. Best of all, Deborah's better health has energized her, and she continues to lose weight. It's no wonder that her vasculopause age went from 70 to 55; Deborah got much younger and healthier once her heart and vascular system were in check.

Hypertension and the Brain

Studies now suggest that the benefits of controlling hypertension seem to go beyond cardiovascular health and may actually help prevent some loss of mental capacity as you age. After age 65, men with uncontrolled hypertension fared worse on short-term memory and verbal ability tests than those with normal blood pressure or those whose hypertension was being controlled.

As your blood pressure increases, so does your cognitive decline. The constricting blood vessels cause a decrease in blood flow and oxygen to the brain. Only the various vascular, hormonal, and nutritional treatments that restore vasculopause and balance to your brain can prevent you from getting dementia. Many of our patients in their 40s and 50s come in with high blood pressure, having been prescribed all sorts of beta blockers, diuretics, and a host of other medications. Just by following my vasculopause nutrient and hormonal regimen, they lose weight immediately, their blood pressure goes down, and their memory and attention improve.

Hypertension and GABA

Hypertension may be linked to copious use of common pain relievers. In one study, women taking acetaminophen, such as Tylenol, or nonsteroidal anti-inflammatory drugs (NSAIDs), such as Advil or Motrin, had a greater incidence of high blood pressure than women who did not take any over-the-counter pain relievers. Pain and emotional distress are certainly age accelerators leading to high blood pressure, and GABA deficiencies leading to pain and anxiety contribute to high blood pressure. If you can boost your GABA, you'll watch your blood pressure drop.

Brain Over Stroke

If you don't take care of your vasculopause with bioidentical growth hormones, estrogen, progesterone, or testosterone—even while keeping your cholesterol levels down—you're still at high risk for brain damage. Strokes and ministrokes occur all the time. Nearly 150,000 people die of strokes annually and 300,000 become disabled.

Strokes occur secondary to either blocked blood vessels in the brain (ischemic stroke) or to a rupture in the brain's blood vessels (hemorrhagic stroke). Most are caused by the former. The toxic effect of stroke occurs as a result of the release of calcium into the cells and the release of the neurotoxic amino acids glutamate aspartate. Literally, the dying cells become petrified.

Symptoms of a stroke come on fast, so it's hard to react appropriately and seek medical attention. They include:

- Sudden weakness or numbness to the face, arm, or leg (usually one side of the body)
- Loss of speech
- Trouble understanding speech
- Dimness or loss of vision (particularly in one eye)
- Unexplained dizziness
- Unsteadiness
- Sudden severe headache

The peripheral vascular system contains the smallest blood vessels and capillaries. Beginning at age 50, peripheral vascular disease (PVD) is a common complication of poor circulation combined with blood clotting, resulting in an insufficient supply of blood to the lower legs and feet. The chief complaints begin with a lifetime of cold hands and/or feet.

PVD is completely reversible if caught in the early stages. However, I am constantly astounded by most physicians' lack of interest in conducting routine ultrasounds and ankle-brachial index (ABI) testing in a physical exam of the arteries. Most doctors are willing to try every type of manual physician's exam including outdated assessment techniques like taking pulses and using tuning forks—methods that were certainly useful in the 19th century but have been far surpassed by more accurate technology. Electrical evaluations, nerve assessment of reflexes, and gauging of muscle pain do not predict the actual internal results that an ultrasound and ABI can. I have been doing these tests for the past 10 years, and now it has finally become "standard practice"—accepted by the medical communities.

Most doctors treat stroke patients as neurological patients, when in fact so much more can be done to reverse the devastating effects a stroke can leave behind. Antidepressants, hormone therapy, sleep aids, better nutrition, and natural supplements can all improve your vasculature AgePrint.

The following are must-have vasculopause tests:

Test	Purpose
Ankle-brachial index (ABI)	Checks peripheral (arterial) circulation; detects blood flow loss and pressure between the arm and ankle
Transcranial ultrasound	Checks blood flow throughout the brain via a transducer held in between the bridge of the nose and the eye; transcranial ultrasound can detect cranial vascular deficiencies
Carotid ultrasound	Checks blood flow to the brain via a probe held up against the neck to

Test	Purpose
Carotid ultrasound *(continued)*	view the large blood vessels that deliver blood to the brain; carotid ultrasound can detect plaque that narrows the artery and may limit the free flow of blood to the brain
Venous studies	Checks blood flow in leg veins returning to the heart; measures structure and motion using both Doppler ultrasonic signal documentation and spectral analysis and/or color flow velocity mapping or imaging
Arterial studies	Checks blood flow in leg arteries moving away from the heart to other parts of the body
Digit studies	Checks blood flow to fingers and toes; hands and feet are most prone to early stages of peripheral vascular disease because they are the farthest from the heart

Talk with your doctor about getting blood tests to check the levels of these substances:

Test	Purpose
Aldosterone and renin	These two hormones are produced by the adrenal glands and are elevated in some patients with high blood pressure.
Urine microalbumin	High blood pressure and diabetes cause protein to be excreted in urine.
Cystatin C	This is a marker of renal function in patients with kidney disease.
Protein C and S	A deficiency causes increased risk for blood clots known as thromboembolism.

Test	Purpose
Antithrombin III (AT III)	A vitamin K–dependent glycoprotein, deficiency causes increased risk for thromboembolic events, including blood clots.
Plasminogen	Decreased levels are found in patients with venous thrombosis.
Fibrinogen	Abnormal levels are linked with thrombosis or bleeding.
Factor V Leiden	Presence of this gene mutation significantly increases lifelong risk for venous thrombosis.
Homocysteine	Increased levels are associated with venous arterial thrombosis.
Anticardiolipin	This antibody is common in lupus; testing for it measures the risk for blood clots in arteries and veins.
Prothrombin	Mutation in the prothrombin gene causes increased risk of venous thrombosis.

The following nutrients will help to improve your vasculopause AgePrint:

- Vitamin E, onions, ginger, fish oil, and willow bark increase circulation and promote blood flow.
- Garlic will help lower blood pressure.
- Arginine, vitamin A, selenium, cysteine, vitamin C, and beta-carotene can assist antihypertensive drugs such as Vasotec, Capoten, and Zestril.

These herbs and spices can help increase circulation:

- Cayenne aids the body to balance pressure levels and resist abnormal bleeding.

- Ginger enhances circulation.
- Garlic aids in circulation and lowers blood pressure.
- Cinnamon increases circulation, especially in arthritic joints.
- Turmeric increases blood flow.

Retinopathy and Congestive Heart Failure

A study in *JAMA* suggested that retinopathy—the inflammation of the retina—is an independent predictor of congestive heart failure even in those individuals without heart disease, diabetes, or hypertension. Participants in the study had a higher incidence of heart failure compared with those without retinopathy, even after controlling for other factors such as age, sex, race, blood pressure, diabetes, glucose level, cholesterol, smoking, and BMI.

To me the reasoning is clear: the eye is a piece of the brain. Arteriosclerosis in one area predicts arteriosclerosis elsewhere. As I tell every patient—you are only as young as your oldest part. If one part starts to fall apart, the rest of you falls apart.

Chelation: A Therapy That Breaks the Vasculopause Code

Many scientists believe that chronic, low-level lead exposure, as well as heavy metals like cadmium, aluminum, and mercury, can also cause hypertension. This is particularly true after menopause, where bone loss may elevate lead levels.

I treat my patients with high lead and metal levels with chelation therapy. Chelation agents travel through the bloodstream "grabbing" onto minerals and metals such as calcium, mercury, cadmium, copper, aluminum, and iron. Once bound by a chelating agent, the metals can

CODE BREAKER: A Younger You Relies on Breaking the Diabetes Code

Life expectancy for people with diabetes is on the average four to eight years lower than for those without.

effectively be released from the body. They are removed from the blood-stream and delivered to the kidneys that excrete them in urine.

Diabetes: The Age Accelerator That Links Obesity to Vasculopause

An estimated 18.2 million Americans have diabetes. One-third of this epidemic have no idea that they are suffering from this disease. What's more, if this trend continues, diabetes and its complications will be the number one cause of death by 2010, surpassing both cancer and heart disease.

Diabetes begins when the body can no longer correctly process the sugars it takes in from carbohydrate-dense foods such as white rice, white flour, and potatoes. The body should be able to break down these foods into simple sugars, or glucose, and use this byproduct as fuel on the cellular level. The hormone insulin should transport the glucose to the cells. However, when the body does not produce enough insulin, the glucose just sits there, building up in the bloodstream, causing a condition called *hyperglycemia* or high blood sugar. This condition sets up a cascade of events that contribute to inflammation and plaque deposition within the vascular system, including high blood pressure. Conversely, high blood pressure and other vasculopause conditions can contribute to diabetes. If this condition has been with you since birth, you suffer from type 1 diabetes. However, if you have developed this later in life, you are suffering from type 2 diabetes.

Diabetes is also closely linked to obesity. Excess weight caused by the overconsumption of carbohydrate-rich foods creates insulin resistance. Sedentary lifestyles also account for much of the diabetes epidemic. However, there is good news. Type 2 diabetes is preventable. The old diet routine—eat less, exercise more—is the prescription.

Take Action: Diagnosing Diabetes

Diabetes is easily confirmed by measuring your blood glucose levels. You may notice many of the following symptoms if you are suffering from type 2 diabetes:

- Blurred vision
- Excessive thirst
- Extreme hunger
- Frequent and excessive urination
- Increased fatigue
- Irritability
- Weight gain

Control Your Blood Sugar and Break the Diabetic Code

By integrating supplements, diet, medication, and exercise, you will have the best chance for beating this disease. Hormone balance is critical for diabetes management; a hormone deficiency can decrease the effectiveness of insulin. Testosterone supplementation for men reduces insulin resistance, raises "good" HDL, lowers blood pressure, and helps to reduce excess weight while building muscle.

Balancing estrogen, progesterone, and testosterone in women also improves glucose control and may alleviate the tendency for older women to gain weight. Human growth hormone (HGH) can help diabetes patients because they have significant muscle wasting. HGH also increases sensitivity to insulin.

Consider the following supplements for normalizing blood sugar:

- Psyllium, guar gum, bilberry leaf extract: slows glucose absorption, prevents blood sugar spikes
- Essential fatty acids: prevents insulin resistance
- Chromium: protects against fatal arrhythmias for people with diabetes
- Fish oil, DHEA: improves insulin sensitivity, optimizes blood lipids
- Lipoic acid: supports healthy nerve function
- Bilberry fruit extract: provides antioxidant and circulatory support

Keys to Disease: Diabetes and Serotonin Deficiency

Patients with both depression and type 2 diabetes have higher mortality rates than patients suffering from either one alone. What's more, if you are sleeping six hours a night or less, you are at an increased risk for impaired glucose tolerance and diabetes. Boost your serotonin and get the rest you need to break the diabetes code.

Rita Broke the Diabetes Code and Got 10 Years Younger

Rita came to my office in dangerous shape. At only 47 years old and 5'5", 168 pounds, she had already been diagnosed with diabetes and hypertension, with symptoms of obesity, fatigue, dizziness, and shortness of breath. Her diabetes put her at an even greater risk for stroke. Upon assessment, I determined that Rita had carotid artery disease, scarily high blood pressure, and a "bad" LDL cholesterol level of 270. A clogged carotid artery puts you at seriously high risk for stroke at any time without warning. I immediately recommended that she start taking a nutrient regimen including policosanol, cholestene, and niacin.

Within one year her cholesterol dropped down to 139, eliminating her need for prescription medications. Her primary care physician was stunned at the change and the fact that we achieved it through natural supplements rather than statin drugs. Rita's carotid stenosis dissipated, and she is left only with mild plaque.

PART 4

The Modulating Systems

9

Thyropause: A Weakening Metabolism

I like to think of the brain-body connection as a golden bowl connected to a shining silver cord. The brain is the golden bowl that transfers electricity to the rest of the body via the silver cord, which begins in the neck and then travels down the spinal column. The cord sends the brain's electrical code through the central nervous system. Like a puppeteer, your brain pulls the strings of your body through your neck.

Within the neck and upper chest, the brain's silver cord first connects to three of the body's great regulators: the thymus gland, which controls the immune system; the thyroid gland, which manages your metabolism; and the parathyroid gland, which controls your bone density and will be discussed in Chapter 13. When they are working properly, you are healthy, free of infections and diseases, and full of vibrant energy.

When any one is compromised, the rest of the body is directly affected. The other organs, which were once adept at fighting off intruders, are now unable to stop small infections from growing or disease from developing. Eventually, a compromised immune system can cause each organ to die off. This is how your brain and body will age through the processes of thyropause and immunopause, which we'll discuss in the next chapter.

Thyropause: The Importance of the Thyroid Gland

The thyroid is an overrated but underexamined gland that controls the rate that your body burns the fuel necessary to keep you and your mood going. It does so by synthesizing the hormones thyroxine (T4) and tri-iodothyronine (T3). These thyroid hormones are necessary in infants for the normal development of the central nervous system, in children for normal skeletal growth, and in adults for normal function of the other organs and systems. Thyroid hormones also affect tissue growth and maturation, help regulate fat digestion, and increase intestinal absorption of carbohydrates.

Thyropause marks the beginning of a metabolic disorder, which can begin as early as birth but typically begins between the ages of 30 and 40 but even more frequently at age 50. The changes that occur are often subtle; without taking your AgePrint, you may not know if you are experiencing thyropause.

Many of the notable symptoms are more "head" than "body" related. These symptoms include:

- Anxiety
- Apathy
- Brittle nails
- Cold intolerance
- Cold hands and/or feet
- Confusion
- Constipation
- Decreased energy
- Delusions
- Depression
- Difficulty concentrating
- Diminished food intake
- Insomnia
- Irritability
- Lethargy
- Manic symptoms
- Memory loss

- Paranoia
- Restlessness
- Weight gain

YOUNGER YOU FACT: Maybe It's Not Your Thyroid
For many patients, the thyroid has no role whatsoever in weight gain.
The brain is the primary determiner of weight. Seventy percent of all
calories are burned by the brain's neuronal activity. It is the core
source of metabolism, and all drugs that treat obesity tend to work
through the brain, not the thyroid gland.

Under or Over?

Thyroid problems can occur in two distinct ways: hyperthyroidism or
hypothyroidism. Both affect the way your body deals with illness and
in many cases are considered autoimmune disorders or self-attacks.
Thyroid-stimulating hormone (TSH) is the feedback loop of the brain.
TSH in the pituitary is low in hyperthyroidism and high in hypothyroidism. Normally, TSH raises with age, but is roughly between 0.5 and
3. Hypothyroidism begins at a TSH over 3, no matter what your age is.
I have seen patients with a TSH as high as 125. Below 0.5 is usually
subclinical hyperthyroidism.

Hypothyroid patients have a host of medical problems, including:

- Constipation
- Dry skin
- Fluid in the heart
- Fluid retention in the body
- Goiter (enlarged thyroid gland in the neck)
- Headaches
- High blood pressure
- Joint aches
- Muscle aches
- Puffiness of the face
- Puffy eyelids

- Thickening of the tongue
- Thinning eyebrows
- Weight change
- Cold intolerance
- Heavy menstrual periods in women

Hyperthyroid patients experience the following symptoms:

- Angina
- Chest pain
- Fatigue
- Frequent bowel movement
- Menstrual irregularities in women
- Muscle atrophy
- Muscle cramps
- Muscle weakness
- Nervousness
- Palpitations
- Rapid heartbeat
- Sensitivity to heat
- Sudden weight loss
- Sweating
- Swelling of the fingers
- Weak nails
- Weight loss

Maybe It's Thyropause

Thyropause is often the cause of many health problems we've been taught to learn to live with. For example, Ella, at 5'7" and 180 pounds, came to see me because she was sick of being overweight and constantly fatigued. However, a complete physical in my office revealed that she was also starting to exhibit symptoms similar to those of multiple sclerosis, memory loss, confusion, and depression. All of these conditions related to an underactive thyroid gland. I started Ella on 1½ grains of natural thyroid hormones (T3 and T4), which restored her thyroid; it is now functioning completely. She dropped to 159 pounds in a period of six months by taking these hormones and natural supplements that support the thyroid, such as carnitine, tyrosine, and phenylalanine, all dopamine supplements. Once her metabolism was back to an age-appropriate state, her memory loss and depression immediately improved.

The bottom line is that there aren't any medical conditions that you should "learn to live with." Illness and discomfort are usually reversible and treatable once you recognize that your health problems are interconnected. Remember the $2 + 2 = 5$ equation? All these patients came to me with multiple, seemingly unrelated symptoms. But by determining their AgePrint, and making a few quick modifications that addressed their primary pause, they disappeared. All of these people got younger, and you can too!

Thyropause Affects the Other Pauses

When the thyroid gland gets out of whack, the rest of the body follows. For example, Eleanor, a 77-year-old patient of mine, had a thyroid AgePrint of 90. However, she was not suffering from any of the classic hypothyroid complaints. Instead, Eleanor experienced shortness of breath, an elevated homocysteine level, high blood pressure, anxiety, and dizziness. I knew from her AgePrint and her blood work that she was experiencing thyropause.

When you take care of a person's thyroid, many aspects of his or her health improve that might not be related to the initial condition. This connection would not have been detected by a general internist who is trained to look for only classic symptoms. Yet I know that thyroid disorders have repercussions that can spread throughout the body. When the thyroid begins to go, each of the pauses will be affected in the following ways:

- Cardiopause: Changes in your thyroid can affect your cholesterol levels, your heart rhythm, and your risk for coronary artery disease. Women with untreated hypothyroidism are twice as likely to have a heart attack.

- Osteopause: Boosting your thyroid gives dramatic improvement for arthritis and joint pain.
- Dermatopause: Increasing thyroid levels will improve dry skin. Aging loss of T3 contributes to the pruning effect of the skin.
- Menopause or adrenopause: A lack of thyroid decreases sexual libido; enhancing it will improve your days and your nights.

Thyroid Disease Can Be Completely Reversed

Any form of thyroid disease can be managed with medication. To treat an aging thyroid, you start with natural thyroid treatment. If it is picked up soon enough, the disease is stopped in its tracks. Taking natural thyroid supplements when you need them works like taking other bioidentical hormones. It's not a crutch. It doesn't make the thyroid weaker but actually makes it less likely to decline by getting its adequate support.

You Can Develop an Old Thyroid at Any Age

Melissa was 12 years old when she started gaining weight for no apparent reason. By 19, she was 90 pounds overweight. Her parents had no idea what happened, but I did. At some point in her childhood, Melissa's brain decided to become old. This is a dopamine brain metabolism disorder that is accompanied by depression, anxiety, mood swings, sleep problems, and dietary selection problems compounded by thyroid problems. The good news is that even seven years after she was initially affected, we completely reversed her thyroid problems. Over the next year, Melissa lost the weight she needed, and we balanced her emotional state to the point where she no longer needs antidepressants.

Rainbow Diet for a Younger Thyroid

Certain foods we eat every day can be extremely healthy yet dangerous at the same time. If your AgePrint shows that you may have thyropause, you need to stay away from a disparate group of foods known as goitrogens. These foods interfere with the function of the thyroid gland. They include all the cruciferous vegetables, including cauliflower, brussels sprouts, broccoli, cabbage, kale, kohlrabi, mustard greens, rutabaga, and turnips. Soybeans and soy-related foods are another group of goitrogens. Peaches, strawberries, peanuts, radishes, spinach, and millet grain are also goitrogens. All of these foods can be dangerous in their raw states; cooking seems to temper their negative properties. However, it's best to avoid them entirely.

Instead, choose foods that are high in iodine, and eat plenty of fish. If your blood pressure can handle it, you should have no problem with iodine-rich salt. Choose foods from this list to boost your serotonin as well:

- Cheese
- Chicken
- Egg yolks
- Lean meat
- Lentils
- Milk
- Molasses
- Sea salt
- Seaweed
- Turkey

Thyropause-reversing meals include:

- Omelet made with low-fat cheddar cheese
- Black bean soup
- Lentil soup
- Japanese seaweed salad
- 4 ounces lean steak, broiled with fresh garlic and basil and a green bean salad
- Organic turkey with lentil sauce

10

Immunopause: When You Can't Fight Infections

Do you remember childhood as one long string of good health, yet your adult life is one sinus infection after another? With every hormone loss or brain chemical imbalance, our immune code is broken. As early as the beginning of puberty, our immune response slowly begins to decline. It then becomes much easier for us to get sick. The immune system provides a layer of protection that keeps viruses and infections from harming the brain and the body. When you enter immunopause, your immune system cannot protect you from the constant attack of viruses and infections that surround you. It's like you are going outside at the North Pole without a jacket. Your survival depends on keeping yourself warm, but how can you manage without the basic outer layering?

As adults, we experience the switching off of the immune system as increased inflammation, which plays a role in every medical condition from heart disease to dermatitis. Serotonin regulates the immune system, and serotonin agents can boost immunity. As inflammation increases, serotonin levels decrease, creating both low- and high-grade fevers as well as sleep abnormalities. Inflammation acts as the immunopause death code, allowing viruses, fungus, and bacteria into every organ of the body.

Meanwhile, aging can be summarized as oxidation—you are literally burning up, including your dopamine. Just as the thyroid is related to dopamine and its control of your metabolism, you need this vital biochemical to suppress illness. For example, that's why adrenaline (dopamine family of brain chemicals) is used as an antidote to an allergic reaction, such as to a bee sting.

Infections Are Alien Invaders

Infections can grow and develop inside the body when the immune system is asleep at the wheel. Tiny microorganisms are let in through the various orifices and work their way into your cells, wreaking havoc along the way. Infections can contribute to further inflammation, and more dangerously, like in the case of AIDS, can destroy your immune system entirely.

Infections that occur in the body can affect our brain. For example, the common flu contributes to Parkinson's disease. When your immune system is compromised, your dopamine level is diminished. That is why Parkinson's drugs like Symmetrel and Flumadine, which build dopamine, can help to alleviate flu symptoms.

Infections can occur anywhere in the brain and the body, sending their own aging code and jump-starting the pauses. It goes like this:

Heart Infections
- Endocarditis: valve infection
- Myocarditis: muscle infection
- Pericarditis: infection of the wrapping around the heart

Sexually Transmitted Infections
- HIV
- Chlamydia
- Genital warts
- Gonorrhea
- Hepatitis
- Herpes
- Syphilis

Infections of the Brain, Spinal Cord, Nerves, Bones, and Muscles

- Parkinson's disease
- Meningitis
- Encephalitis
- Myelitis
- Shingles
- Osteomyelitis
- Lyme disease
- Creutzfeldt-Jacob
- Myositis

Bacterial Skin Infections

- Carbuncles
- Cellulitis
- Folliculitis
- Staphylococcal scalded skin syndrome

Fungal Skin Infections

- Candida (yeast infection)
- Ringworm
- Tinea versicolor

Viral Skin Infections

- Cold sores
- Herpes zoster (shingles)
- Warts

Inflammation

Inflammation is the first sign of aging in any section of your body. There are many subtle markers of inflammation, one of the four core aging killers, the three additional being oxidation, dehydration, and ossification (excessive calcium deposits). Inflammation is a cornerstone of aging. Nodules, cysts, and calcifications found via an ultrasound and numerous blood tests such as interleukins, erythrocyte sedimentation rate (ESR), C-reactive protein, T-helper suppressor ratio, homocysteine, fibrinogen, and others all predict inflammation.

Interleukins

Interleukins are the connections between inflammation and the immune system. Interleukins are the proteins our cells make that stimulate our immune system. When they attack, I see that my patients who already suffer from osteoporosis become more inflamed and frail. Testosterone can reverse this. Most recently, Paul, a 60-year-old patient, told me that no arthritis drug had worked for him. His blood showed low testosterone. When he went on 50 milligrams of dehydroepiandrosterone (DHEA) as well as Androgel (testosterone), a great degree of muscle strength returned, and his overall frailty and weakness improved. Interleukin 6 is now known to be a good predictor because as the immune system deteriorates and our serotonin levels go down, our bone and muscles follow. It's called the aging code cascade in which the brain core code stops the process.

Is Your Immune System Your Best Friend or Your Worst Enemy?

Funny thing about the immune system: as we age it can go awry. Often, it can switch to attack mode. Instead of keeping you healthy, your immune system can ignite inflammation, leading to multiple sclerosis or cancer, or it can switch to viral mode and contribute to frequent colds or infections. This last scenario is often referred to as autoimmune disease. Allergies, for example, occur when your immune system turns against you. So much for loyalty—keep your immune system young and on your side by becoming a younger you.

Immunopause and Cancer

Cancer also occurs as an autoimmune response; good cells are "turned" bad, and they multiply and invade both organs and entire systems of the body. These bad cells cause cancer: eternal abnormal growth rather than eternal normal growth.

Many in the medical community now believe that infections may be the cause of cancer. Research shows that those who have lifelong infections such as hepatitis C are more prone to cancer than their noninfected peers. It has become even more important to protect your immune system, not just for fighting infection, but for monitoring your overall health and risk for cancer.

As with almost every other disease group, cancer seems to favor individuals who are obese, are sleep deprived, are depressed, or have brain chemical imbalances; the biochemical age accelerators are busily at work once again. Some cancers are purely genetic, and others are activated by lifestyle and environment. For example, living in a major urban city, such as New York City, that is heavily polluted obviously feeds all the types of cancer, including lung, breast, and prostate. Cancer cells are anti–stem cells. They create a destructive pattern of mortality. Without our bodies' own stem cells to keep cancer cells in check, we would have even more immune destruction throughout our bodies.

Toxins Cause Cancer and Destroy Our Brain's Signals

It should come as no surprise that our environment—loaded as it is with pollutants—can easily send us into immunopause. Dumping garbage into the environment has the same polluting effects as the garbage we ingest into our bodies. At any given time, the average American has 11 heavy metals, 4 to 6 plastics, and any number of pesticides in his or her body. Worse still, one in three aging Americans have cancer—not because of losing small increments in hormone levels, but because of toxins.

Toxins of all types—especially mercury and lead—have been linked to the destruction of the brain's balance and code. As a result, it triggers cancer as the brain is no longer able to regulate the immune system. The delicate balance of the immune system is dependent on the balanced brain.

Eliminating the effects of harmful pollutants is still one of the most challenging, yet important environmental issues. This is true in both our homes and our workplaces. The following pollutants have been directly associated with cancer:

- Air pollutants from factories, power plants, dry cleaners, cars, buses, trucks, dust, and wildfires
- Asbestos in old buildings
- Lead in paint
- Mercury, often found in deep-water, consumable fish, especially tuna
- Mold found in damp places, especially basements
- Pesticides sprayed on produce and used in our backyards
- Swimming pool chemicals
- Waste, for example, medical waste, garbage, scrap tires, yard scraps
- Water contaminants that may be found even in bottled spring water

CODE BREAKER: Make Friends, Beat Cancer

One of the key components of having a full life is to have healthy relationships. When your brain is well balanced, so is your emotional state, and your ability to let people into your life greatly increases. According to a study done by the University of Iowa, the more friends one has, the less likely the risk for cancer.

The No Sleep–Low Immunity Cancer Connection

Over the years, I have treated dozens of night workers who have cancer. Nationally, night-shift workers have a 30 percent higher incidence rate of cancer. I tell my night owls that they must get at least seven consecutive hours of sleep each day and replace their lost melatonin, a natural hormone your body produces as you sleep. Recent studies have shown that as your melatonin ebbs, you will lose an important layer of cancer protection. Trials in Europe and Canada have shown that melatonin can be useful in conjunction with chemotherapy and radiation, especially for patients who have advanced solid tumors.

Take Action: Early Detection Is Key and the Balanced Brain Is Your Defense

You've already taken the first step toward better health by taking the AgePrint quiz in Chapter 2 and determining what stage your immune system is at. Take these results to your physician, who might recommend some of the following blood tests to determine your risk for immunopause.

Immunopause needs to be more carefully parsed. There are blood tests for various bacterial and fungal infections, as well as other blood work that can see how your white cells are combating disease. There are infection-specific tests if you think you are suffering from a particular illness as well. Many tests can effectively identify early cancer. A combination of the positron emission tomography (PET) scan, blood tests, ultrasound, and magnetic resonance imaging (MRI) can find virtually every type of cancer. For example, in the brain, physicians sometimes make the mistake of trying to find brain cancer using the MRI only, missing the fact that on a PET scan what they thought was a tumor was actually radiation-induced dead brain cells. Many times brain cysts or growths are wrongly diagnosed. These false-positive results are jokingly referred to as "incidentalomas" because they are reporting on something that is not a real tumor. But if it was your head they were operating on, you might not find it to be so funny.

To my mind, three images can break the cancer code: a PET scan lights up with hypermetabolic activity, the MRI gives more detail of anatomy, and an ultrasound gives a good first pass of all nodules, lumps, and bumps. Ultimately, a great cancer exam is a head-to-toe ultrasound with all the blood-testing markers. Cancer ranges from difficult to impossible to treat once it's progressed, so early diagnosis is the key. These screening procedures will get easier, and their costs should become more reasonable.

It's also important to get periodic heavy metal testing and appropriate cancer screening if you are at a genetic or environmental high risk. For example, in New York City, I don't believe that enough patients have had pulmonary function tests, which pick up the first signs of lung disease. Once it's abnormal, we should be following up with chest x-rays and CT scans to identify early lung cancer.

Speak with your doctor about the following tests for infection and about various inflammation markers that might be triggering immunopause:

Blood Levels	Function
Erythrocyte sedimentation rate (ESR)	This is a nonspecific marker of inflammation.
C-reactive protein (CRP)	This is a nonspecific marker of inflammation and cardiac health.
Immune protein electrophoresis (IPEP)	This is a marker of protein elevation.
T-helper/T-suppressor and lymphocyte count	Tells us the fighting ability of your immune system over cancer, fungus, and viruses.
Tumor necrosis factor (TNF)	This is elevated in a person who has cancer and infection.
SMAC	This test checks chemistry, electrolytes, liver enzymes, protein, and kidney function.

Immune Deficiency Tests and Codes	Function
Antinuclear antibody (ANA), anti-DNA Ab, rheumatoid factor (RF), lupus erythematosus (LE)	These are markers for autoimmune diseases such as rheumatoid arthritis or lupus.
Comp C3, 4	This plays a role in immune disorders and is decreased in arthritis, vasculitis, nephritis, lupus, and infection.
Cardiolipin AB	Common in lupus, it is linked to an increased risk for blood clots.

Immune Deficiency Tests and Codes	Function
Interleukin-1, 2, 6, 8	These small proteins regulate immune processes and play a role in autoimmune diseases such as rheumatoid arthritis, systemic sclerosis, and others.

Infection Tests	Function
EBV, antigen, and antibody	These test for Epstein-Barr viral infection.
Hep A, B, C, D, E antibodies	These test for hepatitis, an important killer of the immune system.
CMV antibody	These test for cytomegalovirus infection.
Urinalysis	This tests for infection in the urine.

STD Tests	Function
RPR, MHA-TP	These test for syphilis.
Chlamydia, urine, LCR	These test for chlamydia infection.
Herpes simplex I, II IgM, IgG, Herpes 6 Ab	These test for herpes infection.

Cancer Markers	Function
CA 125, 15-3, 27-29, 19-9, AFP, CEA, PSA	These are markers of early detection of ovarian, breast, pancreatic, liver, colon, and prostate.

Types of Cancer

Every organ of the body can become cancerous, including the bones and skin. Right now there is no cure for any form of cancer. However, there are a myriad of treatment options available that can put these cancers into remission states, where we can extend life for these patients,

The Importance of Pelvic Ultrasounds

The majority of ovarian cancer cases are diagnosed in stage three, when the disease is already advanced. The early symptoms of ovarian cancer, such as fatigue, back pain, and abdominal discomfort, rarely prompt internists or gynecologists to perform an ultrasound of the pelvis, and routine vaginal exams are not sufficient in detecting this deadly disease. If you are experiencing these symptoms, insist on this noninvasive test; it can save your life.

and make their daily lives much more comfortable. Cancer patients who use multimodal treatments have the best results particularly when they augment their brain with a dopamine-boosting antidepressant.

Take Action: Strengthen Your Immune System and Get Younger

It's relatively easy to boost your immunity for a younger you. A multimodal approach including medications, hormones, nutrient supplements, and specific dietary suggestions will help you break the death code of cancer and inflammation that may already be evident by your AgePrint.

You can choose a variety of ways to reverse your immune system. Your choice can be guided by your deficiency. If you are not exhibiting symptoms and your AgePrint was more than 20, you can start with nutrition and lifestyle changes. If your score was between 40 and 60, you will need to address your personal reversal with hormones. At levels greater than 60, you will need medications to reverse your AgePrint to a more normal state.

Growth Hormone

All of aging is a failure to repair, and growth is a form of controlled repair. The absence of growth hormone is a death trigger to the body. Immunopause is linked to human growth hormone (HGH) deficiencies. I have seen astounding results with my patients' use of HGH, including regaining their overall youthfulness, physical strength, as well as a more confident attitude in approaching life's most difficult task: aging gracefully.

The dramatic and scientifically proven effects of this therapy include:

- Decreased blood pressure
- Decreased cholesterol
- Improved memory
- Improved sexual performance
- Increased lean muscle mass
- Increased bone mineralization
- Increased energy
- Reduced body fat
- Slight restoration of hair color and growth
- Strengthened cardiovascular system
- Strengthened immune system

Growth Hormone Does Not Cause Cancer but Aging Does. There has been some discussion over the years that supplementing growth hormone may cause cancer. In my research, I have found that this could not be further from the truth. For example, NBA superstars are born with abnormally high levels of growth hormone, yet these players do not have any significant increases in cancer just because they have unusually high levels of growth hormone. Children with a history of cancer can take growth hormones safely, and children who have taken growth hormone for years do not develop cancer at higher rates. Ironically, young individuals, who have the highest levels of growth hormone in their bodies naturally, have the lowest risks of cancer. Those who abuse HGH, such as some professional athletes, are dying of complications related to contamination and heart-valve problems, not from higher incidences of cancer.

Keys to Success: Growth Hormone and Cancer. Frequently, doctors forget that the radiation during cancer treatment damages the ability of the brain to make growth hormone. Patients can have huge quality of life increases after cancer treatment by restoring their own growth hormone.

Take a look at these longevity-boosting hormones that help strengthen the immune system:

Hormonal Treatment	Suggested Dosage per Day
Testosterone (fights cancer in women)	Women: 2.5–10 mg daily
Estrogen (fights cancer in men)	1–2.5 mg
HGH (fights cancer and improves quality of life)	15–45 mg

Nutrients That Naturally Boost Your Immune System

One of the best things you can do for your body is to make sure it gets the right nutrients, especially when it comes to your immune system. Nutrition and health are intimately linked, and here is no better example. Ironically, when I was doing research at Harvard Medical School back in 1978, the so-called brilliant scholars tried to convince me that nutrition had no role in health care, even though history from the Bible to Egypt and from the writings of Maimonides to Hippocrates disagreed with them. Even then I didn't believe it. I had already been working with Dr. Robert Atkins of diet fame, and he had convinced me of the direct connection between what we eat and how we feel. I'm glad to see that today even Harvard has come around to my way of thinking. We now know that these two parts of our lives are intimately linked and help us keep each one of the pauses at bay.

For example, vitamin D, which we all know keeps your bones strong, is now proven to decrease insulin resistance, regulate cell production, and modulate immune function. According to a recent article in the *American Journal of Public Health*, increasing your vitamin D intake may help lower the risk of breast, colon, skin, prostate, and ovarian cancer by as much as 50 percent.

Yet a vitamin D deficiency may be responsible for thousands of premature deaths each year. If this got as much media attention as mad cow disease or avian flu, people would call it a health crisis. But in this case, we carry the burden of this vitamin deficit on our own shoulders; the necessary increase of sunscreen use coupled with less time spent outdoors leaves many kids and adults deficient in vitamin D. Fortunately, the cure is easy to swallow. Just 20 minutes in the sun every day does the trick. What's more, there's plenty of vitamin D in a well-balanced diet, and a supplement will go a long way toward remedying this silent health crisis.

The following nutrients help break the immunopause code. Consider these natural treatments.

Nutritional Treatment	Suggested Dosage per Day
Probiotics (yogurt cultures)	1 billion–10 billion CFUs
N-acetyl cysteine (NAC)	500–2,000 mg
Zinc	10–100 mg
Arginine	500 mg–3 g
Vitamin A	5,000–25,000 IU
Vitamin C	200–10,000 mg
Thymus extract	500–1,500 mg
Selenium	100–400 mcg

Herbal Treatment	Suggested Dosage per Day
Andrographis	200–2,000 mg
Ashwagandha (winter cherry)	500–1,500 mg
Propolis	500–5,000 mg
Echinacea	4 mL, 3 times daily
Mistletoe	600 mg, 3 times daily before meals
Myrrh	2–4 mL 3 times daily
Licorice root	2–4 mL 3 times daily

Take Action: Rainbow Foods Fight Inflammation

A diet of vitamin-rich, low-fat foods combined with whole grains is an excellent treatment tool for fighting inflammatory disease and immune deficiencies. The Rainbow Diet increases foods in the high-glycemic index: these foods actually reduce inflammation and prevent your immune system from being depleted during an inflammatory response.

Fiber, another mainstay of the Rainbow Diet, is a tremendous age decelerator that impacts everything from colon cancer to inflammation. Along with a high-fiber diet, the best defenses against inflammation are fish oils, vitamin C, lipoic acid, and green tea.

You can start the path to good health by making two or three good food choices each day. As soon as you combine two good deeds into a diet, you get an accelerated health jolt. That is what the Younger You Diet is all about, variety and choices that you can adapt to your lifestyle and preferences.

Inflammation Factor (IF) Rating of Selected Foods

If you want to fight inflammation in the body and boost your immune system, stick to foods that have a high IF rating.

Food	IF Rating
Salmon, 3 ounces	+500
Ginger, ½ teaspoon	+250
Garlic, one clove	+100
Broccoli, ½ cup	+80
Extra-virgin olive oil, 1 tablespoon	+60
Raw almonds, 1 ounce	+50
Bran cereal, ⅓ cup	+40
Veggie burger, one pattie	+40
Flank steak, 3 ounces	+30
10 strawberries	+20

Adapted from The Sinatra Report

Take a look at these Younger You menu ideas for a stronger immune system:

Breakfast Options
- A two-egg omelet with broccoli, peppers, and low-fat cheddar cheese
- 1 cup low-fat cottage cheese, wheat germ, and cantaloupe cubes
- One-half grapefruit with one slice whole-wheat toast
- 2 ounces sliced smoked salmon on top of two slices rye toast

Lunch Options
- 1 cup mashed sweet potato with apricot jam
- 4 ounces baked or broiled cod with sautéed kale and ¼ cup nuts
- 4 ounces baked or broiled chicken breast with ½ cup brown rice and 1 cup grapes
- Spinach salad with carrots, potatoes, and chickpeas

Dinner Options
- 4 ounces braised venison topped with ½ cup apricot and mango sauce
- 4 ounces pan-seared halibut over steamed spinach and tomatoes
- 4 ounces broiled or pan-seared lean steak with ½ cup vinegar cabbage slaw salad

Desserts and Snack Options
- 1 cup mixed fruit salad
- ¼ cup unsalted mixed nuts and dried cranberries
- ¼ cup organic dried papaya and apricots
- Raw carrots and broccoli with a low-fat dressing for dip

And don't forget these cancer-fighting herbs, spices, and flavor-boosting foods:

- Basil
- Chili peppers
- Flax

- Ginger
- Garlic
- Jalapeño peppers
- Onions
- Red clover flower
- Rosemary
- Thyme
- Turmeric

PART 5

Aging Sexuality

11

Menopause: For Women Only!

The hormones associated with sexual and reproductive functions—estrogen and progesterone—are pivotal to our overall health. Like every other organ we've discussed, as we age, hormonal output diminishes, and we first slow down, then break down. Decreases in these hormones affect all of the other systems in the body. The good news, as with the other pauses, is that these decreases are completely reversible. If you can boost these same hormones early enough, the symptoms and conditions related to not only the original sex organ but every other system in the body can be rejuvenated, creating a younger you full of vigorous health.

Sex: It's All In Your Head: The Brain Sex Code

For both men and women, sexual hormone production is governed by your brain. In this instance, your brain controls not only your pause age but your innate sexuality. When you are at the peak of your health, you will want to experience the joys of sex all the time. When your brain is experiencing a chemical deficiency in any of the four primary areas, sex won't seem so enticing and the physical act will leave you lacking. The four phases of sex can be directly correlated to the functioning of the four primary biochemicals:

- Desire is created in the brain by dopamine; when you are low on dopamine, your energy for and interest in sex wanes, as does your performance.

- Arousal is initiated by acetylcholine; when cognitive functioning and internal moisture go awry and your acetylcholine becomes depleted, you will not be able to focus on sex, let alone keep up your attention and stimulation. You will also be uncomfortably dry.
- Orgasm is controlled by your levels of GABA. If GABA becomes depleted, you can't relax and let go, and hence, you can't have an orgasm.
- Resolution is related to serotonin. If serotonin becomes depleted, your timing is off. You're coming to the party either too early or too late.

We Must Have Sex to Beat the Pauses

Some people don't like the idea of combining food and sex, but the two are more intimately related than we think. Oddly, cholesterol is a precursor of all the sex hormones. Estrogen, progesterone, testosterone, pregnenolone, androstenedione, and DHEA all come from cholesterol. So as we get older, and our cholesterol goes up, the ovaries and adrenal glands don't need to make as much of their particular hormones, so estrogen, progesterone, and testosterone production slows. It should not be a surprise then that as our bodies produce less, we feel less sexy and less sexually motivated.

The goal for a younger you is to maintain your best levels of hormone production. Why not start by sparking your sexuality? There's no better way to feel 15 years younger than to be able to have frequent, long-lasting, great sex. What's more, your sexuality is a marker of your overall health. When your interest in sex, as well as your ability, begins to lag, it's more than life just becoming too complicated, too tiring, or too busy. It's a clear sign that you are getting older and that your hormone production is slowing down.

This waning sexual hormone production not only affects your desire to have sex, but it affects all of the other pauses. As soon as your sex hormone production starts to go down, and your brain can't get those levels back up, you start to die. These scenarios are the same for both men and women.

- **Heart:** The heart's ability to pump blood, your peripheral vascular system, and amount of blood getting to your brain are all dependent on your levels of estrogen, progesterone, and testosterone. As sex hormones such as growth hormone decrease, cholesterol increases.

- **Immune system:** Sex hormones are natural immune system modulators. They control autoimmunity and make sure your immune system doesn't go wild. If these hormones get out of whack, your immune system will begin to shut down. Also the decline in sex hormones results in a drop in glucagon and blood sugar control is compromised. This results in an increase in inflammation, oxidation, dehydration, and calcification.

- **Bones:** Each of the sex hormones perpetuates both parathyroid and growth hormone production, while simultaneously maintaining your bone density. When these hormones go down, your bone density goes with them.

- **Skin:** Sex hormones keep your skin young, internally and externally. Many women use creams containing natural estrogen and testosterone supplements on their face to make their skin firmer and keep it looking younger!

- **Brain:** Sexual hormones affect your memory and attention. Testosterone helps your visual memory, and estrogen affects your attention, concentration, and working memory.

Don't Let Your Sex Life Sag

There's no age limit for good sex, so don't fall into the trap that your day has come and gone. For example, Angela was just 41 when she told me about her severely decreased libido. Her AgePrint showed that her menopause age was 65, her blood work showed that her hormonal balances were completely off-kilter, and her bone density scan showed that she already had suffered some significant bone loss.

I started Angela on a few hormonal supplements to try and help her. The supplements worked beautifully, boosting her estrogen as well as her testosterone levels. In no time, her libido was back and she was feeling sexy! Changes in her diet and a willingness to integrate more exercise into daily life meant she started feeling like a 41-year-old again. Angela did not require a massive intervention, but little changes vastly improved her overall quality of life.

Younger Sex Is Frequent Sex

Most divorces are in some way related to sexual incompatibility. Simply, sexually speaking, men are generally "younger" than women and desire sex more often. But women can get younger; I see it all the time. I have had plenty of women who increased both their sexual desire and ability to have orgasms simply by taking bioidentical hormones, including DHEA, human growth hormone (HGH), estrogen, and progesterone. Their husbands, needless to say, are ecstatic. And by the way, so are the women.

You don't need to have sex as frequently as you did in your 20s, but you shouldn't just try to get away with the minimum requirements either. Sexual frequency should never drop below once a week, though ideally it should be around twice a week. The effect an orgasm can have on your brain is like rebooting a computer. There are two ways to reboot your brain—by "turning it on" (like you do when you're having sex or exercising) or "turning it off" (like you do when you are relaxing). Sex reboots your brain both ways at the same time.

Birth Control Pills: An Unnecessary Aging Code

Taking birth control pills is a great way to get old in a hurry. Pregnancy is every woman's age decelerator because by completing a pregnancy you reduce the risk of breast cancer, uterine cancer, and a host of other estrogen-related illnesses. Women who get pregnant even once during their lifetime tend to live longer than women who never were pregnant.

Though the birth control pill tricks your body into thinking that it's pregnant, the results are quite the opposite. Young women have normal estrogen blood levels of 400 pg/mL, and menopausal women have levels anywhere from 0 to 40 pg/mL, yet young women do not experience side effects from their high level of natural estrogen until they take birth control pills. They then develop an increased risk of heart attack, cancer, liver tumors, and possibly lower cognitive function. Blood clots can result, as well as leaving you emotionally unstable.

Birth control pills are supplementing additional hormones at a much earlier age than the body really requires. In all cases, birth control pills are synthetic, and in order to prevent pregnancy they are a combined dose of progesterone and estrogen. All of these factors make the Pill an age accelerator.

Menopause Is an Ultimate Age Accelerator

Menopause is a natural stage of life that every woman must face. The onset of menopause does not have to be an awful experience; in fact, if you are mentally prepared for the challenge, it might be the best years of your life.

Menopause is not associated with any particular age; it simply marks the decline in production of progesterone and estrogen. Many of my female patients had been misinformed, thinking that menopause started during midlife, around the age of 50. But I tell them time and again that by the time you begin to experience symptoms, your pause is already in the middle of its course. Menopause actually begins around the age of 35 and can take as many as 10 to 15 years before it is completed. Hormonal imbalances can start even earlier when brain stress is high.

The following shows the age of ovaries:

Estradiol Levels (pg/mL)	Age of Ovaries
400	20
350	25
300	30
200	35

Estradiol Levels (pg/mL)	Age of Ovaries
150	40
100	45
50	50
40 or less	60
20 or less	75

Women in their 30s are already going into partial menopause. A loss of progesterone can make you cranky and moody and increase the effects of premenstrual syndrome (PMS). By the time you reach 50, it is very likely that you will be beginning to feel the most obvious signs and symptoms, all due to estrogen loss. They include:

- Attention deficiencies
- Bone weakness
- Vaginal dryness
- Failure to ovulate
- Hair loss
- Hot flashes
- Loss of libido
- Mood swings
- Abdominal weight gain

Menopause has acquired lots of labels. The bodily changes that women start to notice in their 50s do not happen overnight, but have been building over a 10- to 15-year span. *Perimenopause* is defined as the beginning of menopausal symptoms, which can occur anywhere from two to eight years before full-blown menopause begins. *Post-menopausal* means past the point of menopause, where symptoms will no longer be noticeable.

Your Bad Mood

Unfortunately, the transition to menopause occurs very slowly, so much so that you might not even notice changes in your mood or your increas-

What Happened to My Flat Stomach?

Increased body fat, loss of muscle tone, and weight gain around your middle are all very common occurrences during menopause. The fall of estrogen and progesterone cause a cascade of rising blood sugars and lower mental activity. Women begin to feel both hungry and tired so often, they eat more junk food to stay alert and they exercise less. The good news is that we now have the ability to give low dosages of natural hormones that will transform not only the way you feel but the way you look.

ing anxiety. However, these symptoms happen to virtually all women. While you may have emotionally adjusted to the lower level of GABA function, it is most likely straining your relationships. Try to stay in tune with those around you, and allow them to help you get the help you need.

Menopause Forces the Other Pauses

Once menopause begins, the rest of the pauses quickly progress, as the imbalances feed on each other. Consequently, your health breaks down. The roll down the hill goes faster and faster, especially if our brains aren't in good shape. The imbalances in the estrogen-progesterone ratio can feel chaotic at best.

When estrogen production flags, the other pauses cascade. Loss of estrogen creates:

- Changes in bone density, leading to osteopause
- Drying of skin and hair, leading to dermatopause
- Heart pump failure, triggering cardiopause
- Increased blood clotting, or vasculopause
- Increased body fat and weight, leading to dopamine biopause
- Increased risk of breast cancer, triggering immunopause
- Interference with thyroid hormone, leading to thyropause

- Loss of memory and other cognitive deterioration, triggering electropause
- Attention failure, leading to acetylcholine biopause

Progesterone to the Rescue

Progesterone is a medical gift from the gods. It is a natural mood balancer, stress reliever, and brain calmer, and it squashes cortisol. It is a natural diuretic, antidepressant, antioxidant, and a precursor of cortisone and necessary for survival. By boosting this one hormone, it will directly affect all the pauses:

- Cardiopause will be relieved through the lowering of blood pressure and prevention of arrhythmias.
- Immunopause will be halted to help prevent breast and endometrial cancers and possibly other cancers.
- Low GABA will be addressed to help decrease appetite.
- Low serotonin depression will be combated by improved mood and better sleep patterns.
- Menopause will be relieved by the restoration of the libido and orgasm by allowing relaxation.
- Osteopause will be reversed through the increase of bone density.
- Thyropause will be slowed through improved thyroid functioning.
- Vasculopause will be relieved through the relaxation of peripheral vessels, which can help circulation.
- Electropause will be slowed through increased GABA, which can reverse seizures and anxiety.

Women May Need Testosterone

Most hormone replacement therapies (HRTs) focus on replacing estrogen, but testosterone is an important component as well. Women pro-

Cortisol: The Stress Hormone

Cortisol is a stress hormone that boosts dopamine-related chemicals, giving us more juice when we are out of brain gasoline.

duce small amounts of testosterone themselves. By supplementing testosterone through natural sources, you will have a balanced approach to hormonal replacement and beat many menopause symptoms as well as control the other pauses. The best way to take hormones is by imitating what the ovaries produce on their own.

Some women should not take testosterone: if you are experiencing baldness or excessive facial or nasal hair, or if you have have an imbalance of sex hormone binding globulin.

Testosterone is needed to prevent:

- Electropause, by improving visual spatial memory or working memory
- Immunopause, because most cancers increase as testosterone decreases with age
- Cardiopause, because testosterone is good for the heart and helps it pump more efficiently
- Osteopause, by building a woman's bone density
- Vasculopause, because of increased blood flow

It's relatively easy to crack the menopause code for a younger you. A multimodal approach including medications, hormones, nutrient supplements, and specific dietary suggestions will help you break the menopause death code that may already be evident by your AgePrint. Menopause is primarily reversed by using bioidentical hormones. However, there are nutrients and medications that can help with your individual symptoms. Virtually all women need all three hormones (estrogen, testosterone, and progesterone) to break the menopause code.

Take Action: Early Detection Is Key

You've already taken the first step toward better health by taking the AgePrint quiz in Chapter 2. Bring these results to your physician, who might recommend some of the following blood work:

Blood Levels	Function
Luteinizing hormone (LH) and follicle-stimulating hormone (FSH)	Pituitary gonadotropins; assess gonadal dysfunction and infertility
Thyroid-stimulating hormone (TSH)	Measures thyroid function
Estradiol	Measures estradiol level
Progesterone	Measures progesterone level
Sex hormone binding globulin	A protein that when bound correctly, allows every sex hormone to be used correctly; when too high, indicates estrogen dominant; when too low, testosterone dominant
Free and total testosterone	Measures testosterone that is stored and utilized by the body

Who's Hot in Here?

Hot flashes and other symptoms of menopause are no joke. While there is no medication that will stop menopause from occurring, many women experience such severe symptoms that medication may be needed to control them. If you are experiencing severe hot flashes (either in number or intensity), let your doctor know. She might prescribe estrogen-containing products, which are the most effective treatment. Prescription drug alternatives include progestogens; the antidepressants venlafaxine (Effexor), paroxetine (Paxil), and fluoxetine (Prozac); as well as the anticonvulsant gabapentin (Neurontin).

GABA and serotonin agents stop the "freak-outs" many women experience as a result of declining estrogen levels. This occurs because you're losing progesterone, the hormone that keeps you calm. Without progesterone, many women experience a general "sinking" feeling. With the right medication, this feeling will go away.

Talk to your doctor about these treatments if you feel like menopause symptoms are aging you:

Antidepressants	Suggested Dosage per Day
Venlafaxine (Effexor)	37.5–375 mg
Parotexine (Paxil)	10–50 mg
Fluoxetine (Prozac)	40–80 mg

Antianxiety Agents	Suggested Dosage per Day
Gabapentin (Neurontin)	300–1,800 mg
Alprazolam (Xanax)	0.25–1 mg
Clonazepam (Klonopin)	0.25–1 mg

Hormone Replacement Therapy Creates a Younger You

Most women have an AgePrint of 100 by the time they are 55. If you take natural estrogen and other bioidentical supplements, then you turn the clock back to age 40 to 45. Staying at age 45 to 50 for the rest of your life is optimal. The secret here is to trick your brain into thinking it is 50 forever.

The only way menopause can be successfully treated is by imitating the body's own mechanisms, which means replacing the hormones that the body naturally has lost. By maintaining and increasing hormone levels, you can restore your health and even reverse the symptoms that have been affecting you. Natural hormones have been found to be capable of doing this without causing negative side effects. This why I tell all of my patients that all hormones are not the same. Synthetic estrogens are made from horse urine and have been known for years to cause an increase in blood clots, heart attacks, stroke, and breast cancer. It has been scientifically determined that women taking estrogen derived from horses (methyltestosterone) have an increased rate of cancer. Other complications associated with synthetic hormones include weight gain. It has also been shown that growth hormone from cadavers causes cancer.

I only prescribe bioidentical, or natural, hormones, which have the exact same molecular structure as those made in the human body. Because of this, they produce the same physiologic responses as the body's natural hormones. Bioidentical hormones are made from plants, not plastics, and have been available for more than 20 years. They are so lacking in side effects that they are frequently sold over the counter as nutrient supplements (melatonin, pregnenolone, vitamin D_3, and DHEA to name a few).

These natural preparations require taking only one tablet nightly, and their only side effect is sleepiness. They have no effect on insulin resistance; if anything, they improve insulin resistance and the response to inflammation. Often, my patients become less arthritic because these natural hormones require smaller doses. These women will also see improvements in their health in multiple areas—they will have better concentration; thicker hair; smoother, more supple skin; as well as reduced inflammation, increased insulin resistance, and an improved sex life. Until we can fix genes themselves, hormones will only be able to turn back the clock 15 years, but it's enough to keep all the pauses in check.

Rita Got Younger When She Went Bioidentical

Rita was a 59-year-old woman when she first visited my New York City office eight years ago. She was active and in good health. She traveled and exercised regularly and kept a jam-packed social calendar. But Rita was beginning to feel that she was always tired and came to me complaining that she lacked her usual pep. She was having increasing difficulty falling asleep and pain during sexual relations, and she had noticed that her skin was becoming dry and her hair unmanageable.

I suspected that Rita's complaints were all related to menopause. When I mentioned this to Rita, she responded vehemently that she was done with "the change" years ago and that whatever she was experiencing now, she was not interested in HRT. She had read about its serious side effects, particularly cancer. She did agree to participate in a comprehensive workup so that we could definitively see what was causing her condition.

The workup confirmed that Rita was in good physical health. Her AgePrint for memory and attention were slightly above her real age, and her hormonal profile was within the norm for her age group. I told Rita that other doctors might be pleased with these results, but I was less than satisfied; I don't believe that we should all be resigned to physical and mental deterioration just because we are getting older. I told Rita that even though she had already experienced menopause, aging was the culprit. If we were able to enhance her hormonal levels, we could reverse her age, and the suppleness in her hair and skin would return, she would enhance her mental acuity, and she would ensure proper sleep that would be able to increase her overall energy levels.

Rita was still hesitant, but I explained that the HRT regimen I would put her on was not the synthetic therapies she had heard about. The micronized hormones that I used did not contain the components used in synthetic versions that cause adverse reactions. I further explained that conventional HRT is frequently not balanced, with estrogen being given without compensating for reduced testosterone. I prescribed a micronized combination progesterone-estradiol-testosterone formulation.

Three months later, the change in Rita was unmistakable. She was animated as she spoke about how much younger she looked. Her skin and hair were noticeably softer and smoother. She was once again experiencing pleasure during sex. Best of all, she was sleeping more consistently and finally had the energy to keep up with her social calendar.

When I saw her again later that year, Rita remarked that along with her better overall health, she was able to concentrate better for longer periods of time. Eight years later, Rita is still following the same regimen and feels "much younger" than what she expected to feel at 67. I was happy for her to do another AgePrint and was delighted to see that she was living like a thriving 50-year-old!

Too Much of a Good Thing

If you screw up one pause, you screw up multiple pauses. If you take too much testosterone, it gets converted to dihydrotestosterone, a substance that can hurt your immune system. When men have too much testosterone, they get prostate cancer, and when women have too much testosterone, they become obese and get polycystic ovaries. When women take the wrong types of estrogen or take too much testosterone, they get facial hair. Follow your doctor's recommended dosages for the most effective and safest way to rejuvenate

The Real Deal on DHEA

DHEA, produced by the adrenal glands, is a sex hormone that plays an important, yet somewhat mysterious, role in sexual physiology for both men and women. DHEA levels peak in our 20s and then begin to decline. By the time we reach our 70s, these levels are down by 20 percent. Recent studies have shown that elderly women can enjoy the enhanced sexual benefits of DHEA treatment when it is aimed at restoring the original youthful levels.

Talk with your doctor about taking these code-breaking hormones:

Hormonal Treatment	Suggested Dosage per Day	Brain Code Action
Progesterone	100–200 mg	GABA, serotonin
Testosterone	2.5–10 mg	Dopamine
Estradiol (E2)	1–2 mg	Acetylcholine
Estrone (E3)	2–4 g	Acetylcholine
DHEA	50–100 mg	Acetylcholine, dopamine
Pregnenolone	10–25 mg	GABA

Vitamin D and Menopause

You can strengthen your overall health by supplementing with vitamin D. The *American Journal of Clinical Nutrition* recently claimed that vitamin D made a big difference for those suffering during menopause. They found that women who were consuming at least 12.5 milligrams of vitamin D from either food sources or supplements had a 37 percent lower risk of hip fractures than women who took less than 3.5 milligrams. Neither milk nor a high-calcium diet was associated with lowering the risks of these fractures.

Typically I prescribe 5,000 units of vitamin D per day as a natural brain builder. We follow with 50,000 units one time per three months, which has a powerful effect on menopausal symptoms and the prevention of osteoporosis.

A Rainbow Diet for Menopause

Weight gain is, unfortunately, a very common side effect of menopause. By following the Rainbow Diet, you'll be able to control your weight and stop the cascade of illness associated with obesity. It's remarkable how carrying as little as 10 extra pounds can significantly affect your overall health.

Increasing your soy and fish consumption are the key additions to tailor the diet for menopause. Soy products are a health alternative to dairy and can be found in choices that go far beyond tofu and tempeh. In most supermarkets you can find a wide selection of soy milks, soy cheeses (hard and soft varieties, even cream cheeses), crackers, enriched whole-grain breads, veggie burgers, and more.

Here are some menu suggestions to help you out even more.

Breakfast Options
- Slice of organic cornbread baked with flaxseeds
- ⅓ cup soy crisp cereal with ½ cup vanilla soy milk
- Sardines on whole-wheat toast
- 8-ounce soy milk smoothie with bananas and strawberries

Lunch Options

- Tofu stir-fry with snow peas and broccoli
- 1 cup tuna fish salad with low-fat mayonnaise on pumpernickel toast
- Veggie burger and a small tossed salad
- Smoked trout pâté on one-half whole-wheat bagel

Dinner Options

- Two-egg vegetable omelet with a whole sweet potato
- 4 ounces broiled salmon steak served with ½ cup brown rice
- 4 ounces grilled mackerel over mixed greens
- Grilled mixed vegetables served over sweet potato pancakes

Herbs and spices are not a powerful antidote for menopause. They have minimal value in raising estrogen. Instead, focus on the bioidentical hormones; they are crucial for women in menopause.

12

Andropause: For Men Only!

Men usually don't notice when their body is changing, except when it comes to sex. As men age, we turn into those cantankerous old coots who throw temperamental fits. It's not that we've hit the wall; we are experiencing a decline in our hormone production that affects all the same parts as menopause does in women. Andropause, the male equivalent, affects our mood, memory, thinking, and, most of all, our health. Andropause typically begins for men at age 40 and is marked by a decline in production of the hormone testosterone. Male menopause is different from female menopause in that men can cycle in and out of andropause. This occurs in the cases of high stress, depression, excessive athleticism, or drug use.

Testosterone

Men do need their testosterone. At age 20, men's testosterone levels are around 1,000 nanograms per deciliter in blood (ng/dl). By age 30, they hover around 900, by 40 they're at 800, age 50 at 700, age 60 at 500, age 70 at 400, age 80 at 300, and then age 90 they're at 200.

The Aging Male Sex Code

All of your hormones play some role in healthy sexual function. Your brain sends its electrical signals as hormonal messengers to your aging liver, thyroid, pituitary and adrenal glands, and many other organs to give them an additional jump start. As we get older the brain needs to increase the number of these chemical messengers to get the same job done, the result of which is ultimately toxic to your brain. When those stimulating hormones keep rising because the organs are dying, a death code is sent to the rest of the body—and to the brain itself—that it's time to die. As we age, hormones such as follicle-stimulating hormone (FSH) and leutinizing hormone (LH) increase in a desperate attempt to stimulate sexual organs. The hormones are toxic to the brain, accelerating dementia and other health problems as well.

What's more, the diseases of the body affect your sexuality, with diabetes and obesity being the worst age accelerators and alcohol and drug abuse not far behind. Diabetes kills all the nerves in your penis, which literally stunts your ability to feel. Without these nerve endings, it is impossible to be sensual or in touch with your partner. Obesity affects your heart muscles and blood flow, making sex (which should be quite vigorous) much more difficult. Fragile bones may hinder your performance; if you are afraid of hurting yourself during active sex, it can't be much fun. Last, skin lesions all over the body may make the experience quite painful.

The Fix Is the Easy Part to a Younger You

As you've seen already, we often can fix other pauses by increasing your sex hormone levels. By doing so, good health in every section of the body becomes pervasive. For example, when we treat men who have osteoporosis with testosterone and parathyroid, the two hormones augment each other. By fixing the sexual pauses, we wind up fixing bone density, and the two together are synergistic.

For example, Hal was a 60-year-old patient of mine who had suffered from a stroke. That was nine years before he came to see me, and he had not had an erection since. After going on my hormone revitalization program consisting of human growth hormone (HGH), natural testosterone, and dehydroepiandrosterone (DHEA), he was finally able to repeatedly achieve orgasm.

Andropause and Sex

Sex isn't just about recreation or procreation. The inability to have sex is definitely disappointing, but more important, it can trigger the rest of the body to age. When the brain gets tired, the signals to the body get weaker, and you will produce less testosterone. As this hormone drops, it in turn signals the body and the brain to begin shutting down.

The biological cascade of reactions that occur as a result can cause a number of different symptoms beyond sexual side effects. These are directly related to the pauses. Decrease in testosterone can lead to:

- Increased fatigue, weight gain, as well as loss of desire for sex, attention deficiencies, and memory lapses plus poor lubrication, reduced quantity of semen, and genital shrinkage leading to electropause
- Loss of height and muscle strength, resulting in osteopause
- A metabolic syndrome that leads to diabetes, a precursor state to cardiovascular disease, triggering cardiopause
- Decline in cognition and an increase in sexual dissatisfaction and increasing unhappiness

Andropause and Addiction

Andropause and addiction often go together. It's called the reward deficiency syndrome. As we age and experience declining dopamine levels, we often look to self-medicate with either prescription or recreational drugs in a desperate attempt to find reward. It can be a dangerous cascade that can be avoided by balancing testosterone. And we often turn to the one thing we simply cannot handle. For example, I once treated a prominent 54-year-old physician whose dopamine was so out of whack that he was abusing cocaine and binge drinking every night and was unable to perform sexually. He tried Viagra and Cialis, but nothing seemed to work.

His andropause age code was 70. His blood work showed that his problem was a combination of diabetes and deficiencies in both testosterone and growth hormone. He also had chronic anxiety and panic attacks. I put him on a therapy program of niacin, fish oil, natural testosterone, DHEA, and HGH. Within two months he was off alcohol and cocaine and was genuinely enjoying his sex life. By balancing his brain through raising his mood and reducing his anxiety, I was able to cure his addiction problem. Now he feels younger than he has in years. The male brain balanced with testosterone has many more productive ways of living.

There has been an explosion on the market of drugs to treat erectile dysfunction. The tremendous volume of sales has demonstrated the magnitude of this problem. It's a shame that men have fallen into the pharmaceutical trap of believing that the only way to fix their problem is with a prescription. They are willing to risk serious side effects instead of seeking alternative methods.

The truth is that the majority of erectile dysfunction is due to a loss of testosterone. Male sexual dysfunction is therefore more effectively treated with testosterone supplementation. The loss of testosterone also results in low satisfaction, motivation, and drive to do the activities they once found enjoyable, for example, sex and exercise.

Take Action for a Younger You

It's relatively easy to get your groove back on. A multimodal approach including medications, hormones, nutrient supplements, and specific dietary suggestions will help you break the death code of andropause that may already be evident by your AgePrint.

You can choose a variety of ways to reverse your aging body. Your choice can be guided by your deficiency. If you are not exhibiting symptoms and your andropause age code was greater than 20 years more than your chronological age, you can start with nutrition and lifestyle changes. If your score was between 40 and 60 years more than your chronological age, you will need to address your personal reversal with hormones. At levels greater than 60 years more than your chronological age, you will need medications to reverse your AgePrint to a more normal state.

To find out if you are approaching andropause, talk with your doctor about these blood tests:

Blood Levels	Function
Luteinizing hormone (LH) and follicle-stimulating hormone (FSH)	This will measure the brain's electrical and chemical messenger to the testicles; 50 percent of men in andropause have high LH or FHS and 50 percent have low or normal levels.
Testosterone, free and total	There are two kinds of testosterone in the body; *total* is the reserve and *free* is what the body is using.
Sex hormone binding globulin	This is a key modulator between male and female sexual hormones. When elevated, this test identifies male menopause relative to himself even if he appears normal when compared to others.

Every Erection Has a Resurrection

These well-known prescription medications restore, and possibly enhance, erectile function by increasing your blood flow to the penis. The results are exactly what you've heard. However, there are serious side effects to consider, including upset stomach, headaches, and loss of vision. What's more, I've found over the years that blood flow to the penis is rarely the originating problem of erectile dysfunction. So before you order these drugs from Mexico, get yourself properly tested. Your problem may lie elsewhere.

Raising the level of neurotransmitters in the brain is critical to treating andropause. Dopamine improves libido, acetylcholine provides moisture, GABA helps you relax, and serotonin will make it fun. When your brain is balanced and you still have trouble with sexual performance, the issue might be in your vasculature system. If you do have a vascular problem, medications such as Levitra, Cialis, and Viagra can be helpful but should remain as a last resort. If you want something natural, arginine (500–2,000 mg) may be helpful for improving sexual function.

Conventional Treatment	Suggested Dosage per Day
Levitra	5–20 mg
Cialis	5–20 mg
Viagra	50–100 mg

Stop Andropause for a Younger, Sexier You

You can reverse a flagging sex drive and return your overall health to the same level as those younger boys. When you take a combination of bioidentical growth hormone and testosterone, multiple pause areas begin to work better. You could again be 60 years old with a 40-year-old memory, a 30-year-old lung capacity, and a testosterone level of a 28-year-old.

For example, Steven was 55 and discouraged and depressed about his sexual dysfunction. I changed his antidepressant, put him on a CES device, and started him on my sexual rejuvenation hormone program. He went from having sex with his wife once a month to six times per week.

Go Bioidentical for Male Sexual Hormones

The synthetic methyltestosterone now has a black box warning that it may contribute to liver cancer. Fortunately, there is no similar black box warning on the natural, micronized testosterones. Natural testosterones treat hypogonadism by restoring your testosterone to its normal range. A variety of natural testosterone is available in the form of pills, pellets, creams, patches, and gels. Androgel delivers natural testosterone in a gel that you simply rub into your skin—no patches or injections to worry about.

I have been using testosterone and HGH replacement therapies for my male patients for more than 10 years, which has enabled these men to maintain brain function as well as physical stamina and libido. A study reported in the *Journals of Gerontology* showed that men ages 65 to 87 who used testosterone transdermal patches for one year also improved their memory and concentration abilities. Androgel is now ranked as the easiest delivery system.

So remember that depletion equals andropause. Try these boosting hormones.

Hormonal Treatment	Suggested Dosage per Day
Testosterone (bioidentical)	100 mg
DHEA	50–100 mg
Androgel	Consult your doctor
(most effective form)	
Testim	1%
Testoderm	6 mg/d patch
HGH	5–60 mg

Younger You Foods That Let You Lose Weight and Still Eat Like a Man

Suggestions for men are quite different from those for women. To reverse andropause, you need to beef up. Follow the dopamine diet outlined in Chapter 3, including lots of meats and poultry.

The following tips will augment this particular eating regimen:

- Look for foods that are high in copper and zinc to aid hair growth; sources include barley, beets, garlic, nuts, pecans, soy, radishes, raisins, and seafood.
- Fish provides essential fatty acids that keep hair healthy.
- To improve stamina (circulation), eat vitamin C–rich foods such as beet greens, black currants, mangoes, sweet peppers, and pineapple.

Being in Shape Means More Great Sex

Even moderate weight loss results in significant improvements in sexual functioning and satisfaction. And those who regularly exercise have higher levels of desire and enhanced ability to be aroused and achieve orgasm. If you are overweight, losing between 8 to 20 pounds will help you look younger and feel sexier.

And, check out the following manly meal menu options:

Breakfast Options
- Omelet made with two eggs, low-fat cheddar cheese, and green pepper
- 8-ounce smoothie with yogurt, soy milk, and ground flaxseeds
- One-quarter pineapple and 1 cup cottage cheese
- 3 ounces lean bacon and two scrambled eggs

Lunch Options
- 4-ounce slice of meatloaf, made using whole-wheat bread crumbs
- One baked sweet potato and 8 ounces beef soup
- 1 cup beef and soybean chili
- Grilled cheese sandwich on multigrain bread

Dinner Options
- Seafood paella with ½ cup brown rice
- Grilled turkey legs and pan-roasted brussels sprouts
- 1-pound lobster, steamed, served with whole-wheat pasta and broccoli
- 4-ounce lean pork chops served with grilled apples and quinoa

PART 6

Your Aging Frame: Bones, Muscles, and Skin

13

Osteopause: Reversing the Frame of Old Age

As we get older our bodies dry out, and we will begin to feel achy. Internal dryness directly affects our bones and muscles, which both require lots of moisture to remain flexible. Without the proper amounts of moisture, our bones will become weaker and more brittle, and our muscles will become tense and painful.

This internal dryness does not begin overnight. Like most other signs of aging, it's a code that begins before we notice any symptoms. Bones inevitably begin to weaken after age 30, especially for women. It cascades to a set of symptoms including frequent broken bones when we are younger to a loss of height, joint pain, and compression fractures as we get older. Ultimately, your brittle skeleton will not be able to support your body, leading to a painful and debilitating condition known as osteoporosis.

Eighty percent of all patients with osteoporosis are women, yet one-third of all men will experience its symptoms by the age of 75. It is a painless disease that progresses slowly until your bones are no longer able to do their job, which is keeping you upright. The injuries that can occur from this disease may erode your quality of life, as the simplest tasks become difficult to manage without bone strength. What's more, osteoporosis is often compounded with a hormonal problem. This is especially true for postmenopausal women, whose estrogen and progesterone levels decrease, significantly affecting bone loss.

Your bones and muscles are affected by three separate pauses: osteopause, parathyropause, and somatopause. Each of these pauses is governed by particular brain chemicals and their hormonal counterparts. Each sends its own death code to the rest of the body to shut down. And each is completely reversible.

Maria, a spunky 62-year-old, came into my office complaining of an increasing number of annoying aches and pains. A bone density scan revealed significantly low bone density for a woman her age. This was surprising, given that she exercised frequently by taking long walks around her neighborhood and running after her active grandchildren. She usually made wise food choices and followed a diet any physician would be proud of. Maria was doing all the right things to keep her postmenopausal body, particularly her bones, healthy. Yet for some reason, they were failing her.

When I broke the news to her that she could very well suffer a hip or other fracture, Maria was frightened. She had already lived through her mother's hip fracture, from which she never quite recovered. Even though I wrote Maria a prescription for bioidentical supplements, she chose not to fill it. Instead, Maria chose to alter her lifestyle. She began to step more softly, and she stopped caring for her grandchildren and left her house less. In a few weeks Maria noticed that her aches and pains were dissipating, but so was her quality of life. Maria was lonely and unhappy.

I saw Maria eight months later and tested her bone density again. The results were still the same. What had changed was her weight and body fat. In just a few months Maria had gained the equivalent of 7 percent of her overall body weight and increased her body fat by 3 percent, both of which multiplied her risk not only for poor health but for more bone fractures as well. After this startling news, Maria decided her course of action wasn't working, and she would consent to medical treatment for her bones. I recommended that she start parathyroid treatment to lower her slightly elevated parathyroid hormone levels and to increase her bone density. Parathyroid is one of the few hormones that increase with age. When an injection of parathyroid is given, the gland normalizes its own level.

After one year on Forteo, Maria had her bone density rescanned and there was significant improvement. Perhaps more important, Maria was back to her old self; she was once again walking daily and enjoying her grandchildren. Maria's choice resulted in her becoming younger so that she could fully enjoy her family and her life.

Musculoskeletal Test

Musculoskeletal aging is subtle business. Everyday events can slowly yet directly affect the health and wear and tear of your frame. Answer these questions to see if you are beginning to feel the effects of this type of aging code:

1. Do you stand or walk on hard surfaces for more than four hours daily?
2. Do you participate regularly in any physical sport (basketball, baseball, tennis, golf, bowling, etc.)?
3. Have you ever injured your knee, back, or neck?
4. Are you having trouble exercising?
5. Do your shoes wear unevenly at the heels or toes?

Osteopause: You've Got Old Bones

Osteopause refers to the weakening of the bones and is more commonly thought of as osteoporosis, or loss of bone density. When this occurs, the bones throughout the body—but primarily within the spinal column—begin to weaken. A younger brain and body help postpone osteopause; younger brains send more biochemical messengers to produce hormones naturally, and younger bodies can better absorb the nutrients and hormones the bones need to stay supple.

Your bone's age is affected by a host of variables, including proper amounts of hormones, vitamins, and minerals, as well as age, weight, drug use, and genetics. All of these factors determine how fast or how slowly our bones "get old." Just because your chronological age is 30 does not mean you are young. You are only as young as your oldest part.

Calculating Your True Bone Age

Your bone age can be determined by your AgePrint. It can also be measured by determining its density. Bone is living tissue that is composed of a soft, porous center encased in a hard outer surface. Osteoporosis occurs when the density of the porous center is much less than the outer surface, and the bone literally collapses on itself. This causes us to lose height with age. The vertebrae, composed almost entirely of the softer, more porous bone, compact as they lose density and shrink.

Height loss shows up well after the loss of bone density occurs. My patients are often surprised at how much damage can be done before they notice any symptoms. They are constantly amazed at the findings from bone density tests; I often find multiple vertebral compression fractures that are the cause of height loss. Twenty percent of the women I see are suffering from vertebral compression fractures, as are 10 percent of the men over the age of 70. Most of these people are asymptomatic, completely unaware that there is a problem.

Your bone age is calculated in pluses and minuses; +1 would equal 40-year-old bones, +2 would be 50-year-old bones, +3 would be 60-year-old bones, and so on. I have seen patients with +4 bone density in their 40s who have the equivalent of 70-year-old osteoarthritis.

Bone Mineral Density	Age
−1	20: firm, stiff bones
0	30: ideal, no bone loss
+1	40: beginning bone loss
+2	50: osteopenia
+3	60: osteoporosis
+4	70: severe osteoporosis with possible fracture
+5	80–90: dead bones, likely to fracture
+6	90–100: almost 50% bone fracture rate per year; death or severe dehydration

This Time, You Can Blame DNA

Perhaps you are not what you eat, despite what your grandmother may have told you. Though the foods you choose contribute to bone formation and maintenance, a shocking amount of us are born with genetically fallible parts. Some of us take plenty of calcium and vitamin D supplements, yet our genetic bone structure is weak, just as many of us eat properly but still gain weight because we come from a family with slow metabolism.

Or You Can Blame Your Brain

Bone and muscle health are also intimately related to a loss of acetylcholine. All acetylcholine deficiencies lead to the dehydration of the brain and body. Once your brain starts to dry out, it can no longer regulate your immune system. Further, as we age and begin to lose acetylcholine, the aging brain triggers the joint system to age prematurely (arthritis). The brain then calls on the calcium resources in the bones to add moisture to the system, thereby drying up the bones as well (osteoporosis).

You can boost your brain by increasing your acetylcholine production and get younger. If you can keep your brain young, you can manage this aging process and recover the use of atrophied muscles and bones. I have seen patients who have gone from crippling bed-bound lives to regaining full movement. A powerful, healthy brain can manage osteoporosis better than the failing one. But without hormonal replacement, sooner or later even the strongest brains will give out, as the foundation of the brain's home falls apart.

Meet the Cousins: Arthritis

Arthritis is another low-acetylcholine condition that occurs when we internally dry it. It affects the cartilage that is supposed to protect the tips of our bones, separating them from one another. When this cartilage dries, it begins to wear thin and eventually disintegrates. Without the cartilage that keeps your bones apart, they will begin to rub together.

Rubbing is really an understatement; the bones actually grind against each other, causing pain and stiffness.

Arthritis is the number-one cause of movement limitation among the elderly and a leading cause of disability. Almost everyone over the age of 50 has it to some degree, unless they've been smart and have been taking care of their bones all along. Arthritis in the hands is actually a predictor of later knee and hip problems.

But we do not have to suffer with painful joints; there are effective supplements I prescribe all the time that give long-lasting relief to my arthritis sufferers. Topical pain killers such as Zostrix are helpful, as is the supplement glucosamine. Fish oils and other natural anti-inflammatory foods that are packed with vitamin D will help ease the pain as well. Virtually all arthritis is a combination of bone loss, dehydration of joints, inflammation, and calcification and will end with the new treatments available today for aging bones.

Francis, a 72-year-old female, came to me complaining of joint, knee, and back pain. I put her on a hormonal program consisting of hormonal replacement therapy (HRT) (natural estrogen, progesterone, and testosterone), vitamin D, fish oils, and serotonin-boosting nutrients and medications, which all resulted in her being able to move again with ease. Some can find relief from arthritic pain with estrogen replacement only, and some require a total osteoporosis-reversing program.

To decode your bone health, get these blood tests:

Blood Levels	Function
Calcitonin	Hormone involved in calcium metabolism; helps maintain bones
Parathyroid hormone	Produced by the parathyroid gland; regulates the amount of calcium in body fluids (blood levels under 30 are ideal)
Urine telopeptides	Marker of bone resorption; increased in some patients with osteoporosis and metastatic bone cancer

Blood Levels	Function
Vitamin D$_2$, D$_3$	Helps to maintain normal blood levels of calcium
Boron and strontium	Low boron and strontium levels contribute to osteoporosis
Vitamin K	Has calcium binding properties in blood
Osteocalcin	Protein found in blood, a marker of bone turnover
Ionized calcium	Physiologically active forms or calcium
T-helper/T-suppressor	May mark inflammation in the bone
Antigliadin Abs IgG, IgA	Markers of celiac disease and calcium malabsorption

Cognitive Decline and Osteopause

Have you ever seen a heavy Alzheimer's patient? The answer is no, because cognitive decline and osteopause are both acetylcholine issues. When the brain loses its moisture, it loses its energy (electropause), and cognitive deterioration begins. When the body loses its moisture,

Brain over Back Pain

Mind over Back Pain is a classic lay medical book written by Dr. John Sarno. He provides a great fix for chronic back pain, including relaxation techniques that can help lower your body fat, enhance mood, decrease stress level, clean arteries, and improve diabetes. He also discusses how to improve your immunity and sex life and how to sharpen your mind. But in reality, he's not teaching mind over back pain; it's brain over back pain. Brain health simply builds better overall health. No matter what the source, we don't have to live with pain from osteoporosis or disk problems.

Old Bones Are Fat Bones

By the time we're 30, more than half of our bone cells have turned to fat. Those of us with high osteopause AgePrints have more fat in our bones than those with younger bones. As much as 5,000 IU of vitamin D$_3$ will help convert this type of fat back into bone, reversing the bone code.

osteopause begins and we become thin and frail. As we age, cognitive deterioration, arthritis, and bone loss often occur simultaneously. The brain is instructing the body to draw stored moisture in its bones and muscles for its reserve. You simply cannot have a decrepit frame and be at the peak of your mental edge.

Here's the fix. A study reported that potassium intake was higher in subjects with normal cognition compared to those with mild cognitive impairment. A diet containing carbohydrate sources that are high in potassium, such as fruits and vegetables like oranges, tomatoes, bananas, and potatoes, may help improve cognitive function.

The Pauses Contribute to Osteopause

If your AgePrint shows that your bones are aging faster than you are, or if you had or currently have any of the following disorders or deficiencies, you may be experiencing the early stages of osteopause. As you'll see, many of the precursors to osteoporosis are linked to specific pauses, making them part of one larger cascade of disease.

- Adult body weight less than 127 pounds regardless of height, often caused by electropause
- Occurrence of diabetes, triggering vasculopause
- Early onset of menopause, with premature loss of estrogen
- Frequent alcohol consumption and smoking, leading to dopamine biopause

- Hyperparathyroidism caused by a calcium deficiency, which leads to parathyropause
- Loss of thyroid hormone, which leads to thyropause
- Long-term steroid therapy, rheumatoid arthritis, organ transplantation, triggering immunopause

Osteopause Is Aging You

Fragile bones are bad for our overall physical and mental health. Emotional stability is dependent on musculoskeletal health. Once your muscles and bones start to deteriorate, the rest of the body is not far behind. The cascade that starts with osteopause goes like this:

- **Heart:** Weak bones and muscles mean a more sedentary lifestyle, which is bad for the heart and the waistline.
- **Vascular system:** Bone loss may increase lead levels resulting in an increased risk of high blood pressure.

Osteoporosis Is Not Just a "Women's Health Issue"

Male osteoporosis is an epidemic. Approximately 2 million of the 10 million Americans afflicted with osteoporosis are men. Yet most men don't realize they are at risk for osteopause. In fact, research has shown that very few older men with hip fractures indicative of osteoporosis are tested or treated for the bone-thinning disease, even after they are treated for their fractures. Thirty-two percent of the men studied died within a year of their fractures from ailments linked to the weakening condition of being immobilized. Those deaths might have been preventable with treatment for osteoporosis or the underlying conditions that can cause it. A simple 15-minute scan can identify those at risk. *Now* are you going to schedule a bone density test? Good, I thought so.

- **Immune system:** Bone loss is linked to certain cancers, including gastric cancer.
- **Cognitive function:** Loss of acetylcholine is directly related to memory and attention issues.
- **Skin:** Loss of bone and muscle will cause your skin to sag away from your frame, from your face all the way down to your arms and legs.

Bone Loss Is Not Inevitable

Bone density values do not follow any age-related norms. Any bone deterioration is considered abnormal, at any age. The same applies to loss of memory, loss of muscle mass, and other declines too often accepted as inevitable consequences of aging. We now have the knowledge to diagnose and treat all of these breakdowns, or pauses, that occur in the aging body.

Optimizing peak bone mass in early adulthood is your best defense in preventing osteoporosis later in life.

Parathyropause

Parathyroid hormone is the most important endocrine regulator of calcium. This hormone is secreted from cells of the parathyroid glands and finds its major target cells in the bones and in the kidneys. Its job is to maintain calcium levels throughout the body.

Parathyropause can begin as early as age 30, when the parathyroid gland begins to slow down, contributing to premature aging and a loss of bone density. The parathyroid comprises four purple glands that surround the thyroid gland but are not related in function. As we age, our parathyroid hormone levels elevate because the gland loses its ability to pulse its hormone to the rest of the body. When this happens, hormone production increases, causing the bones to be unable to absorb calcium. The calcium then flows into the bloodstream, acting like a sponge, seeping up fluids and cementing the body's organs. This process wreaks havoc as it pushes the rest of the pauses:

- Electropause occurs when calcium plugs up the brain causing dementia.
- Cardiopause occurs when calcium fills the coronary arteries causing heart attacks.
- Vasculopause occurs when calcium fills the carotid arteries, causing stroke.
- Osteopause occurs when low calcium in bones leads to low bone density
- Dermatopause occurs when additional calcium dries out the skin, leading to more wrinkles.

Yet the fix is quite simple. By injecting a bioidentical version of this hormone in a pulsing manner, calcium and parathyroid levels can be normalized. Parathyroid injections lower the parathyroid levels, relieving the gland of its excessive work and returning it to its normal levels of hormone production. By doing so, the bones' ability to absorb calcium returns, and each of the other pauses stops; the body begins to return to a more age-appropriate state.

We have also been treating osteoporosis with a combination of parathyroid hormone plus human growth hormone (HGH). We have

The Parathyroid Fix

Bioidentical parathyroid hormone supplementation is an increasingly popular option for treating osteoporosis. It is proven to increase spinal, hip, and total bone density over the long term, because it directly mimics how the body's natural hormones work.

For example, Carrie S. had a 20 percent reversal of her bone density in just three months when I treated her with a combination of parathyroid and growth hormone. These hormones provide better bone density reversals than any of the drug therapies ever can produce. Parathyroid actually activates growth hormone inside the bone, which is why they work so well together.

successfully reversed bone and muscle age by as much as 20 years. This combination of hormones yields significantly better results than the antiresorptive agents like Actonel and Boniva, which can only reverse about 4 years of bone loss. With natural parathyroid and growth hormone, my patients report that their strength is better, their mood is better, and, best of all, their normal brain speed returns.

14

Somatopause: Aging of Muscles and Loss of Muscle Mass

Somatopause refers to a decline in growth hormone that affects your muscle growth. Between the ages of 20 and 90, 20 to 40 percent of muscle mass can be lost, particularly if you do not exercise. Because it is governed by the biochemical acetylcholine, symptoms of somatopause can include loss of memory as well as a loss of muscle strength. The hormones that stimulate muscle growth also stimulate nerve connections. Growth hormone prevents dementia.

The Warning Signs of Somatopause
- Nighttime muscle cramps
- Decreased energy
- Decreased well-being
- Depressed mood
- Increased anxiety
- Poor social interaction
- Social isolation
- Reduced sleep
- Increased body fat, particularly abdominal fat
- Decreased lean muscle mass and functional strength
- Thin skin and increased wrinkles
- Decreased hair and nail growth
- Cool hands and feet

- Decreased bone density
- Decreased sweating
- Wounds take longer to heal

Growth Hormone Is the Key to Improving Muscle Mass

Growth hormone links the spinal cord and skeleton with brain activity. It also controls the receptors that are found throughout the entire brain, affecting memory, sleep, and your emotional well-being. So it's not just your bones that benefit from this particular hormone, it's your whole body, brain, and mind. When you make sure your growth hormone levels are young, you are taking care of all the pauses:

- Improved bone density helps prevent osteopause.
- Improved sexual desire and performance fights off menopause.
- An increased libido helps delay andropause.
- Improved memory and brain processing speed fend off electropause.
- Lower blood pressure, increased coronary blood flow, and reversal of heart failure help fight cardiopause.
- Improved retinopathy and increased blood flow fights vasculopause.

The Entire Body Requires Growth Hormone to Stay Youthful

Routine exercise is the best way to prevent most muscle loss. Supplementing with human growth hormone (HGH) and other vital amino acids is also beneficial. While boosting all the brain's biochemicals can help, dopamine is the most stimulatory to muscle growth.

HGH's Beautifying Benefits

HGH therapy not only helps improve muscle mass but also has a positive effect on the aesthetic bone structure of the face. Facial bone struc-

I've Fallen, and I Can Get Up

A study conducted on patients over the age of 60 who had suffered an accidental hip fracture confirmed that growth hormone and improved muscle mass were integral to returning these patients to their prefracture mobility.

ture changes dramatically with age, resulting in sagging skin. Taking HGH can help preserve your organic facial structure, which is better than anything a plastic surgeon could offer.

Take Action: Early Testing Is Key to Reversing Your Aging Muscles and Bones

Catching any of the musculoskeletal pauses—especially the loss of muscle mass—is easier than ever before. Using a new scanning technology, called micro-CT, doctors can now examine bone density and muscle mass with 100 times more detail, and they can assess the effectiveness of drug and hormone therapies for restoring bone health, providing yet another weapon in the antiaging arsenal. Insurance companies often claim that these tests are medically unnecessary. Fight back, and insist on these life-saving tests.

Natural Treatments

Take your vitamins for strong bones, muscles, and teeth:

Natural Treatment	Suggested Dosage per Day
Calcium	1,000–1,500 mg
Magnesium	400 mg
Vitamin K2	Consult your doctor
Copper	1 mg

(continued)

Natural Treatment	Suggested Dosage per Day
Manganese	1 mg
Zinc	15–90 mg
Boron	1 mg
Silica	20 mg
Vitamin K1	1–100 mg
Vitamin C	200–10,000 mg
Strontium	400–800 mg
Omega-3	500–3,000 mg
Omega-6	500–3,000 mg
Ipriflavone	200–600 mg

Rainbow Foods to Improve Bone and Muscle Mass

You need to eat lots of calcium-rich food to keep your bones strong. But did you know that some of the foods you choose are working against you? This time it's not the carbohydrates and junk foods. Instead, it's protein. A diet high in animal protein washes calcium out of your blood so your bones don't get the chance to absorb this important nutrient. A purely vegetarian, high-fiber diet isn't the answer either. Too much fiber and not enough protein can bind important nutrients, so they are excreted before they get absorbed.

Rainbow foods are high in anti-inflammatory proteins called flavoproteins. This diet is high in calcium, potassium, and vitamin D. Look for lots of dairy products that help metabolism, build bone, and improve muscle mass. The following is a list of foods you might not have realized are high in calcium and vitamin D.

Food	International Units (IU) per Serving	Percent of Recommended Daily Value
Cod liver oil, 1 tablespoon	1,360	340
Salmon, 3½ ounces	360	90

Food	International Units (IU) per Serving	Percent of Recommended Daily Value
Mackerel, 3½ ounces	345	90
Tuna, 3 ounces	200	50
Sardines, 1¾ ounces	250	70
Milk (nonfat, reduced fat, and whole), must be vitamin-D fortified, 1 cup	98	25
Margarine, fortified, 1 tablespoon	60	15
Prepared puddings made with vitamin-D fortified milk, ½ cup	50	10
Ready-to-eat cereals (check labels for more information)	40	10
One egg yolk	20	6
Beef liver, 3½ ounces	15	4
Swiss cheese, 1 ounce	12	4
Watermelon	33	9

Check out the following sample meal suggestions to help build those muscles:

Breakfast Options
- ½ cup organic yogurt topped with granola and strawberries or trail mix consisting of nuts and seeds
- An 8-ounce smoothie made from blended strawberries, mango, guava, wheat germ, orange juice, and soy milk
- One-half sesame seed bagel toasted with a slice of low-fat cheddar cheese
- One-third cantaloupe filled with low-fat strawberry yogurt

Lunch Options

- Red leaf lettuce salad with tomatoes, radishes, and green peppers, tossed with almond slivers and a dressing made with olive oil, balsamic vinegar, and herbs
- Spinach salad with tofu squares and unsalted mixed nuts in a strawberry vinaigrette
- Vegetable soup served with one whole-grain roll and 4 ounces hard cheese
- Tuna melt made with low-fat mayonnaise and low-fat Swiss cheese on two slices whole-grain bread

Dinner Options

- 4 ounces beef liver with onions and peppers, served with string beans and toasted sesame seeds
- Spinach chef salad with one hard-boiled egg, grated low-fat cheese, chickpeas, and tuna
- 4 ounces grilled sardines served with spinach and tomatoes
- 4 ounces grilled herb salmon with broccoli

Desserts and Snack Options

- 1 cup fruit salad made with strawberries, bananas, mango, and cantaloupe
- 2 ounces of your favorite cheese on whole-wheat crackers
- ¼ cup whole almonds
- An 8-ounce smoothie made with guava or mango and low-fat yogurt

Follow Your Gut, Not the Pack

Improving your bones and muscles will involve prioritizing your health, but the results are well worth it. The fix for this pause above all others is in your hands. You will need to carefully incorporate the right foods, exercise diligently, and insist on the proper testing and supplement therapies. By following this protocol, I know that you will look and feel 15 years younger within the first year of treatment.

15

Dermatopause: Restoring Aging Skin for a Younger Face and a Firm Body

Beauty and youth are not interchangeable. In fact, the old saying is true: beauty is only skin deep. Youth, however, goes to the core. It is not by accident that younger people have youthful-looking and supple skin. The skin has a dynamic interaction with the health of the rest of the body. Skin depends on its tone the same way that our muscles are toned. Frail body is equated with frail skin. Furthermore, the skin assists with the entire neurosteroid cycle that relates to male and female menopause. Vitamin D, one of the most common nutrients that decreases with age, is essential to the well-being of the skin, bones, and muscles. Healthy skin is glowing as a result of a healthier internal body.

This book is about reversing internal aging, or internal plastic surgery repair of the body, or beautifying your body from the inside out. When you have addressed all your pauses and begun the process of reversing your illness, you'll be able to see how much better you look on the outside because you will be feeling better on the inside. That's getting to a younger you.

However, there's nothing wrong about wanting to look younger on the outside. Unfortunately, we live in a world where we are judged by how we look, and youth is a premium. We all want to be young and look young. And the condition of your skin is the universal measurement of youth.

Other doctors are more than happy to talk about how to rejuvenate your face with plastic surgery or Botox injections. To them, turning back the clock means fixing the face from the outside. But even the best face-lift does little if you are not addressing the aging that is going on inside the body. To truly look and feel young, you have to start from within and, most important, with the brain. Boosting your brain's biochemicals and restoring your body's natural hormone levels enables it to tell your body to feel good, tell your organs to run efficiently, tell your skin to tighten up. Then you'll reverse your aging skin and truly look 10 to 15 years younger. Better still, you'll be 15 years younger, and have more time to enjoy the new you!

Beauty from the Inside Out

There are no beauty contests for the most beautiful thyroid. But the fact is that external beauty cannot occur without internal beauty first.

Healthy Skin Can Last Your Lifetime

Youthful skin is full of collagen, the fat that resides just underneath your skin that plumps up our face and hands. Without it, your skin will lose its elasticity and begin to sag. I refer to this change as dermatopause. Your life begins with skin that's like a beautiful piece of fruit. When you are young, your skin is soft to the touch, smooth as silk, fleshy, and firm—a perfect plum. As you age, your skin dries up, gets coarse and wrinkled, and loses its firmness—you've turned into a prune.

Everyone's skin begins this transition from age 30 on, because of the loss of growth hormone. Often, you've helped the process along by just plain living, perhaps indulging in the common early 20s lifestyle of smoking, drinking, and not sleeping. A few years later, depression and

Expensive Creams Won't Erase Wrinkles

No cream in the world can erase wrinkles, no matter how much you spend. No wrinkle remover can penetrate the skin beyond the first few layers. Youthful skin can only be achieved by taking care of your skin from the inside out. There are some studies, however, that suggest using Retin-A (a modified form of vitamin A) beginning at age 20 can slow the process of collagen and elasticity loss as well as protect against radiation and repair sun damage.

anxiety give you frown lines. Crow's-feet, freckles, moles, and weathered hands are already on their way by age 20 because of sun exposure.

But we can't live in a bubble, and the party years can't be taken back. Your AgePrint is a great indication of how well you've maintained your skin. If you haven't done a good job, there's no better time than the present to start. Like every other pause we've covered, you need to identify and treat your problems as soon as possible so that they don't send death codes to the other organs.

Your Brain, Your Skin

While the age and condition of your skin is regulated by genetics, it is also affected by its overall level of hydration: water content. Remember acetylcholine discussed in Chapter 4: moistness = youth. As we age, everything dries up, starting in your brain and continuing throughout the body. So the younger your brain is, the higher the water content. Aside from vanity (and there's nothing wrong with that), you need to pay attention to your skin and keep it healthy because your skin is the organ that prevents the most dehydration. Ultimately, hydration is what makes your skin look younger. And no amount of plastic surgery or creams will prevent dehydration.

Inflammation, dehydration, structural damage, and oxidation are the brain's four codes that cause the skin to age. When your brain is low on dopamine, your skin burns up, causing inflammation; red, blotchy patches; and rough, bumpy skin. For example, you can always tell a serious drinker by the size and color of his or her nose; often it looks red and swollen compared to the rest of the face. Remember, dopamine loss and addiction go hand in hand.

When we dehydrate from a loss of acetylcholine, we get wrinkles. Acetylcholine provides the moisture to the body, so when it goes, we dry up from the inside out. No amount of moisturizer is going to replace your acetylcholine.

Without serotonin, we can't sleep. And without sleep, our face swells up. A bad night's sleep is slapped on your face the very next morning with puffy eyes, a sallow complexion, and dark circles. You can place cucumber slices on your eyes to remove the puffiness, but you'd be better off snacking on them instead and going to bed a bit earlier. The aging brain triggers the aging face. The youthful brain triggers a youthful face.

Esther Is 68, But Her Skin's Age Is 40

Esther had sagging, dry skin, wrinkles, and dark circles under her eyes. She told me that even though she was full of energy her friends said that she always looked tired. After one year using topical Retin-A and vitamin K (for prevention of dark circles), taking alpha lipoic acid (for decreasing inflammation), using fish oils and natural estrogen replacement (to lubricate her skin from the inside), and eating foods that were

Lip Service

That little pot of gloss you religiously apply does a great job of protecting your lips, but if the damage is already done, you're going to have to call in the big guns. You need to switch to an emollient that actively rehydrates your pucker that also contains a gentle exfoliator to slough off the dead skin. This combination will keep your lips in kissable condition.

high in antioxidants (to slow free radical damage to the skin), she is now feeling great about herself. At parties, people always comment on how sexy she looks. Esther never had plastic surgery and is living proof that my protocol is an effective way to turn back the clock.

The Brain Is Wrapped in Skin

The skin that surrounds the brain is called the meninges. Its cells, along with the spinal cord cells, are also wrapped in myelin sheaths, which are similar in structure to skin. This internal skin also needs to be maintained, another reason why we need to take care of the skin from the inside out, to get total age reversal. When the pauses begin, the skin responds as well. You can't fix the skin without fixing the internal aging of every part of the body, but when you do, it's like turning a prune back into a plum.

Your skin receives the code from the other pauses and sends you a clear signal that your health is failing; you just need to know how to break the code. Here's how you can take a cue from your skin that something else is wrong.

- Dopamine biopause: Obese, addicted smokers often have psoriasis and other skin disorders. A diet of fatty, fried, and unhealthy foods can contribute to a host of skin disorders, especially acne.

- Acetylcholine electropause: Dry, wrinkled skin may be a clue that your memory is fading as well. Remember, acetylcholine is a marker of dementia; when the moisture in the skin goes, it's gone in the brain as well.

- GABA biopause: A wrinkled face is literally full of stress. If you are starting to get frown lines and deep creases between your eyebrows, you are holding in a lot of stress, a sure sign of a GABA deficiency.

- Serotonin biopause: Lack of sleep—another function of electro-pause—causes inflammation, a swollen-looking face, and dark circles.

- Menopause: When you lose estrogen, the skin loses elasticity and suppleness, drying out the hair and nails as well.

- Immunopause: Skin disorders, including acne, chicken pox, viral rashes, and allergic hives, all point to a failing immune system. The worst-case immunopause scenario is skin cancer.

- Osteopause: Have you ever seen a woman crippled with arthritis yet her face looked radiant? Have you ever seen a man with horrible posture whose skin looked good? Your skin is made of collagen that also supports your bones. If your skin is sagging, your bones are next.

- Vasculopause: Fungus under toe- and fingernails grows when circulation is limited. And don't forget that varicose veins and age spots are all vasculopause related.

- Somatopause: Your muscle tone supports your whole body, including your cheeks. Sagging jowls suggests aging muscles everywhere.

Don't Worship the Sun, Worship Longevity

If you want to stick around for the long haul and have great look-ing skin, limit your sun exposure now. Besides the skin cancer risk, sunbathing is a wrinkle guarantee. Too much sun is not pretty and not healthy, and it's nearly impossible to reverse. You need about 20 minutes of sun every day to get your necessary amounts of vitamin D, but a less wrinkle-producing way is to eat lots of foods rich in this nutrient. One day in the sun provides you with only 10,000 IU of vita-min D and a lifetime of skin cancer.

Beautiful Skin Starts with Internal Plastic Surgery

Your skin is as alive as every other organ inside the body. What's more, every internal system has a direct connection to the skin and contributes to the appearance of a youthful body and a younger you. The process by which the skin ages is intricately linked to your AgePrint. By maintaining and enhancing each of the pauses, the results will reflect in younger, healthy skin.

The brain lives in the skin. Our skin is filled with neuronal connections stemming from the brain, which is why it responds to touch so quickly. This sensory experience puts skin in the category of sexual organs and identifies why we are aroused by the caresses we receive to the face and entire body. Yet the sensations we feel when we are touched diminish as we age, as the nerve endings in the skin lose sensitivity. It's therefore so important to our sexual as well as our overall health to keep the brain as young as possible and maintain the brain-body connection.

The skin contains an abundance of blood vessels, making it vascular in nature. These blood vessels promote circulation, blood flow, cleansing, and cleaning of the skin. When our cardiovascular system clogs up, our skin is affected. It loses its pink, youthful appearance. You may have noticed that beyond wrinkles, the skin tone of older people is often sallow and pale.

The skin's collagen and other proteinlike structures interconnect with bone, cartilage, and all of the other tissues of the body. Collagen gives skin its structure, and it is essentially a "flexible bone." As osteoporosis sets in and your bones deteriorate and calcify, the skin loses its flexibility as well.

Skin Cancer: The Ultimate Skin Code

Almost 10,000 people die each year from melanoma, the most serious form of skin cancer; 48,000 more are diagnosed. If not caught in the earlier stages, melanoma is almost always fatal, spreading quickly and often affecting the lymph nodes, lungs, liver, brain, or bones. Fair-skinned individuals who already have freckles and moles are most at risk. A thorough head-to-toe skin check needs to become part of your yearly physical from age 20 on.

Positron Emission Tomography (PET) Scan

Dozens of lives have been saved with a PET scan with its ability to identify internal melanoma before it even surfaces to the visible layers of the skin.

Find Your Freckles

If you notice new freckles or moles, see a dermatologist immediately. He or she will examine you either by sight or with a head-to-toe ultrasound. Dermatologists are trained to find four distinct irregularities of freckles or moles that may be cancerous.

Glowing Skin—It's in the Blood

Anemia, a blood disorder that develops when the body's level of healthy red blood cells drops too low, can be one reason why you keep looking a little ghostlike. Red blood cells contain hemoglobin, which is responsible for carrying oxygen to your tissues. A lack of oxygen can cause stress on organs; if anemia goes untreated, common symptoms include mild skin paleness and dizziness or light-headedness.

Don't love the skin you're in? Find out if there's a deeper problem using these blood tests

Blood Levels	Function
Vitamins A, B$_1$, B$_2$, B$_6$; alpha linolenic; selenium; magnesium	Risk for skin disorders such as rosacea, eczema, dry skin, brittle hair, dermatitis

Blood Levels	Function
Linoleic, gamma linolenic, elcosapentaenoic, docosapentaenoic acid	Risk for lipomas, fatty skin, dry skin, psoriasis, brittle nails and hair, eczema
Apolipo-A, B ratio, liproprotein A	
Zinc, copper	Risk for inflammation, actinic keratosis, dandruff, slow wound healing, loss of elastin and collagen
Lead, cadmium, aluminum, mercury	Presence could indicate risk for dermatitis and toxicity to the skin
Homocysteine, fibrinogen	Risk for decreased blood flow
Electrolytes, plasma amino acids, red blood cells	Blood flow, indicates pink healthy glow of skin
RAST allergy profile	Determines if itchy skin is allergy related, can identify causes of allergies, red blotchy skin especially on the neck, loss of pigment, melasma (changes in pigment)

Take Care of Your Health and Your Nails Will Follow

A most unwelcome sign of dermatopause is a common side effect of peripheral vascular disease: ugly, yellow nails, especially on your feet. It will take a lot more than a pedicure to fix this fungal problem. Talk to your doctor or dermatologist about various medications you can try, such as Spranox and Lamasil. Natural treatment that restores good circulation and blood flow to the nail beds includes zinc, boron, vitamin A, calcium, and even hydrolyzed collagen now available in powder form.

Take Action: Preserve Your Skin for a Younger You

A younger you begins with knowing exactly what's going on inside your body at all times. That means early and frequent testing. Many types of blood work can show exactly what's affecting your aging skin, as well as other physical tests and treatments to control environmental problems.

For example, toxic metals still remain a very serious problem in our society, particularly in urban areas. Heavy metals such as lead and cadmium are toxic to the brain and body, especially the skin. Heavy metals, especially lead, damage free radicals causing more cancer-causing cells to develop as well as discoloration to the skin. I still see patients with elevated lead levels, despite the fact that blood lead levels have fallen dramatically since the 1970s. Lead has been successfully removed from gasoline and paint but still exists in older buildings with lead pipes and peeling, lead-based paint, or contaminated soil. An analysis of toxic mineral levels in the body is a worthwhile test to preserve or reverse skin issues.

If you don't love the skin you're in, find out if there's a deeper problem using these blood tests:

Blood Levels	Function
Vitamin A, B$_1$, B$_2$, B$_6$; alpha linolenic acid; selenium; magnesium	Risk for skin disorders such as rosacea, eczema, dry skin, brittle hair, dermatitis
Linoleic, gamma-linolenic acid (GLA), elcopentaenoic acid, docosapentaenoic acid	Risk for lipomas, fatty skin, dry skin, psoriasis, brittle nails and hair, eczema
Apolipo-A, B, Apo A1/B ratio, liproprotein A	
Zinc, copper	Risk for inflammation, actinic keratosis, dandruff, slow wound healing, loss of elastin and collagen

Blood Levels	Function
Lead, cadmium, aluminum, mercury	Presence could indicate risk for dermatitis and toxicity to the skin
Homocystein, fibrinogen	Risk for decreased blood flow
SMAC, plasma amino acids	Blood flow, indicated pink healthy glow of skin
TSH	
RAST allergy profile	Determines if itchy skin is allergy related, can identify causes of allergies, red blotchy skin, especially on the neck, loss of pigment, melasma (changes in pigment)

Take Action: Treatments That Can Improve Your Skin

You can choose a variety of ways to improve the condition of your skin, through either prescription medications, bioidentical hormones, or nutrients, supplements, or diet. Your choice can be guided by your deficiency. If your AgePrint for your skin was greater than 20 years more than your chronological age, you can address it with nutrition and lifestyle changes. If your score was between 40 and 60 years older than your chronological age, you will need to address your personal reversal with hormones. At levels greater than 60 years older than your chronological age, you will need medications to reverse your AgePrint.

To clear up skin disorders, talk to your doctor about these treatments:

Conventional Treatment	Suggested Dosage per Day
Retin-A: form of vitamin A that abrades the skin	0.1% cream
Tri-Luma: a combination of Retin-A with a small dose of a steroid and bleaching agent	4% cream

Conventional Treatment	Suggested Dosage per Day
Metrogel: treats acne rosacea	1% gel
Glyquin-hydroquinone bleaching agent for treating pigmentation	4% cream

Hormones Break the Brain's Skin Code

Natural hormones reverse many of the pauses, including dermatopause. For women, one of the most likely suspects in the skin damage lineup is menopause. Bioidentical estrogen can slow the aging process in the skin by slowing collagen loss and affecting the skin's ability to retain moisture. I've seen dozens of perimenopausal women with facial sagging use hormones to replenish their skin. Replace your lost hormones and reverse the signs of aging, guaranteed!

CODE BREAKER: Time May Not Heal All Wounds, but DHEA Will

Produced by the adrenal gland, dehydroepiandrosterone (DHEA) is the precursor to the sex hormones estrogen and testosterone. Recent studies suggest DHEA as a treatment for accelerating wound healing in elderly patients. Many of our patients find DHEA more effective when combined with N-acetyl cysteine (NAC).

Talk with your doctor about the following skin-toning hormones:

Hormonal Treatment	Suggested Dosage per Day
Human growth hormone (HGH)	5–45 mg
Estradiol	1–2 mg

Improve Your Skin with Nutrients

Supplementing your diet with vitamins is a great way to fight the skin battle. Here are some of the most effective treatments and the science behind them:

- **Vitamin C, estradiol, and L-lysine** stop the spread of skin cancer by inhibiting the enzymes produced by cancer cells that are used to attack collagen. They also are essential for the production of collagen, so you can replace this important fat that compresses with age.
- **Vitamin D** also prevents and reverses skin damage. As your skin ages, it can no longer synthesize vitamin D coming from the sun. If you notice that your skin is not healing like it used to, extra vitamin D may be the key.
- **Zinc** promotes wound healing and is beneficial to hair and skin health, particularly for those who suffer from dermatitis and dandruff.

Leora Took Her Vitamins and Got Younger Skin

Leora was an attractive 60-year-old woman who wanted to perk up her skin. She had brown spots, dull skin, wrinkles, fine lines, and sagging. She had already gone through one face-lift but was not happy with her results. When she came to see me, we did a head-to-toe physical. Her overall AgePrint showed that she was in good health, but her skin's age was 70. I placed her on Retin-A, which reduced her wrinkles and tightened her skin. Additionally, I suggested that Leora take natural estrogen, progesterone, DHEA, and HGH to thicken, moisturize, and improve the overall integrity of her skin. Alpha lipoic acid, vitamins A and E, and fish oils rounded out her regimen to decrease inflammation and give her a beautiful healthy glow. Finally, she was prescribed Tri-Luma, which reversed her brown aging spots.

Leora came back three months later; her new AgePrint showed that she was already reversing her skin's age. She was ecstatic by how much younger and healthier she looked. Leora told me that she secretly regretted her face-lift, especially now that she knew that had she fed her body the right nutrients, it would have repaired itself.

Starting to Sag?

Although natural hormones are most effective in bringing back the elasticity of the skin, nutrients may have some minimal beneficial effects.

Proper DHEA Use

Too much DHEA can cause acne because of its powerful internal moisturizing effect. Be sure to have your DHEA levels checked by your doctor.

Natural Treatment	Suggested Dosage per Day
Vitamin C	200–10,000 mg
Vitamin E	100–1,000 IU
Omega 3	500–3,000 mg
Omega 6	100–500 mg
Alpha lipoic acid	25–1,000 mg
Beta-carotene	10–50 mg
Zinc	10 mg

Rainbow Foods for Beautiful, Younger Skin

My friend Dr. Nicholas Perricone has developed an outstanding food regimen to promote and protect the skin. His diet is high in salmon, a nutrient-rich, antioxidant food. Luckily, he loves fish! He supports this diet so much that he promotes eating fish for breakfast, lunch, and dinner, every day.

While I agree with Nick that antioxidants are important not only for your skin but for your overall health, my diet allows for a bit more diversity. To keep your skin healthy and young, you also need to control inflammation. For this reason, stick with foods that have a high inflammation fighting (IF) rating. The IF rating is the total value of all nutrients in a food to fight swelling, autoimmunity, and inflammation. And eat lots of salmon, too.

The best defenses against inflammation are supplements containing fish oils, vitamin C, lipoic acid, and green tea. Here are some other great suggestions:

Food	IF Rating
Salmon, 3 ounces	+500
Ginger, ½ teaspoon	+250
Garlic, one clove	+110
Broccoli, ½ cup	+80
Extra-virgin olive oil, 1 tablespoon	+60
Raw almonds, 1 ounce	+60
Bran cereal, ⅓ cup	+50
20 strawberries	+40

Adapted from The Sinatra Report

Herbs and Spices That Help the Skin

Herbs and spices are an important supplement to a healthy diet but may not have a significant impact on the integrity of your skin. Bioidentical hormones will have the greatest impact, but do add these to your diet:

- Basil
- Bay leaves
- Chamomile
- Hyssop
- Juniper
- Lavender
- Rosemary
- Thyme
- Turmeric

The following herbs or oils can be used to clean your skin:

- Aloe vera
- Jojoba
- Primrose oil
- Tea tree oil
- Green tea

Here are some sample meal options to help you get that beautiful youthful skin:

Breakfast Options
- 1 cup fruit salad with yogurt; use brightly colored fruits
- 1 cup oatmeal topped with fresh strawberries and cinnamon
- 1 cup bran cereal with sliced strawberries and skim milk
- Two poached eggs over 2 ounces smoked salmon

Lunch Options
- Grilled vegetables with ginger and balsamic vinaigrette dressing
- Seven-grain seeded bread sandwich with alfalfa sprouts, avocado, tomato, and carrots
- Spinach salad with 4 ounces grilled salmon
- Veggie burger on a whole-wheat bun

Dinner Options
- 4 ounces basil chicken curry with toasted almonds and ½ cup brown rice
- 4 ounces grilled tuna steak served with ½ cup gingered mashed sweet potato
- 4 ounces broiled flank steak served with one-half acorn squash and almond slivers

Desserts and Snack Options
- ½ cup organic granola with mixed berries and yogurt
- ½ cup guacamole and salsa with whole-wheat pita chips
- ½ cup dried cranberries (Craisins)
- An 8-ounce blueberry smoothie

The Importance of Color in Your Diet

People who eat diets rich in tomatoes have increased protection against the sun's damaging UV rays. Tomatoes contain carotenoids, a powerful enzyme found in fruits and veggies with a red or orange hue, such as carrots. Eat a variety of them if you find yourself in the sun often. And don't forget the sunscreen and sunglasses. A high-carotenoid diet may also prevent certain cancers. Alpha-carotene found in carrots and pumpkin; lycopene found in red fruits, such as watermelon, grapefruit, and tomatoes; cryptoxanthin found in peaches, mangoes, and oranges; beta-carotene found in all the foods mentioned as well as sweet potatoes and cantaloupes; and lutein and zeaxanthin, which are found abundantly in red peppers, pumpkins, and dark green vegetables (the yellow-orange pigments are masked by green chlorophyll), will also help improve the look and feel of your skin.

The Skinny on Skin Care Products

Skin care products do have their place, once you've made the necessary corrections from the inside out. But be careful: skin care is not a one-size-fits-all approach. Many products contain ingredients that are drying agents, and if your skin is dry, it will only make things worse. Talk to a licensed dermatologist—not the woman in the lab coat at your favorite department store—to find out what type of skin you have and what product is right for you.

If you know you have dry skin, stay away from products that contain the following:

- Alcohol or SD alcohol
- Ammonia
- Benzalkonium chloride
- Benzyl alcohol
- Bergamot
- Camphor
- Citrus oils
- Cornstarch
- Essential oils
- Eucalyptus

- Fragrance
- Lemongrass
- Menthol, menthyl acetate, and menthyl PCA
- PABA
- Phenol
- Sandalwood oil
- Sodium C14-16 olefin sulfate
- TEA-lauryl sulfate
- Witch hazel

The Younger You Facial for Glowing, Radiant Skin

Washing your face with supermarket bar soap is not going to cut it once you are past 30. Instead, you need to gently and thoroughly cleanse your skin and then lock in your skin's natural moisture. Call it a facial if you're fancy, but this morning routine does not have to be expensive or elaborate. These four steps are all it takes:

1. **Wash your face:** Combine warm (not hot) water and a dollop of gentle, nondrying cream or gel cleanser. With the tips of your fingers or a soft, cotton towel (one use only), cleanse your face and neck, using gentle, circular motions. Rinse and pat dry with a second clean towel.

2. **Exfoliate:** Once a week (or more often if you have oily skin) add an exfoliating cleanser that contains natural fruit acids such as alpha and beta hydroxy. Natural fruit acids slough off dead skin cells and diminish areas of darker pigmentation and uneven coloring. Follow the same directions as in Step 1: warm water, gentle pressure, rinse.

3. **Tone:** A toner is a liquid that you splash or spritz onto your face that seals in the moisture from your clean skin. You can buy a toner anywhere that skin care products are sold. Never choose one

that contains alcohol; it will only dry your skin out. A great home-made treatment uses brewed green tea (the more potent the better: green tea tightens the pores, has anti-inflammatory properties, and is a powerful antioxidant against environmental toxins). Make the tea at night, and let it cool completely. Then, right after you've washed your face and it still has that dewy feeling, splash or blot face and neck with soaked cotton pads. Or fill a small spray bottle and spray your face. Whatever method you choose, do not rinse or wipe away; allow the tea/toner to dry on your face.

4. **Moisturize:** Apply moisturizer liberally to continue hydrating your face all day (or night). For daytime use, choose a moisturizer with SPF sunscreen 15 or higher. Look for ones that contain dimethylaminoethanol (DMAE), alpha lipoic acid, vitamin E, or green tea. Research suggests that DMAE and alpha lipoic acid help restore collagen, thus preventing future wrinkles from developing.

Release Tension with Acupressure

Skin is a place where people hold a lot of tension. Acupressure works in much the same way acupuncture does, without the needles. Acupressure relies on fingers to touch on specific points throughout your body to release energy or tension that may be blocked. Next time you feel particularly tense, apply very firm pressure for a full minute to each of these three sights:

1. The base of the skull, one finger width to each side of the spine
2. The pad between the joint of the thumb and index finger
3. The sole of the foot, one-third of the way from the toes

A Whole Life Plan

Every year, new breakthroughs in antiaging medicine are allowing us to prolong life. This book has brought together all of the most recent findings, which I have incorporated as part of my medical practice with each of my patients. This cutting-edge research and new discoveries are the hallmark of the Younger You Plan.

These new discoveries are not for the glory of science, but they are for you! Just by reading this book, you have taken the first important step toward achieving longevity and looking and feeling younger. You now have been introduced to a complete health program that explains how each part of your body ages and what needs to be done to stop and reverse this process. You've learned that by improving your brain chemistry, you can enhance your health and extend your life. By identifying your aging parts and treating them appropriately, you will stay healthy. What's more, by reversing the age of your oldest part, you can begin the healing process before further deterioration has begun.

Next, we need to lobby our doctors and health insurance providers and insist on full coverage for the latest tests and tools to be used during our yearly physicals. My 21st-century physical incorporates the minimum requirements that should be met for each one of us. Bring these lists of blood tests and physical scans to your physician, find out which are covered under your current plan, and insist on using them. Preventive testing is the only way to discover what is going to ail you and the best way to keep feeling young into the future.

The AgePrint is the cornerstone of the Younger You Plan. You have already used it to identify your weakest parts and address your health issues. Bring this information to your physician, and together you will be able to devise a program to reverse your aging code. You might require hormone therapy; if so, insist on only bioidentical hormones. You might require medications; if that is the case, make sure that they are compatible with any other medication that you might currently be taking. If your AgePrint shows only the mildest discrepancy between your real age and your pause age, first see if you can rectify the problem yourself with nutrient supplementation and diet before the discrepancy is able to widen.

Every day, the path that medical science is taking is changing. This constant barrage of changing information is confusing, but it is also critical. Make sure that your physician is up-to-date with the latest research and is on board with your goals: to look and feel 15 years younger now. As I've said before, if he or she is unwilling to work within the Younger You Plan, it may be time to find a new, more open-minded and informed doctor.

Where (and When) Are You Going to Break?

All of us are caught up in hectic schedules and busy lives, and our health is not always at the top of minds. However, our busy lives are causing us to miss the subtle changes that are happening to our minds and bodies. The key is to be relentless in checking your health out and finding your oldest part before it finds you. That's where the AgePrint quiz comes in.

If you take your AgePrint quiz today and find that your real age is compatible with all of your pause ages, consider yourself lucky, at least for now. Like death and taxes, we are all guaranteed to age sooner than we would like. Repeat your AgePrint testing every six months, and you will be able to catch the slightest changes in your health. By doing so, you will be able to break each death code as it appears, without suffering unnecessary symptoms. This is the best way to stay young.

Good Things Come to Those Who Wait

Creating a younger you takes time. To completely reverse your bad health, you'll need to make changes in small steps. Remember, your mind and body has aged little by little; reversing it should be just as gradual. Fifteen years younger is an achievable goal, but it won't happen in the first year. It's a stepwise process; institute a new diet, start taking nutrient supplements, begin and continue a realistic exercise program, and develop a personal headfirst health program, all at a pace you're comfortable with.

The Brain Is the Ultimate Code Breaker

Looking and feeling 15 years younger won't mean a thing to any of us if we can't enjoy the time we've earned. I've seen it a million times. Many of my patients get too narrowly focused on many aspects of their lives, including their health. If you find yourself becoming too literal, too closed in, or too critical of others, you may end up with dementia. You need to learn to let go; these feelings can overtake the entire brain and its connection to the mind and body.

It's all about balance, and we need to include all facets of a healthy existence into our lives every day. This means making time for work and play, activity and rest, passion and focus, and talking and listening. You don't have to be a Rastafarian to be able to be personally free and enjoy your life. Express yourself in terms of the imaginative world, and share your creative ideas with others. When your life feels like you are getting stuck in too many ruts, make changes. Keep exercising your mind with constant learning on topics that introduce you to new, engaging ideas. And remember that happiness lies within a positive attitude, enjoying where we are in life and finding our daily existence compelling. My goal for each of you is to extend your life as long as possible, fully enjoying your future with vitality and a sharp mind.

Every code signal test or symptom of aging has an antidote. *Younger You* will break your aging brain and extend not just the length of your life but the quality as well.

Index

Abdominal ultrasound, 39
Abdominal weight gain, 156, 218, 219
Abstract IQ, 91
ACE inhibitors, 159, 164, 165
Acetylcholine
  age acceleration and, 9, 84–85
  AgePrint quiz on, 43
  Alzheimer's disease and, 10
  asparagus and, 99
  bone/muscle health and, 243
  brain speed and, 7, 85, 87–88, 91, 95
  cognitive decline and, 87–93
  creative IQ and, 91
  exercise and, 32
  fish oils and, 19
  heart disease and, 156
  importance of, 84–85
  lifestyle choices and, 86–87
  memory and, 10–11, 82–84, 88–89
  Mona's story, 81–82
  sexual arousal and, 214
  somatopause and, 251
  turmeric and, 99–100
Acne, 262, 270
Acupressure, 275
Addiction
  as age accelerator, 9
  andropause and, 231–32

food, 57–58, 68–69
  stress and, 112
Age, chronological
  brain speed and, 88
  hormone changes and, 9–10
  organ or system age versus, xvii–xviii, 5, 13
Age reversals, xix–xx
AgePrint, defined, 40
AgePrint quiz
  defined, 40, 41
  instructions, 41–42
  pauses and, 50–53
  repeating, 278
  scoring, 42
  worksheet, 50, 51
AgePrint quiz sections
  brain, 42–44
  cardiovascular system, 45
  modulating systems, 46
  musculoskeletal aging, 48–49
  sexuality, 47–48
  skin, 49–50
Aging. *See also* Pauses
  differences in, xv
  exercise and, 32–33
  faulty brain code and, 8–9
  pauses and, 4, 5
Aging code
  breaking, xviii–xix
  defined, xiv, xv, 4